Praise for
OWN YOUR HEALTH

"This is a fabulous book! It's filled with life-saving information presented with crystalline clarity. And as hard as this may be to believe considering this is a book about nutrition, it's also side-splittingly funny. I found myself laughing out loud on nearly every page. This book is for you if you want to be healthy for the rest of your life—and if you don't mind laughing a lot."

—John Robbins, Author of *Diet For A New America*,
and other best-sellers; and President of
Food Revolution Network

"*Own Your Health* is one great book! It is engaging, thought-provoking, and persuasive. It's different than a lot of vegan books—in a good way! The real hook for this book is Glen Merzer's humor weaved through every page. As a special bonus, Chef AJ contributes an amazing set of recipes to live by. Glen and AJ are a dynamic duo, and the reader is the beneficiary!"

—Brenda Davis, R.D., co-author,
Nourish and Becoming Vegan: Comprehensive Edition;
author, *Kick Diabetes Essentials*

"Take Glen Merzer's wise nutritional advice, add Chef AJ's fabulous recipes, and you've got the formula for health."

—Neal Barnard, M.D.,
President, Physicians Committe for Responsible Medicine

"*Own Your Health* is the funniest book on diet you'll ever read. And it's the diet that's right for the planet!"

—Ed Begley, Jr., actor, environmentalist

"Glen Merzer writes like a regular guy who can really tell a story. In this passionate personal manifesto, this very smart regular guy takes you on a fast-paced journey away from doctors, hospitals, medicines, and misery—and points you directly toward health, life, vitality, and your better future. *Own Your Health* is a terrific read. Don't miss it! And don't miss out on Chef AJ's latest and greatest recipes!"

—Douglas J. Lisle, PhD, Founder of Esteem Dynamics, Esteemdynamics.com; Author, *The Pleasure Trap*

"Glen Merzer has written yet another essential book to add to your nutritional library. *Own Your Health* is loaded with important information about how you can actually take control of your health destiny. It features Merzer's dazzling wit, along with amazing recipes from legendary Chef AJ. A must-read!"

—Jeff Nelson, Founder, *VegSource*

"We highly recommend taking your health into your own hands today and truly *Own Your Health* for the rest of your life. This book will support you on this journey so that you can start reaping the benefits immediately!"

—Alona Pulde, M.D. and Matthew Lederman, M.D., *N.Y. Times* Best Selling Authors of *The Forks Over Knives Plan;* Cofounders, *Kinectin.com*

"I wish *Own Your Health* had been written 40 years ago. The savings in my health care costs would have me on easy street today. It is never too late to do the right thing. Many thanks to Glen Merzer—you have outlined universal health care at an affordable price."

—Howard Lyman, author, *Mad Cowboy*

"The real truth about healthy eating and living, spiced with humor and no-holds-barred good sense. Oh—if you think the plan seems spartan, check out the recipes from Chef AJ: this is comfort food even your arteries can love."

—Victoria Moran, author, *Main Street Vegan*;
host, *Main Street Vegan Podcast*

Own Your Health

How to Live Long and Avoid Chronic Illness

by
GLEN MERZER
with recipes by
CHEF AJ

Copyright 2020 Glen Merzer
All rights reserved.

Cover designed by Jeannine Elder

ISBN: 9798670357029

Hail to the Kale Publishing

TABLE OF CONTENTS

ACKNOWLEDGMENTS

First, my thanks to Chef AJ, who has added more than seventy-five amazing recipes to this volume, and with whom I had the pleasure of working on her books *Unprocessed* and *The Secrets to Ultimate Weight Loss*. Now we've got a trilogy! Thanks as well to her wise and trusty husband Charles Shrewsbury, whose advice I make a practice of taking. Thank you to the other great chefs and cooks, friends and followers of Chef AJ, who contributed recipes to this volume. Thank you to Dr. Pamela Williams-Russo for contributing the Foreword; I didn't see that coming when we were housemates in San Francisco. I want to thank my vegan editor, Jeff Melton, for an attention to detail that I'm sure no meat-eating editor could match. Thank you to Jeannine Elder for the cover design. To the text's early readers: John Tanner, Arlo Vegan, Benji Kurtz, and Merrilee Jacobs—I appreciate your notes and your insights. My gratitude to Thomas Calabro and Dr. Steve Lawenda for letting me tell their stories. An unanticipated thank you to Gary Taubes, whose views on nutrition vary widely from my own but who answered my queries with civility and openness. Finally, to the love of my life, Joanna Samorow-Merzer, thank you for letting me tell your story as well, for keeping me healthy, and for putting up with me.

FOREWORD

I first met Glen Merzer in 1980, when I joined a vegetarian household in San Francisco. I was a vegetarian medical student, and Glen was a vegetarian aspiring stand-up comic. Every day when I returned home from school, Glen would pull out his shirt pocket pad, read me a new joke, and ask me, "Is this funny?" I was proud to serve as Glen's official joke arbiter.

Glen gave up the stand-up career because he couldn't take the nightclub cigarette smoke, and went on to write plays, screenplays, television shows, books on health and the environment, and one very funny novel about a vegan candidate for president. I went on to finish medical school and earn a master's in public health, did a residency and fellowship, and became board certified in internal medicine and rheumatology. I saw patients in hospitals and in clinics, led NIH funded research, and taught medical ethics. The vast majority of my patients were on Medicaid or without insurance, and their health—and their ability to control it—was daily assaulted by poverty, unstable or unhealthy housing, discrimination, lack of safe places to walk and exercise, and food insecurity—what we now call the "social determinants of health." My inability to change their individual situations led me to leave clinical medicine and work at the Robert Wood Johnson Foundation, pursuing the mission of creating a culture of health.

My medical school offered an elective course in nutrition, taught by Marion Nestle—the only nutrition education of the entire four years, and optional. As part of the course, we had to keep a one-week food diary, and then calculate the percentages of our diets that came from carbohydrates, protein, and fats. I was convinced that my diet was healthy, what with my large quantities of homemade yogurt and my consumption of cheese rather than meat. I was stunned when my diet turned out to be over 60% fat. I then turned to Glen for some advice, which at that time was to increase vegetable, fruit, and whole grain consumption, and pull way back on the dairy-based fats.

Over the years, Glen and I kept in touch. He turned vegan, and we would occasionally dine together at vegan restaurants in N.Y.C. and Los Angeles. He kept asking me, the way he used to ask me "is this funny," if I had become vegan yet. He shared his books and his wife Joanna's recipes. But, although I had given up milk for plant-based alternatives once I figured out, after three years of daily morning abdominal pains, that the milk in my coffee and cereal was the culprit, I was still a big fan of cheese. When I went for my annual physicals and labs, my general internist kept on mentioning that my cholesterol was borderline high, with a non-desirable HDL/LDL ratio. I kept rationalizing that my health had to be good because I don't smoke, I don't have diabetes, I don't have a family history of cardiovascular disease, and I exercise. Finally, two years ago, the results were worse—and my internist suggested statins.

At that point, I could have had a long discussion with him about going on statins, and debated the risks of taking a drug that might give me abdominal distress, muscular pains, and other side effects. I could have called on any number of brilliant colleagues for their opinions. But I had a better option. I called Glen. He turned me (finally) not only into a vegan, but into a healthy, low-fat vegan. In three months, my cholesterol was down 25%, down into the normal range, and has continued to drop.

Do I mind that Glen, in the pages of *Own Your Health*, lambastes the medical profession? No; he's too often right, particularly about the overwhelming effect of culture and the assumption that to ask patients to make such a "radical" change in their diet would be asking too much of them. Medicine too often seeks a silver bullet—diet takes more work. Like Glen, I believe in prevention—whether it is primary prevention, such that you never develop the pathophysiology, or secondary prevention, meaning that you can decrease your risks or even return to a normal state by changing your diet once diagnosed. Ben Franklin had it right: "An ounce of prevention is worth a pound of cure."

Is *Own Your Health* funny? Yes, it is. But it's also provocative, timely, cogently argued, and a dose of medicine that my profession may well need. It could also save your life.

Pamela Williams-Russo, M.D., M.P.H.
Robert Wood Johnson Foundation

Chapter One:
What You Need To Know About What Doctors Don't Know

AUTHOR'S NOTE: Most of the text of *Own Your Health* was written before the current Covid-19 crisis ravaged populations and economies across the world, creating a public health emergency more profound and devastating than anything any of us has ever witnessed. This book has nothing to do with the Covid-19 crisis—and, in a way, it has everything to do with it.

Let's start with how it has *nothing* to do with it. The body of the text does not explore the nature of the virus or the nation's collective response to it. But I would be remiss not to say here that the medical community in America (and around the world) has met the challenge of the coronavirus with a selflessness, dedication, and heroism that inspires awe. Doctors, nurses, and allied healthcare professionals have risen to the occasion with extraordinary bravery, despite often being shamefully deprived of sufficient personal protective equipment by a negligent federal government that cannot seem to act with the focus, urgency, and moral clarity required to meet the moment. These health professionals work around the clock, in what is truly a wartime setting, risking their own lives to save the lives of others. Rightly, most of us feel the kind of reverence now for the medical community that we felt towards the first responders after the 9/11 tragedy in 2001. We salute them.

But, again, the pandemic is not the subject of this book. This book concerns the ongoing, if far less acute, public health crisis in America that revolves around such conditions as obesity, diabetes, hypertension, cardiovascular disease, and cancer. That crisis will still be with us, unfortunately, after the pandemic is, with the help of science, resolved. And in dealing with the ongoing health crisis that stems almost entirely from diet, the American medical community earns far lower marks, at least from me. It has quite simply failed, year after year, to stem the rising tide of chronic disease, ignoring clear and convincing scientific evidence of the way these conditions can and should be addressed.

Now allow me to mention how this book has *everything* to do with the Covid-19 crisis. First of all, we know that the novel coronavirus takes a far more deadly toll on those suffering from obesity, diabetes, hypertension, and cardiovascular disease than it does on those of us who are healthy. *Own Your Health* is all about how to take your health into your own hands and avoid obesity, Type 2 diabetes, hypertension, or cardiovascular disease. If America's population were healthier—if the medical community had risen to the challenge of meeting our ongoing health crisis with a fraction of the urgency and effectiveness it displays now, facing down the pandemic—the death toll from Covid-19 in America would be greatly reduced.

And then there is the very cause of the pandemic itself. Like other emerging infectious diseases—Ebola, HIV, H1N1, MERS, SARS and more—it came from animals. Raising animals for food is an inherently dangerous activity that risks pathogens jumping from animals to humans. There is no greater threat to the collective health of humanity than putting human beings—even a small number of human beings—in contact with unnaturally crowded populations of animals. Further, our prolific, indefensible use of antibiotics to fatten animals contributes to the emergence of antibiotic-resistant bugs.

If everyone around the world ate the diet this volume advocates, there would be no Covid-19 outbreak. Add that to the list of benefits of the low-fat, plant-based diet detailed throughout this book. -- GM

* * *

You may have read the boilerplate disclaimer on one of the front pages of this book: "It is recommended that you consult your physician before making any dietary changes." I wish I could also recommend that you ignore that advice, but when I suggested doing so, my lawyer threw a fit, and since he bills his fits in five-minute increments, I couldn't afford it. He also didn't go for my proposed alternative: "It is recommended that you consult your plumber before making any dietary changes."

Here's my thinking: doctors generally receive little in the way of nutritional education during their four years of med school—less than twenty hours, on average, over four years of medical education.[1] That's about five minutes a week, rarely integrated in any way with clinical practice. Twenty hours is less time than someone could spend reading, say, two or three weight-loss books. And I'll bet the average plumber has read at least three or four weight-loss books. So it really makes as much sense to ask your plumber for nutritional advice as it does to ask your doctor.

Consult with whomever you trust on the subject—just don't imagine that there's any sound reason to expect nutritional wisdom from your doctor.

Nor, I readily acknowledge, should there be any logical reason to expect me, of all people, to have anything remotely useful to say on the subject of health. I have no formal medical education. I never even *wanted* to be a doctor. Biology was my least favorite subject in school, and I'm squeamish around blood.

The subject of medical care always raised tensions within my immediate family. My mother readily put all her trust in doctors; my father couldn't stand them. As it turned out, with astounding luck, their respective biases played themselves out in such a way that they saved each other's lives.

My mother's moment of glory occurred when she and my father were in their mid-sixties. She announced to my father that she urgently needed to visit the dermatologist in order to have the varicose veins in her legs examined. My father undoubtedly sighed, probably argued a little, maybe feigned some admiration for the little purple tributaries animating her limbs, then reluctantly drove her to the dermatologist's office. He waited in the waiting room while my mother went in to see the skin doctor.

"What seems to be the problem, Dorothy?" the doctor asked.

"My husband," my mother said.

"What's the problem with your husband?" the doctor asked, confused.

"He's in the waiting room. Please bring him in here, I beg you."

The doctor complied. He stepped out into the waiting room, and politely escorted my father into his office.

"Look at that thing on his cheek!" my mother cried, blocking the door. "Don't let him run away!"

There was indeed a dark, irregular growth on my father's cheek about which he had repeatedly been dismissive. The doctor insisted that my father allow him to biopsy it. My father gave in, unhappily. He didn't like being tricked, and he didn't like wasting money. And did I mention that he wasn't fond of doctors?

It was melanoma. Surgery was scheduled, and the deadly cancer was successfully excised from my father's face, without leaving much of a scar. The cancer never returned. My father would live for another twenty-five years.

I went into Manhattan with my parents on the day of the surgery. When my father emerged from the hospital into the light of a bright autumn day, he embraced my mother right on the street. "Dotty," he said, "I'll remember every day for as long as I live that you saved my life. I'll never forget what you did." And he gave her a passionate kiss.

"Okay, not here," my mother said.

Cut to about four years later. By then, my parents had retired to a condo in Delray Beach, Florida, and, during one of my visits there, my mother must have said or done something—undoubtedly minor—that left my father peeved, and he raised his voice at her. It was just a typical, annoying little spat between spouses, but I couldn't stand the sound of it.

I tried to patch things up between them. "Pop," I said, "remember that day when you came out of the hospital in Manhattan and you kissed Mom on the street and you said you would remember every day for the rest of your life how she saved your life?"

My father stared hard at me for a long time, squinting.

"Doesn't ring a bell," he said.

But his own opportunity to return the favor would soon come. My mother had suffered since her early fifties from a heart condition—angina—and she had a new cardiologist in Florida, the son of a childhood friend of hers. The doctor performed an ultrasound, and declared that my mother had a severe, 90% blockage of one of her carotid arteries, and required an immediate, emergency angioplasty. There was no time to lose.

"Don't do it, Dotty!" my father said, right in front of the doctor. "He's just trying to make money."

"I resent that. I'm trying to do what's best for the patient!" the cardiologist protested.

"If you let him do it, I'll divorce you!" my father shouted. "Don't be a sucker! The man's going to kill you!"

At this point, the doctor was royally pissed off, and he turned his back on my father to plead directly with my mother. It was her decision to make, after all. "Who are you going to listen to, him or me? He's not a doctor! Your life could be at stake!"

My mother was in a tough spot. The doctor, after all, was the son of her beloved childhood friend; her husband, on the other hand, was the father of her now-and-then beloved children. The doctor clearly had more medical credibility. But she didn't have to live with him; she had to live with my father. Unless, of course, he would really divorce her over an angioplasty. It was hard to know if he was bluffing. Still, the doctor said her life could be at stake, and *he* definitely wasn't bluffing. My mother never liked to make tough decisions, and this one must have challenged her to the hilt. But she trusted her instincts and came up with her answer.

"I'm sorry, I don't want to get divorced," she told the doctor. "I couldn't handle it, emotionally. We just got new furniture."

And so she passed on the procedure. Instead of allowing a balloon to be inflated in her carotid artery and a small piece of metal mesh implanted there, she talked to me about how she should change her diet.

She was summarily fired by her doctor. Absolutely true. He refused to ever see her again. My father was delighted. He felt like he had won the lottery.

Now it's impossible to know for sure how things would have played out had my mother undergone that urgently recommended invasive procedure. But we do know with certainty how things played out for her *sans* angioplasty. She died two months shy of her ninety-ninth birthday (outliving my father by nine calendar years, and ten years of lifespan), having enjoyed relatively good health for most of the thirty years or so that she lived after refusing the angioplasty. Until she was ninety-five, she was ambulatory, fairly independent, and mentally active. She would read a novel or two a week. In her late nineties, some delirium and dementia kicked in, exacerbated by urinary tract infections related to a prolapsed bladder. The prolapsed bladder was the unfortunate consequence of childbirth (and for that I must, of course, blame my sister). My mother suffered no cardiovascular events until the stroke—at least we think it was a stroke—that eventually killed her.

Had she undergone that angioplasty in her late sixties and lived to be nearly ninety-nine, the cardiologist would surely be touting her as one of his greatest success stories. It would have been, I guarantee you, the signature accomplishment of his medical career.

But angioplasties have a spotty track record. About one percent[2,3] of patients die on the table, and once you go down that route, other interventions routinely follow. There's considerable danger of becoming a perpetual patient. At the time my mother declined the intervention, the risk of restenosis—the recurrence of the narrowing of the artery that brought about the angioplasty in the first place—was high, nearing fifty percent. (That risk has in subsequent decades been reduced, but only by the use of drugs that carry their own formidable risks.) Restenosis, and the even more catastrophic stent thrombosis (a blood clot developing at the site of the stent), remain serious risks even today, and can lead to repeat angioplasties or (for those with occluded coronary arteries) to coronary artery bypass surgery. Blood thinners become part of the daily survival regimen, making falls particularly hazardous. My mother must have fallen a dozen times in the last two decades of her life, but thankfully she wasn't on a combination of blood thinners, so the falls didn't do much damage.

Some may call it an exaggeration when I say that my father saved my mother's life by pressuring her, in his own less-than-woke way, to disobey her doctor, but I strongly doubt she would have lived for thirty more years had she begun subjecting herself to profoundly invasive medical interventions in her late sixties. And if my father hadn't resorted to his extreme gambit of confronting and alienating the stunned doctor, and turning the situation into a him-or-me choice, I doubt she would have refused the operation.

One of my parents' dear friends was felled, some years later, by an angiogram. Her aorta was nicked in the procedure, which had been undertaken to discover the extent of her heart condition. Her extraordinarily kind and decent husband, my father's closest friend, probably came to wish he had ranted and raved in the doctor's office the way my father had.

My mother always credited me with lengthening her life. That was simply because I told her what she should and shouldn't eat, and because, in her last decade of life, after I moved my parents to California so that I could take care of them, I often did their food shopping. She became, willy-nilly, a low-fat, whole-foods vegan. She outlived her five siblings and virtually all of her friends. In her mid-nineties, she would sometimes say to me, "Why am I still here?"

"Because I do your shopping," I would say.

I like to think that my parents left behind a health legacy: an object lesson in when to permit medical procedures and when to eschew them. When there are no real risks to a medical intervention that could improve or even save your life—and such is clearly the case with a sensible, indicated dermatological biopsy—then by all means do it, get the damned biopsy! When a medical procedure involves significant risks and there is an effective—perhaps even more effective—risk-free alternative, such as eating the way human beings are designed to eat, then run from the white coats and take your health into your own hands.

Some friends began asking me for my health advice over the years and, alarmingly enough, I often found that I was able to help them considerably more than their doctors could. Given the fact that their doctors were expensive and I was free, I guess folks felt that they had nothing to lose by hearing me out.

Take my friend Thomas Calabro, for example. As an actor, he is perhaps best known for playing an evil doctor on the show *Melrose Place*. (Let me make clear that I don't believe that most doctors are evil, but the doctor Thomas portrayed apparently was. I wasn't watching. Please don't tell Thomas. He thinks I loved the show.) Thomas, who is a very fit, athletic guy and a skilled practitioner of yoga, was troubled by his stubbornly high serum cholesterol count, over 200. There's a history of heart disease in his family, and his doctor strongly recommended that he start taking a statin to lower his cholesterol. So did his sister, who is also a doctor. Yet, before capitulating to the seemingly inevitable, he asked me to weigh in. I told him to try a vegan diet instead, and gave him instructions on how to do it.

A few months later he called me. "Glen, bud, I tried it, and it just didn't work for me. I've got lousy genes, man. I've been 100% vegan for three months, and I just had my cholesterol checked, and it's still 201."

"You're doing something wrong," I said. "I'll be right over."

When he let me in, I headed straight for the refrigerator, and opened it up. "What do you got in here? What the hell is this?" I picked up a plastic container of something called *Earth Balance*, a butter substitute.

"That's totally vegan! We use it to bake cookies now."

"Where's your garbage?" I said. "Did I tell you to eat fake butter?"

"No, but—"

"Where's your garbage?"

He showed me, and I threw out the *Earth Balance*.

"Hey, schmuck, can't you at least ask first?"

"I did. I asked where your garbage was."

"No, I mean—"

"And what the hell is this?"

"Vegan sour cream."

"Give me a break."

And so we rid his refrigerator and freezer of vegan junk foods, including the vegan ice creams, and then I asked him about the vegetable oils on his countertop.

"Mostly we use organic cold-pressed olive oil," he said. You could hear the defensiveness in his voice.

"Did I tell you to use organic cold-pressed olive oil?" I asked.

"No," he admitted.

"What did I tell you?"

"You said no oil," he mumbled, sheepishly.

"That's right, no oil. So give it another month. No oil, no fried foods, no junk food. No vegan cookies. Eat only real plant food for a month. Oatmeal for breakfast every day, with oat bran added and cinnamon and whatever fruit you want. Then check your cholesterol again."

A month later, Thomas sent an email. Not just to me, but to almost everyone he knew. He had eaten correctly for a month, and now he didn't need to go on medication. His serum cholesterol was 131. He no longer had to worry about the heart disease that plagued his family. He knew that he wasn't condemned by his "lousy genes" to a future spent fighting the side effects of pharmaceutical drugs. Fair to say he was ecstatic.

Now, you may ask, how come a know-nothing like me was able to do that for Thomas (who, I note with pride, has gone on to help many of his friends lower their cholesterol), but none of his doctors could do the same?

It's a good question. I'm at a loss for words to describe the extraordinary nutritional ignorance of the majority of medical professionals in this country.

Now don't get me wrong. Doctors sometimes save lives, as my mother proved to my father. If you get banged up in a car accident, American doctors will do a bang-up job of patching you up and repairing your injuries. If surgery is required, most often you will find yourself in able hands. If you have a malignant tumor growing somewhere in your body, America boasts, from shore to shore, an abundance of skilled surgeons to turn to, who are likely to provide you with your best shot at survival. If you are a pregnant woman, turning to medical professionals to monitor your pregnancy and assist in child-birth undoubtedly makes sense (although you'll want to steer clear of doctors who turn C-sections into the norm). And goodness knows, doctors are heroically saving the lives of many Covid-19 patients today, in the throes of a frightening pandemic.

But what if, like a significant majority of the adult American population, you suffer from a condition either wholly caused by, or aggravated by, your diet? What if you suffer, that is, from obesity, Type 2 diabetes, cardiovascular disease, high blood pressure, autoimmune disease, constipation, Crohn's disease, nonalcoholic fatty liver disease, or metabolic syndrome?

For these chronic conditions, unfortunately, most doctors can do nothing for you but put you on a pharmaceutical regimen that is likely to lead to a downward spiral in your health. Most doctors have little to offer but futile attempt after futile attempt to manage your symptoms. The overwhelming majority of doctors are useless in helping you overcome conditions brought on by the Western diet.

They are generally bright people. They are generally well-meaning. They are often brave. They generally do their best, often struggling against a medical bureaucracy of provider organizations and insurance companies that constrain both their time and their choices. Doctors certainly know a thousand times more than I do about anatomy, a thousand times more than I do about a range of diseases, a thousand times more than I do about the pharmaceutical drugs that have been developed to fight those diseases, and a thousand times more than I do about the side effects of those drugs. Naturally, they've also studied, as I have not, the best drugs to use to counteract those side effects, as well as the best drugs to use to counteract the side effects of the drugs used to counteract the side effects of the original drugs.

It's just that they have no clue how to help you stay healthy, or return to a state of health when you have eaten yourself into disease.

That's where I—like, I should add, an untold number of my brothers and sisters who have joined the whole-plant-foods movement that promotes the idea that human beings should eat human food, the food we were designed by nature to eat—seem to know a thousand times more than doctors do.

How do we know for sure what human food is? We'll get to the science later on in the book, but it all points in the direction of plants, and away from dead animals and the lactation of other mammals.

The best way to own your health is to create a diet centered around the bountiful world of whole plant foods, so that you don't get sick in the first place.

The truth is, medication is about as likely to "solve" an illness caused by the Western diet as it is to "solve" an illness caused by alcohol or drug use. Nobody expects a pill to cure alcohol abuse, but for some reason people expect pills to cure conditions that are caused by food abuse.

It's on the single pillar of diet, a subject on which the public is hopelessly confused, that doctors fail us right and left. And that's because they are as confused as the public. They flail about in a state of cognitive dissonance because they know that they're supposed to know this stuff—patients, after all, ask them what they should eat to address their conditions—and they also know that they were never really taught a damned thing about it. So they're left repeating nonsense that they may have heard on the morning news or talk radio, or nonsense gleaned from a misleading scientific study, and they advise their patients to choose "lean meats" and "skinless chicken," get "plenty of protein," eat "low-fat" dairy, and avoid "carbohydrates," and they make fools of themselves spouting pablum while dooming their patients to deterioration.

In her last decade of life, my mother had a very experienced doctor in her sixties, a wonderful, caring woman, and undoubtedly a woman of great intelligence, who monitored my mother's care and prescribed medications for her recurrent urinary tract infections and her fluctuating blood pressure. Aware of my background as an author, this same doctor once started a conversation with me about nutrition. It turned out that she thought that there was cholesterol in carrots. Really. I felt almost embarrassed in setting her straight. It was an awfully elementary error, and I found myself hoping she hadn't spent four decades of practice steering her patients with heart disease away from carrots.

Imagine how you would feel (assuming you are not a doctor) if a medical office, short of personnel one day, outfitted you with a doctor's robe and stethoscope and enlisted you to help them out by pretending to be a doctor and consulting with a few patients. And the first patient came in and right out of the gate asked you if her dosage of *Quinapril hydrochloride* should be adjusted because she'd been feeling dizzy.

You'd feel like the fraud you were, right? You wouldn't know what to say but you'd have to say something because of the outfit you were wearing and the patient's expectations. If you had any conscience at all, you'd of course regret having let anyone talk you into pretending to be a doctor.

That's how actual medical doctors must feel every time their patients ask them the sensible question of how they should modify their diet. They know no more about it than you know about *Quinapril hydrochloride.*

They'd be better off—and, more importantly, their patients would be better off—if they spoke the truth, and admitted that they don't really know anything about nutrition and aren't qualified to answer, and advised their patients to consider picking up a book. And there are indeed plenty of helpful books out there, books by the likes of Dr. Neal Barnard, Dr. Michael Greger, Dr. Caldwell B. Esselstyn, Jr., Dr. Dean Ornish, Dr. Garth Davis, Dr. Matthew Lederman, Dr. Alona Pulde, and Dr. John McDougall. See what those authors all have in common? They're all doctors—and unlike (probably) your doctor, they happen to know what they're talking about when it comes to nutrition. And, on the larger questions involving nutrition, they have all arrived, in deference to the medical and scientific evidence as well as their own clinical and/or research experience, at the same fundamental conclusion: eat plants; spurn flesh foods, dairy, and eggs; and do your utmost to avoid oil. They agree on those matters simply because they follow the evidence; they did not start their careers with the opinions they now hold. Not one of them was raised in a vegan household or in a community of animal rights activists. Their opinions on meat, dairy, and oil are shared, I would venture to say, by nearly all serious researchers who view the scientific evidence without cultural or financial bias. Unfortunately, probably a minority of researchers fit that description. The resulting confusion in the world of nutritional research has likely left your doctor as flummoxed on the subject as your plumber.

Your doctor isn't going to tell you to pick up a book, though. She or he is going to tell you to strive for a balanced diet, get plenty of protein, eat lean meats, favor white meat over red, eat sweets in moderation, go easy on the pasta, order the chicken salad in restaurants, don't drink too much soda pop, make sure to start the day with a healthy breakfast, monitor your salt intake, watch your carbs, limit coffee to two cups a day, don't go overboard with buttered popcorn, and try not to eat right before going to bed.

None of that is going to solve your problem.

All doctors are trained in the field of sickness. Few know anything about health. If you want to have your best shot at a long, healthy life, you're going to need to learn how to take your health into your own hands.

Once you do so, you may still choose, as I do, to see a doctor on occasion. I usually visit once a year for an annual physical, mainly just to say hi and see how my doctor is feeling. I get my bloodwork done and make sure that my "radical" health program of eating human food is still working.

So far, so good.

CHAPTER TWO:
MY STORY

As a child, I learned about the grandparents I never knew. My parents told me what they were like, and how they died. My mother's mother was an obese woman who died of a heart attack before I was born; my maternal grandfather also died of one before I was old enough to know or remember him. My father's mother died of cancer when my father was twelve (and she was about thirty-five); my grieving and embittered grandfather then apparently canceled my father's Bar Mitzvah and banned any mention of God in the house. My grandfather would perish about fifteen years later, in his mid-fifties, shortly after my parents married; he suffered fatal cardiac arrest when someone pulled a knife on him in a dispute over rent. I often wondered how the thug who wielded the knife reacted when he realized that he had killed a man without needing to actually use it. He may have learned the lesson that heart disease is a formidable weapon in itself. Or, you know, he may have just run.

Most of the men on my father's side of the family died in their mid-fifties of heart disease. Almost all of my father's many uncles were gone before I was born. His closest cousin died young of a heart attack when I was in college. The women on his side of the family (other than his mother) fared a little better, but not much. Nobody lived to a ripe old age.

My mother had two brothers. When I was sixteen, they both died of heart attacks. One was in his fifties; the other, his late forties.

That was when I started to think about becoming a vegetarian. It seemed clear to me that if I ate the way the people around me were eating, I'd be middle-aged at twenty-five.

Perhaps my family could have been diagnosed with a condition called "Familial Hypercholesterolemia"—high cholesterol running rampant in the family, a result (allegedly) of unfortunate genes. There's a website of something called the FH Foundation that explains, "Familial hypercholesterolemia (FH) is a common life-threatening genetic condition that causes high cholesterol. Untreated, FH leads to early heart attacks and heart disease."[1] The website also explains the intractable nature of this "genetic" condition, scoffing at the contribution of dietary cholesterol: "FH is inherited high cholesterol; it is not caused by eating too many burgers!"[2] Yet it also says, "Usually, your LDL-cholesterol levels and family medical history are enough for a clinical diagnosis of FH."

Now think about that: it's apparently a *genetic* condition, not a condition caused by diet, but the Foundation doesn't ask you to prove you have it by taking a genetic test; rather, you prove it with a cholesterol test and a family history. Since you can get a diagnosis of FH just from your LDL-cholesterol levels and family medical history, then most everyone in my family, including me, surely would have qualified. And how would the FH Foundation have known how many burgers we were eating, or how much better we might have fared if we gave them up? In short, what makes the FH Foundation so sure, in any given case, that diet isn't the problem?

I spoke with the "Community Relations Lead" of the FH Foundation[3] and asked her why the Foundation doesn't recommend a genetic test to confirm the condition that it contends is genetic and that it calls Familial Hypercholesterolemia. She told me that genetic testing is very complex and potentially inaccurate because there could be genetic variants and mutations that aren't yet discovered, so the best way to establish that one has the unfortunate condition is through family history and LDL readings. She told me that diet and lifestyle changes will generally have "only about a 10-15% impact on lowering your LDL cholesterol." (Of course, in my own experience, and in the experience of countless others who have embarked on a plant-based diet, that's simply not true.) She told me that people with FH have to take lipid-lowering medication because they are genetically predisposed to high cholesterol and they'll always have high cholesterol, regardless of their diet.

Established in 2011, the FH Foundation didn't exist when I was a teenager, so I didn't have the glorious opportunity to allow it to convince me that I was a victim of my own god-awful genes, and send me down the route of medical intervention. Instead, I looked for some light and hope. Surely there was a path to a long, healthy life that my relatives had missed. Instinctively, I knew that I could optimize my chances for longevity with diet.

I was a fan of the late, great comedian Dick Gregory, who advocated a vegetarian diet. Gregory had made several profound transitions in his life: from high school track star to obese stand-up comedian (at one point weighing 350 pounds) to a healthy vegetarian and political activist. I was in high school when he gave a talk in my hometown on Long Island and I got to see him in person. At the time, he was on a juice fast against the Vietnam War; he weighed less than a hundred pounds and was still jogging five miles a day. As I recall,[4] he had gone more than a year without eating solid food. What I remember vividly is that when America finally pulled its troops out of Vietnam, he held a press conference to announce the end of his fast. He was asked, "Mr. Gregory, would you fast again if America got involved in another Vietnam?" He replied, "I wouldn't fast again if they were fighting in my living room."

So, with Dick Gregory as my inspiration, I resolved to take the plunge into vegetarianism on the first day of summer vacation before my senior year (1973-74) in high school. I awoke that morning a newly minted vegetarian, and prepared for myself an English muffin with jam for breakfast. The phone rang; it was my buddy Dave.

I said, "Congratulate me, man, I've become a vegetarian."

Dave said, "Hey, that's great! Since when?"

I said, "Well, you know . . . since breakfast."

He laughed at me.

It was a stroke of luck that Dave laughed at me because I've now gone forty-seven years without eating dead animals since that English muffin breakfast. Which is not to say that I would have lapsed into meat consumption without Dave's help, but certainly the memory of his mocking laughter proved a great motivator over the years. There was no way I was going to let his derision go unpunished.

I should note, as an aside, that a mere twenty-seven years later, Dave himself became a vegetarian after seeing the movie *Chicken Run*. He was just morally outraged at the treatment of those claymation figures.

Fact check: actually, to be precise, after seeing *Chicken Run*, Dave initially became a *pescatarian*. For the next few years, he continued to eat the occasional fish. Until he saw *Finding Nemo*.

Back to 1973: the next person I informed of my newly established vegetarianism was my mother, and that's when I learned a curious fact about her pregnancy with me.

I said, "Mom, guess what? I'm a vegetarian."

Unlike Dave, she didn't congratulate me. Instead, in a challenging tone, she said, "*What took you so long to figure that out?*"

It was an odd reaction, to say the least, but my mother could sometimes be puzzling. I said, "Huh? What does that mean?"

She said, "I never told you, but when I was pregnant with you, I was determined to raise you as a vegetarian. Unfortunately, my doctor talked me out of it. He said you wouldn't grow up strong and your bones would be fragile. He said you wouldn't get enough protein and your brain would never develop fully. He scared me to the point that I gave up on the idea."

So that unknown doctor goes down in my book as the first one whose stupefying nutritional ignorance would prove a nuisance in my life. The son-of-a-bitch actually managed to harm me before I was born. Kudos, doc.

Still, the whole thing was odd. I said, "Wait a minute, Mom. You're not a vegetarian. Dad's not a vegetarian. Sheila (my older sister) isn't a vegetarian. Why in the world were you planning to raise me as a vegetarian?"

Her explanation came matter-of-factly. "Because, Glen, when I was pregnant with you, you felt like a vegetarian."

I had learned, when my mother said things like that, to just let them slide. "Okay, Mom," I said. "Now it's all coming into focus. But were you ever planning on informing me that I was destined to be a vegetarian?"

"I was waiting for you to figure it out," she said. "*What took you so long?*"

My father didn't react very strongly to the news bulletin that his son had gone vegetarian. My old man believed in moderation in all things. His favorite expression was, "Too much of anything is no good," a truism he'd repeat at least a dozen times a day. In any case, my newfound vegetarianism was fine by him. He said he'd heard positive things about the diet, and he thought it would prove a valuable experiment for me, as long as I ate meat once in a while.

By contrast, an obese aunt and uncle were immediately thunderstruck by the news. "Where will you get your protein?" they fretted. They were visibly distressed, alarmed that I wouldn't survive my drastic dietary gambit. It was my first experience with a feeling of wonderment that would recur often for years to come. "*You're* worried about *me?*" I was thinking. "*Look at yourselves!*"

But, of course, you can't say that.

Even today, close to half a century later, America remains a nation of fat, sick people sworn to the supremacy of protein. They are nothing if not loyal to a macronutrient they wouldn't recognize if it took human form and slapped them upside the head.

"I'll get my protein from cheese," I reassured my quivering aunt and uncle. It seemed like a good, sound answer, and it was one that I would use for years to come to ward off the skeptics—and, yes, stupidly, to comfort myself that I hadn't taken any extreme risk with my health.

And so, for the next nearly two decades, while I rigorously abstained from red meat, fowl, fish, eggs, milk, and butter, I made sure to eat cheese of all kinds. Cream cheese, cheddar cheese, and brie were favorites, and of course mozzarella on pizza.

And then, in my mid-thirties, something started to go wrong, I suspect (admittedly without proof), with my heart, or the arteries surrounding it. Over a period of months, on at least a dozen occasions, and with increasing frequency, I experienced what I can only describe as an electric shock in the vicinity of my heart. Each time, it was powerful and frightening, and each time it was over as soon as it came. I didn't know (and still don't know) what it was, but I knew I was scared—scared that my vegetarian diet hadn't protected me from my damned genes.

It was clear what one of my options was—the one that I suspect most people in my boat would have chosen. I could try to find out what was happening to me by scheduling an appointment with a cardiologist, who would run tests to diagnose my issue by measuring exactly how clogged my arteries were, or whether I had some rhythmic malfunction of the heart. But I am my father's son. I have an instinct to run away from, rather than toward, medical professionals. What can I say? It's a gift.

Or I could try to figure out for myself what was causing my problem, without necessarily needing to know the extent of the damage. And I didn't have to think too hard to come up with the answer. I'd been eating cheese all my life, and determinedly for the prior two decades, initially to satisfy the protein concerns of my obese aunt and uncle (and then of so many others who would echo their concerns), even though I knew that dairy protein came attached to mountains of saturated fat and cholesterol—the very same substances I was trying to protect myself from by abstaining from meat. Cheese truly is "liquid meat." It was as if, from my body's point of view, I wasn't really abstaining from meat at all, just eating it in a form that could melt or be served on a cracker. And so, after experiencing a dozen lightning bolts around my heart in my mid-thirties, I took control of my own health: I gave up cheese and became a vegan in 1992.

I still don't know what those "electric shocks" were. I can't even say for sure if they were truly an indicator of cardiovascular disease. I'll never know, and I don't need to. I just know they never happened again, once I gave up cheese. It would seem unlikely that that's a coincidence.

I've never regretted for a moment giving up meat, but continuing to eat cheese for nineteen years after doing so was the single worst mistake I ever made. And eliminating cheese, however belatedly, was the single most crucial and beneficial dietary decision I ever made. Had I not made it, I might not be alive today. I would quite possibly have fallen victim to heart disease in my forties or fifties, and people would have teared up at my funeral and said it was my rotten genes, and proof that even a vegetarian diet cannot overcome them. Well, I'd like to think they would have teared up. Anyway, whether they teared up or not, the main point is that they would have blamed it on my genes.

But my genes are actually fine. It's the dairy that would have killed me, not my genes. And, to be perfectly fair, even if nobody teared up, some people might have felt sad. At least a few people. A little sad, anyway. Keep in mind that I owed some people money.

If you're wondering where I get my protein today, here's the answer that I wish I'd been informed enough to give my aunt and uncle back in 1973: *from food*. Protein, you see, is found in virtually all types of food. It's even in fruit, although most fruits are comparatively low in protein. I say *comparatively* because protein is found in abundance in every other type of human food: vegetables, fungi (mushrooms), grains, nuts, seeds, and, especially, legumes. There is also, of course, a serious and potentially harmful *excess* of protein in the non-human foods that people make the mistake of eating: meat, eggs, and dairy. The idea that protein is difficult to obtain and required in great quantity is utter nonsense on both counts.

Protein deficiency has a name: *kwashiorkor*. It is in fact a serious condition that affects millions of malnourished people around the world. You've undoubtedly seen pictures of starving children in Africa with distended abdomens. They suffer from kwashiorkor. They don't get enough protein because they don't get enough food. As long as you take in enough calories, and those calories come from actual food—not, say, lollipops—protein deficiency is the last thing you need to worry about. If you live in America, and have never traveled to famine-stricken parts of the globe, I'll bet you've never encountered anyone suffering from kwashiorkor. I would estimate that the number of Americans who are not malnourished and yet suffer from a protein deficiency is zero or very close to it. A fruitarian who makes a point of not eating nuts and seeds might be at some risk. A fruitarian who eats nuts and seeds would not have a protein problem (though it's not a diet I'd recommend). A vegan who eats anything resembling a normal amount of healthy food is at no risk at all, and it is an ignorant slander to suggest otherwise.

Do you know anyone who ever died of a stroke or a heart attack, or was hospitalized for one? I'll bet you do. Do you know anyone who was ever hospitalized for a protein deficiency? I'll bet you don't. And yet people worry about getting enough protein, and not about the protein-rich foods (meat, dairy, and eggs) that send them to the hospital or the grave with strokes and heart attacks.

If you have clean air to breathe, you don't worry about where you'll get your oxygen. Similarly, if you have enough food, you don't need to worry about where you'll get your protein. It's a total non-issue, so naturally it's what the media and medical professionals concentrate on.

Nobody needs protein more than an infant. As a consequence, mother's milk has been designed by nature to contain ample amounts of protein. Still, breast milk contains about five times as many calories from carbohydrate as from protein[5]; all in all, about seven or eight percent of the calories in mother's milk come from protein. So if an infant doesn't require a higher percentage of calories as protein than that, surely an adult can get by with that percentage or less.

I stopped concerning myself with protein when I turned vegan, and haven't looked back. I couldn't tell you how many grams of protein I eat per day, except I know that it's more than enough, since I eat plenty of food, and legumes almost daily.

A few years after turning vegan, I was introduced to Howard Lyman, an icon of the vegan cause, at a restaurant in Santa Monica by a mutual friend named Marr. Howard's life story has a wonderful arc: he was a fourth generation Montana cattle rancher turned vegan and animal rights activist. Marr pitched to me the idea of writing a screenplay based on Howard's life.

Although I was sorely tempted to say yes, I was constrained by my understanding of dramatic structure. I said, "Howard, I hope someone can make a film based on your life because I'd love to see it. But I don't know how to write it, because, you see, in the third act climax . . . when you order the stir-fried vegetables . . . I'm sorry, I don't know how to make that work."

There was a silence at the table, and then Marr said, "How about a book?"

That made more sense to me. A work of non-fiction doesn't require a third act climax. I said I could try, and Howard and I went on to collaborate on *Mad Cowboy*.[6] In *Mad Cowboy*, we predicted that mad cow disease would come to America, and when it did, we followed the book up with what I like to call our I-told-you-so book, *No More Bull!*

Writing those two books with Howard was a professional highlight of mine, and working with him brought me into contact with many of the leaders of the plant-based food movement. Some are animal rights activists; some are environmentalists; many are doctors and nutritionists. That's because the diet that's right for our bodies turns out to also be right for the environment and the animals. Getting to know these good people reinforced my will to advocate the dietary path that I had initially chosen on instinct, merely to save my own life.

I did not know, when I was seventeen, that the stakes were as high for the planet that we all go plant-based as they were for me that I do so for my own health. And there are those who would argue that the planet is even more important than I am. (Out of a sense of fairness, I'll recuse myself from that debate, though naturally I have strong opinions on the matter.)

When I decided at seventeen to abstain from meat-eating, I never considered for a moment the possibility that my resolve would ever lapse. The thought honestly never crossed my mind—not then, not since. The truth is, there was really no way such a lapse could happen, whether Dave laughed at me or not. While I had turned to vegetarianism for health reasons, the whole idea of eating dead animals had begun to upset me, and it upsets me still. To anyone who will listen, I would offer this advice: think about what's involved in the cruelest of human professions, the raising of animals for slaughter—think about the horrid circumstances of the animals' confined lives, their grisly factory-automated deaths and dismemberments, the soul-destroying work that humans are put through in managing the whole mess in the slaughterhouses—and then decide simply not to be a party to it.

Raising bovines for their lactation is not any prettier; it is among the most bizarre and inexplicable of all human endeavors—right up there with the running of the bulls in Pamplona, but leading to far more death and destruction—and it is part and parcel of the raising of bovines for slaughter. It's all the same inhumane industry, and that industry (animal agriculture) contributes more than any other to global warming—according to a report by the U.N.'s FAO, more than all forms of transportation combined.[8] In a rival report produced by *The Worldwatch Institute*, the U.N.'s FAO report was famously disputed—not for overstating the risk from animal agriculture, but for understating it. The *Worldwatch* report instead pegged the contribution of animal agriculture to greenhouse gases at an extraordinary 51%—more than all other sources of greenhouse gases combined.[9] The *Worldwatch* study factored in livestock respiration, as would seem logical; the FAO scientists had apparently chosen instead to assume that all livestock are holding their breath, hoping not to be sent to the slaughterhouse.

The cattle industry warms the planet while serving no other purpose than destroying human health. The notion that there could be a health benefit to humans in drinking the lactation of bovines defies common sense. It's ludicrous on its face. I know that we've been sold the idea that milk is nutritious, but we should know better than to believe the inane notion that a substance designed by nature for bovine calves could be healthy for humans. It's patently absurd to drink cow growth hormones, unless for some reason you want to grow to be the size of a cow. Similarly, you wouldn't drink rat milk, even if it would be more likely to make you petite. So, again, make the decision to not be a party to that cruel and destructive industry. Make the decision, act upon it in that instant, and take pride and delight in joining the side of the angels.

It is in the nature of decisions, especially any decision as sensible as the decision to forego food that harms us, harms the planet on which we live, and degrades our humanity, to simply not be subject to reversal. Never look back from the wise determination to renounce animal foods. Go into it with the same certainty I possessed at the age of seventeen. Wherever my certainty came from, it has proved a blessing.

As I write these words, I am sixty-three years old. My invocation of the year of my transition to vegetarianism, 1973, would have the same echoes to a college student today that any invocation of the year 1927, when Babe Ruth hit sixty home runs, would have had to me when I entered college. Which is to say, it would seem unimaginably distant, legendary, barely believable as real. But I remember 1973 keenly. I remember it like I remember last week. The decision I first enacted on the hallowed morning of the English muffin would change my life and give me my only true shot at longevity. I was as alive then as I am now, as conscious, as committed to health, as dismissive of societal norms that wither in the light of reason. And my instincts in 1973 were absolutely right. I just didn't go far enough.

I exist now in the netherworld between middle-aged and old. With the exception of the occasional antibiotic, taken sometimes with good reason and sometimes perhaps unnecessarily, I have never in my life taken or needed any drugs. My blood pressure is consistently excellent. My serum cholesterol, despite a bad case of what would easily pass for Familial Hypercholesterolemia, last clocked in at 163. I weigh 148 pounds (I am five-foot eight), the same as I weighed in my twenties. I have enjoyed excellent health virtually all my life.

By now, I have had friends, roughly my age, survive, and not survive, heart attacks and strokes. I have had friends undergo emergency open-heart surgeries. I have had friends schedule angioplasties like dental check-ups and speak of the wire mesh in their arteries as a natural part of the normal process of aging.

It isn't.

There is nothing natural about what has become normal.

I propose to everyone reading these words the same commitment I made as a teenager in 1973.

Just make sure, when you give up meat, to give up dairy and all other animal foods at the same time.

And welcome to the side of the angels.

CHAPTER THREE:
CARBS VS. ROADKILL

Jane E. Brody has been the Personal Health columnist for the *N.Y. Times* since 1976. That's quite a run. Surely you can't hold that position on the *newspaper of record* for that many decades without knowing, for example, what a carbohydrate is.

In the fall of 2017, Ms. Brody wrote a piece for the *Times* called "Unlocking the Secrets of the Microbiome";[1] it's a helpful overview of the role of the human microbiome in the causation, and potentially the cure, of a wide range of diseases. She makes the point that, "A diet more heavily based on plants—that is, fruits and vegetables—may result in a microbiome containing a wider range of healthful organisms." Then, in her final paragraph, she concludes, ". . . people interested in fostering a health-promoting array of gut microorganisms should consider shifting from a diet heavily based on meats, carbohydrates and processed foods to one that emphasizes plants."

So, with gut health in mind, she seems to be advising people to eat a diet centered on plants, while shifting away from (among other things) carbohydrates.

That's like advising the public to take vacations centered on cruises, while shifting away from boats.

Surely apples are a fruit that Ms. Brody, like everyone else, would recommend. Every apple contains a healthy complement of three or four grams of fiber. By weight, apples are about 86% water; it's always a good idea to eat foods that help keep you hydrated. (Plant foods best animal foods by a country mile on this score.) As for the caloric content of apples, they are about 2% protein, 2% fat, and 96% carbohydrate.

Whoops! 96% carbohydrate! Are apples the kind of "carbohydrate" that Jane Brody suggests we shift away from?

A cup of strawberries has about 49 calories. 45 of them are carbohydrate. Should we avoid strawberries, too, in our campaign against carbohydrate? Peaches, plums, pears, cherries, grapes, kiwis, and papaya are all between 90-96% carbohydrate. The same is true for virtually all fruit except the rare fatty fruit (avocado, coconut, olive).

So what in the world does Jane Brody mean when she suggests that we shift away from carbohydrates while emphasizing plant foods?

It addles the brain to attempt to interpret a statement so clearly preposterous and self-contradictory, but I'm going to hazard a guess. Although she should know better, I'm guessing Brody was using the term "carbohydrates" to mean "foods made from flour." That would align with her caution concerning processed foods. Foods made from flour—pasta, bread, muffins, bagels, pancakes, waffles, cake, cupcakes—are commonly disparaged and lumped together as "carbs." They are all, to one degree or another, processed foods, although a whole grain bread will generally be a lot less "processed" than a cake. Flours are broken grains, and grains that have been pounded into flour will all contain some measure of carbohydrate, protein, and fat, although the preponderance of their calories, as with most plant foods, will come from carbohydrate. As a general rule, cakes, cupcakes, muffins, and waffles can be counted upon to contain a lot of fat, usually in the form of oil, but sometimes in the form of butter or margarine or milk or eggs. That fat content is what, along with sugar, makes these foods unhealthy; their carbohydrate content derives in the main from one type of flour or another (and some flours, like white flour, are going to be more refined and therefore more problematic than others) and often from sugar or some other sweetener. The sweeteners, especially sugar (white or brown), can be addictive, and can do a lot of damage to your health, and certainly represent one reason that "carbs" have a bad reputation.

A chocolate croissant, for example, would be unhealthy because of the following ingredients it would likely contain: butter, eggs, milk, sugar, and cocoa butter. The butter, eggs, and milk are of course all animal ingredients high in saturated fat and cholesterol; the refined sugar is deleterious to everything from your teeth to your heart; and the cocoa butter in the chocolate adds significantly to the saturated fat content of the treat. The croissant would also contain refined flour, but the flour would be the least of the insults to one's health. It's not hard to imagine a person who ate even one chocolate croissant per day putting on weight, and then saying, "I've been eating too many croissants; I've got to cut out the carbs." But most of the calories in the croissant would be coming from eggs, milk, butter, and cocoa butter—in other words, from the fat. It would be more logical, though still inaccurate, to call a chocolate croissant a "fat" rather than a "carb."

In the interest of clarity, let us stipulate that bread, cakes, cupcakes, muffins, pancakes, pastas, and waffles are not "carbs"; they are processed foods that contain a mix of ingredients varying in their content of carbohydrate, protein, and fat. Treats like cakes and cupcakes may contain more calories from fat than from carbohydrate. Some breads and pastas may be surprisingly high in protein. So if Jane E. Brody, or anyone else, wants to suggest that people avoid flour-based foods, that's fine with me. Flour-based foods are certainly not among the most nutritionally dense foods you can eat, but they are calorically dense, and even the least objectionable products made with flour are by no means indispensable to good health, although I choose to eat some whole grain breads as well as some gluten-free pastas made from flours derived from such ingredients as lentils, buckwheat, and mung beans.

Let's just cut out the nonsense of labeling processed foods that are by no means pure carbohydrate—not even close to it—"carbs," and then using that linguistic trope to disparage the macronutrient that is the natural, primary fuel of the human body, and that no diet that is not biochemically insane can hope to avoid: carbohydrate. Carbohydrate is the predominant (but of course never the sole) macronutrient in virtually every food that is universally touted for its health benefits, from cauliflower to beans to berries to onions to mushrooms.

Until we stop hearing this foolish term "carbs" bandied about in the media, I suggest that those of us who eat a diet composed of human food—a low-fat, plant-based diet—employ our own term of choice concerning all flesh foods, and the term I would suggest is "roadkill." Doing so will be a lot more justifiable and reasonable than labeling cakes "carbs" and then, with absurd logic, advising people to shun carbohydrates.

Consider a dead squirrel in the middle of the road, freshly run over by a car. We would all agree to call that poor rodent "roadkill." Yet not even the biggest meat-eaters among us would ever consider eating it.

Frankly, I don't see why not.

First of all, there is no science at all to suggest that squirrel meat is any worse for you than the flesh foods from animals commonly eaten: cows, pigs, sheep, turkeys, chickens, or fish. The selection of animals people eat is not determined by science; it is determined by economics: these are the animals easiest to husband (or catch, in the case of fish) and slaughter for profit. Some people do eat squirrels, and they're even served in restaurants in England, where controlling the grey squirrel population is a matter of public concern. You probably won't find squirrels served in any restaurants stateside, as wild "game" cannot be served in restaurants unless it's been inspected by the USDA's Food Safety and Inspection Service, though that seems a little unfair considering the mere second (or even one-third of a second) that the same agency allots to its inspectors to inspect each chicken for pathogens.[2]

A newly-run-over squirrel is sure to be cleaner than most chickens you can find packaged under cellophane in a grocery store or served in a restaurant.[3] Factory-farmed chickens (i.e., almost all chickens that Americans eat), pumped full of antibiotics, live out their short lives in hellish warehouses that may house as many as twenty thousand of the birds. They spend those lives breathing air poisoned by ammonia-laced excretory fumes. Chicken excrement is everywhere, including, naturally, on the chickens themselves. Unsurprisingly, in these unnatural conditions, salmonella and other pathogens run rampant.

The Food Safety and Inspection Service has set for itself an extraordinarily low bar for chicken "safety": they consider it acceptable if no more than 15.4% of the chicken parts (wings, for example) that they sample at the end of a slaughterhouse's kill line are infected with salmonella.[4] How in the world did they come up with the figure *15.4%*? Well, I suspect they gave some serious thought to the prospect of *15.5%* of chicken consumers becoming violently ill, and decided that would be a wee bit too much. Still, in the slaughterhouses they oversee, they regularly fail to meet their own lax standard.

Wouldn't a *free-range* squirrel, freshly crushed by a Goodyear tire, be more appetizing, and less likely to make you sick, than the strips of salmonella-tainted factory-raised chicken you may find in your chicken salad in even an upscale restaurant? It simply makes sense that roadkill would be, at least in terms of cleanliness, a step up from the spoils of factory farming. That may be why the state of Montana has considered the harvesting of roadkill for food.[5]

Of course, one would have to be careful not to eat squirrel brains or any squirrel spinal fluid, as it could contain the prion associated with Creutzfeldt-Jakob disease (CJD—essentially mad cow disease in humans), but after all, it would be equally wise to avoid eating any animal's brain tissue and spinal fluid, which could easily be sent flying in a slaughterhouse.

Admittedly, the health quotient of the roadkill would depend in large part on how long it was dead in the road before you found it. But do you know how long ago a fish was caught before you spotted it in a deli counter at the supermarket? Not only do you not know that relevant fact, but you don't even know what kind of fish you may be buying: a study found that forty-three percent of fish in New York City supermarkets was falsely labeled.[6]

So if you happened upon a squirrel freshly crushed by a Toyota, then surely, for health reasons alone, you should prefer eating that to a chicken raised in fetid conditions on a factory farm, or a fish of dubious identity that may have been caught weeks ago.

That's why I say it's hardly unfair—it's probably even too kind—to label all flesh foods "roadkill." Most of the flesh foods people eat are, after all, filthier than fresh roadkill, and come from animals that were sicker while alive. Like dead animals on the highway, they're simply animal carcasses, but it seems only proper and right to call them all "roadkill," since "carcass" might sound unappetizing.

So to those omnivores who are critics of the low-fat, vegan diet, please stop saying that we eat too many "carbs." We don't eat carbs; we eat plants. Fruits and vegetables and grains and legumes and nuts and seeds. All of which contain protein and fat and fiber and water, in addition to carbohydrate. Fruits and vegetables and grains and legumes and nuts and seeds are not "carbs"; they are human food.

To Jane Brody and so many others in the media who blather on illogically about "carbs," I've got to confess, I've often wondered what the hell your problem is.

But now maybe I've got a handle on it.

It could be that you've been eating too much roadkill.

Chapter Four:
Gary, Meet Steve

Perhaps the most prominent ideological opponent of veganism whom those of us who dine on the side of the angels had no choice but to tolerate for many years was the late Anthony Bourdain, who tragically took his own life in June of 2018. The man was a conundrum: highly intelligent and literate, he could be charming; he seemed to have a healthy curiosity about people, to enjoy his friends, and to celebrate culture; he was politically progressive in many respects, a kind of anti-racist populist; and yet his animus toward vegetarians and vegans knew no bounds. He was positively fixated on attacking us, regularly deriding vegans in particular. In the book that brought him to prominence, *Kitchen Confidential,* he famously wrote, "Vegetarians, and their Hezobollah-like splinter-faction, the vegans, are a persistent irritant to any chef worth a damn. . . . Vegetarians are the enemy of everything good and decent in the human spirit . . ."[1]

Now it's hard to think of anything more Orwellian than comparing the gentlest of people, who object to the unnecessary killing of animals for food, and to the torturous conditions generally endured by those animals for their entire lives, to haters who wantonly commit mass murder. But Bourdain attacked us repeatedly, in a way that seemed almost unhinged. He also sometimes turned his television show, which at its best could be thoughtful and civilized and engaging, into a sick snuff show of animal sacrifice: on air, he might be seen literally wringing the neck of a chicken or slitting the throat of a pig. He celebrated the killing of animals because he believed that their sacrifice to fill our stomachs was a sacred and necessary part of the circle of life.

That would of course be true if we were carnivores.

We are not. Anatomically and physiologically, as we shall see in Chapter Seven, we're not even omnivores; we're herbivores.

No animals have to die for vegans to live, and that reality generated cognitive dissonance in a man famous for eating such delicacies as bushmeat, warthog rectum, fetal duck eggs, maggot fried rice, bull testicles, bunny heads, fermented shark, seal eye, and the live heart of a cobra. The man would eat anything that moved, and so it's likely that he hated to confront—as the vegan presence compelled him to do— the possibility that his culinary philosophy was wrongheaded from the word go. Bourdain did not shrink from the central fact embedded in the act of eating animals: the brutality required to kill them first. By personally killing animals and then cooking and eating them, he could feel superior to the masses who acquire their meats prepared for them and wrapped in cellophane, allowing them to willfully overlook the source of their food. But it was harder for him to feel superior to people who do not need to sacrifice animals at all in order to thrive. And so the peculiar jaundice and vitriol he exhibited toward vegans may have been the price he paid, and we paid, for him to justify his life's work.

To my knowledge, nobody at CNN, the network that aired his show, objected to his persistent attacks on vegans. We may be only three percent of the American population, but we are not, apparently, a protected minority.

I was less surprised than most by his suicide because he always seemed to me to be a man who was not well—a man who embraced death, or at least had no healthy dread of it. No one who compares vegans to terrorists and revels in killing animals should be considered mentally stable.

Many iffy speculations have been bandied about in the press for a suicide that appeared so counterintuitive. Bourdain, after all, seemed to have everything in life that one could ask for: celebrity, wealth, accomplishment, a creative life spent doing exactly what he loved to do, and a young daughter he surely loved. He had long ago kicked a drug habit; there was no evidence that it had returned to haunt him.

Allow me, then, to add another iffy speculation to the list. We know that flesh consumption leads to inflammation,[2] and the man ate all manner of flesh. We also know that inflammation brought on by diet is not contained: it can affect all the tissues of the body, including the brain. And we know that brain inflammation can bring on depression.[3]

It seems to me altogether possible, therefore, that the man who derided vegans wound up a tortured victim of his own meat consumption.

It's just a theory; it may well be off-base. If you disagree with me, fine. But *you* try eating warthog rectum and see what it does to *your* mood.

In any case, with Bourdain gone, we vegans may have lost our harshest critic, but not our last. Perhaps our most prominent nutritional adversary today is one whose tone (though not his diet) is less inflammatory: the journalist and author Gary Taubes, a big critic not only of the low-fat, plant-based diet but also of mainstream nutritional science, and a big fan of beef and lard and all manner of fatty animal foods.

Taubes is a kind of only-in-America story. He received his bachelor's degree from Harvard, where he studied physics. He then became a science journalist and turned his attention to nutrition. Although he has a background in science, he has no academic credentials in medicine or nutrition, and so—credit where credit is due—he appears to be an amateur like me. Nonetheless, unlike me, he came to national attention as a widely respected nutrition expert thanks to a cover story he published in the New York Times Magazine in July, 2002, entitled, "What if It's All Been a Big Fat Lie?"[4]

The premise of the piece was that the American medical establishment had been urging Americans to eat "less fat and more carbohydrates," which was exactly the opposite of what we should have been eating. We should have instead been following the advice of the (now) late Dr. Robert Atkins to eat "steak, eggs and butter to our heart's desire." Taubes argued that the obesity epidemic developed during decades in which Americans were subject to "the rise of the low-fat dogma," and that the percentage of fat in the American diet had been decreasing while obesity had been increasing.

It's probably fair to say that the article, which caused a sensation, catapulted Taubes, at the time, to second place in America among the advocates of eating fatty animal foods, behind only the obese Dr. Atkins, whose work he touted in the article. The timing proved auspicious for Taubes, as within a year, Atkins, who suffered from heart disease and hypertension that he persistently denied was diet-related, would perish (allegedly from injuries sustained after slipping on ice; his widow refused to permit an autopsy that might well have pointed inconveniently to a stroke), leaving Taubes to reign, as it were, as the King of Fat ever since.

Spearheading a war on carbohydrate, contending that carbohydrate is the source of obesity and so many of our health problems, places one in a strange and, I would think, intellectually uncomfortable position. It is effectively an attack on the natural fuel of the human body; our brains run on glucose, after all. So it's possible to make the case that the argument, if sincerely believed and acted upon, is a kind of self-reinforcing foolishness.

Carbohydrate, let's not forget, is simply the bonding of carbon, the stuff of life, with water, the stuff of life. What exactly is there to hate?

Taubes appears to believe that one can essentially eat as much fat as one likes—ample servings of pork chops and beef and lard (which he seems to favor over butter)—without consequence to one's waistline or health. In his universe, it's as if calories from fat just disappear into the ether. All calories from carbohydrate, by contrast, as he explains in his book, *Why We Get Fat*,[5] somehow drive fat into the cells, and since plant foods, with few exceptions, are high in carbohydrate, that means that Gary Taubes has a problem with, for example, apples. He has a problem with virtually all fruit, and he's not terribly high on many vegetables, and he cautions against whole grains, and he's even skeptical of beans. He seems to be okay with green leafy vegetables, and that's about all the "carbohydrates" that he can stomach. He recommends a diet composed mostly of animal foods.

A delightful 2018 article, entitled "The Struggles of a $40 Million Nutrition Science Crusade," published in *Wired Magazine*,[6] tells the amusing story of Taubes' highly expensive failed attempts to do the impossible: to scientifically vindicate fat from its indictment as the cause of fatness.

Back in 2012, Taubes launched his non-profit *Nutrition Science Initiative*, dedicated to research explicating the true cause of obesity. (Hint: it wasn't likely to turn out to be meat or dairy or anything else fatty.) The ostensible purpose was to dramatically reduce (by more than half, no less) the rates of obesity and diabetes in this country by 2025, by accurately revealing their cause. (Perhaps a hitherto unknown, secret cause?) A foundation set up by a fabulously wealthy former Enron energy trader named John Arnold apparently committed to putting some $40 million into the non-profit's coffers to help it achieve its ambitious goal of contradicting all established nutritional science on the subjects of obesity and diabetes. It appears, however, to have come up some $11 million short[7]—perhaps deciding to pull the plug after the first $29 million turned up no good news about fat, diminishing the *Nutrition Science Initiative's* appeal as a good use for all that not-very-hard-earned money.

According to the article in *Wired*, Taubes and his colleagues at the *Nutrition Science Initiative* hired professional researchers, and worked with them on their research study design—then, predictably, found themselves frustrated with the results, and blamed the study design. So, tens of millions of dollars later, they have not proven that excessive fat doesn't make you fat and sick, and of course they haven't had any effect on the skyrocketing rates of obesity and diabetes in America. On the positive side, their operation is now skeletal, so at least they've cut the fat in their budget.

It's strange that Taubes' 2002 *Times Magazine* cover story made such a splash and brought its author so much prominence, because its case is so thin and frankly silly. It's premised on the kind of vague, imprecise use of the term "carbohydrate" that Jane E. Brody might approve of, but that the rest of us should know better than to take seriously. Taubes argues that the rise in obesity in the United States is the unfortunate consequence of American consumers, whom he implicitly believes are scrupulously attentive and health-oriented, heeding the terrible advice of the medical establishment to discourage fat consumption and to instead encourage carbohydrate consumption.

Really. That's the argument that caused a sensation. I'm not making this up; you can find the article on the web. Others in the Taubes camp have made a similar case. Dr. Dean Ornish responds to those arguments in Michal Siewerski's admirable documentary, *Diet Fiction*, this way: "We may have been told to eat less fat, but every decade since 1950, we've been eating more fat, more sugar, more calories and more meat—and a lot more. So, not surprisingly, we're fatter . . ."[8]

Did Taubes really believe in 2002—and does he believe now—that Americans have, *en masse*, been heeding the advice of advocates of a low-fat, plant-based diet like Dr. Neal Barnard and Dr. Caldwell B. Esselstyn, Jr.? The CDC estimates the mean fat intake for Americans today at over one-third of calories; that is hardly a low-fat diet! Beyond what has become, for me, an instinctive caution when I eat fatty plant foods, I don't pay any real attention to the percentage of fat in my own diet—I just eat fruits, vegetables, whole grains, legumes, nuts, and seeds, and let the macronutrients fend for themselves—but if I try to analyze it, I find that my fat intake comes to about ten to fifteen percent of my total caloric intake. A low-fat diet by definition needs to be in that vicinity, and never in my lifetime has the American diet come anywhere close to it. The average American is probably eating about three times the fat that the human body can healthfully accommodate.

The Pew Research Center has analyzed how the American diet has changed between 1970 and 2010, as the obesity and diabetes epidemics have mushroomed.[9] The findings? Our overall average daily caloric intake has increased by a whopping twenty-three percent, going up from 2025 average daily calories to 2481. Now if you do the math, given that there are nine calories in a gram of fat and four calories in a gram of carbohydrate, it would be pretty close to impossible to increase total caloric intake by twenty-three percent while at the same time switching (as Taubes alleges we have) from highly caloric fats to less caloric carbohydrates. The truth is, forty years later, we're getting the same minimal amount of calories from vegetables—about 100; the same minimal amount of calories from fruit—less than 100; the same minimal amount of calories from legumes—well below 100; the same significant amount of calories from flesh foods—about 400; with the biggest increases coming from fats and oils, and the second biggest increase coming from grain products—but keep in mind that those "grain products" are more likely going to be unhealthy crackers tainted with oil than bowls of brown rice, for example. Sugar and sweetener consumption, which has always been unnaturally and unhealthily high, has gone up modestly. Chicken and cheese consumption have doubled.

Astonishingly, about 85 million Americans consume fast food every day.[10] The rise in fast food consumption is universally (unless Gary Taubes wishes to exclude himself?) recognized as one of the contributing factors to the explosion in obesity. When was the last time anyone had a low-fat, vegan fast-food meal? Can you run into *McDonald's* for a quick bowl of chickpeas, buckwheat, and steamed veggies? A *Double-Whopper* at *Burger King* contains an astonishing nine hundred calories, with fifty-eight grams of fat (about as much as I'd eat in two days) and twenty grams of saturated fat (about as much as I'd consume in two weeks). Then there's the *Triple Whopper with Cheese*, with a mind-blowing 1140 calories, seventy-six grams of fat, and a heart-stopping twenty-nine grams of saturated fat. And yet Taubes would likely consider this a slimming, heart-healthy meal, as long as you ditch that damned bun.

(An aside here: in response to environmental awareness, especially among young people, *Burger King* and other fast food franchises are now featuring plant-based burgers like the *Impossible Burger*. For the environment, this represents a real improvement. And all plant foods are of course a wiser choice than all animal foods if we're concerned about avoiding future pandemics. Health-wise, the *Impossible Burger* is also an improvement over beef, but it's still awful: one *Impossible Burger* has a horrific eight grams of saturated fat, stemming from the use of deadly coconut oil. It's considerably less terrible for your heart than the beef *Whoppers*, but that's about the best you can say for it.)

If the percentage of fat in the American diet has come down at all over the last few decades, it's been only the most modest of decreases, and it isn't because Americans are eating less fat; it's because they've added more sugar to sweeten a spectacularly, insanely, preposterously, suicidally fatty diet. And, although you'd never know this from reading Taubes' article, there is no real dispute over sugar: almost all nutritional experts (plant-based or not) agree that it is harmful. Taubes makes it sound like the advocates of a low-fat, plant-based diet have been promoting sugar as a substitute for beef; again—*come on, Gary!*—we're promoting fruits and vegetables and legumes and whole grains. Sadly, these are not the elements of the American diet that have seen a significant increase in consumption in the last decades.

Vegans constitute about three percent of the American population, and a lot of those—I'd estimate more than half—are "junk food vegans" who have adopted the vegan cause on behalf of animal rights; they are not on a low-fat diet. You can be a vegan and find yourself fatter than you thought possible by feasting on the *Impossible Burger*, fries, and sugary soft drinks. Vegans on a healthy, low-fat diet probably constitute no more than one percent of the population, so with obesity rates approaching forty percent in America, it's a little nutty to blame it on us.

In his book, *Why We Get Fat*, Taubes acknowledges that the *keto-genic* diet he proposes—in which carbohydrates are restricted to almost zero and the body is forced to burn fat instead of glucose as its fuel—may bring on, at least temporarily, some unpleasant side effects: "weakness, fatigue, nausea, dehydration, diarrhea, constipation"[11] and even orthostatic hypotension, which can cause you to pass out from a sudden drop in blood pressure when standing. He dismisses all this suffering as mere "carbohydrate withdrawal."[12]

If anyone's keeping a scorecard, the low-fat, plant-based diet does not come with side effects. Standing up to get a second helping of rice and beans will not be fraught with danger.

"Carbohydrates are not required in a healthy human diet," Taubes writes,[13] thereby establishing that having any plant food at all is optional, at best—and that must mean that fiber is optional, too, since only plant foods have fiber. And I'm deducing that may mean that bowel movements are optional, too, although Taubes doesn't say.

Taubes' nutritional rationales always make it sound like people have a choice to sit down with a bowl of carbohydrates, a bowl of fat, or a bowl of protein—and he recommends the bowl of fat, and warns you to dodge the bowl of carbohydrates. But, to state the obvious, food does not come to us in monolithic macronutrient containers. Oatmeal, for example, is seventy percent carbohydrate, fifteen percent protein, and fifteen percent fat. How does he feel about oatmeal? He doesn't say, but despite the fact that it has healthy complements of both fat and protein, Taubes would most likely consider oatmeal a "carb," and would have a jaundiced view of it. He is enthusiastic only about animal foods. Any foods that contain carbohydrate—all plant foods—are reduced in his mind to their predominant macronutrient; they become "carbs." He does believe that certain carbohydrates (sugar and other sweeteners, and anything made of refined flour, as well as starchy vegetables like potatoes, rice, and corn, along with what he calls "liquid carbohydrates"—beers, fruit juices, and sodas) are worse than others. He generally seems to absolve the carbohydrates in non-starchy vegetables, though he does note that "some people may be so sensitive to the carbohydrates in their diet that even these green vegetables may be a problem."[14] Without providing any detail, he suggests that "it's a good bet that most fruit will make the problem [of obesity] worse, not better."[15] Beyond his condemnation of carbohydrate, his work is remarkably free of recommendations about which foods to eat. The man wants you to eat lard, but how does he feel about your having the vegan lentil soup made with carrots and celery? That's anyone's guess, but given that the soup is made from plants and is not fatty, he's probably against it (even though lentils are high in protein), believing it would make you fat because it contains, yup, those deadly *carbs*.

Those who argue for the low-fat, plant-based diet can and do speak with clarity: By all means, we say, enjoy the lentil soup with carrots and celery. Eat legumes (beans, peas, lentils), whole grains, fruits, and vegetables. Avoid all animal foods, avoid oil, avoid sugar (in its many forms). Be careful not to overdo fatty fruits (avocado, olive, coconut), nuts and seeds (also fatty), and dried fruit (which is high in sugar). To minimize sugar consumption further, avoid or minimize fruit juice consumption, and of course don't drink soda. We're very clear. The King of Fat has trouble being clear, as all his arguments are about macronutrients and not about food as we encounter it in the real world.

It's possible that his views are softening, though. Five years after bringing out *Why We Get Fat*, Taubes came out with a book called *The Case Against Sugar*,[16] in 2016. In it, he writes of ". . . the likely possibility that the difference between a healthy diet and one that causes obesity, diabetes, heart disease, cancer, and other associated diseases begins with the sugar content. If this is true, it implies that populations or individuals can be at the very least reasonably healthy living on carbohydrate-rich diets, even grain-rich diets, as long as they consume relatively little sugar."[17]

Wow. Whereas, in his earlier book, he argued that all carbohydrate makes you fat, and is "not required in a healthy human diet," he now—after the humbling failure and near collapse of the *Nutrition Science Initiative*—appears to be acknowledging that you can eat that darned apple, after all. Taubes denies that this represents a departure in his thinking,[18] but it certainly seems like a significant concession to reality that he hadn't made in *Why We Get Fat.* Anyway, since I've been eating nothing but plant food for more than a quarter-century now, you can imagine my relief at learning that one can be *"at the very least reasonably healthy"* if one eats human food. And hey, if Taubes decides to dedicate himself, from this point forward, to making the case against sugar, and cuts out the insane attack on the macronutrient known as carbohydrate, then we will be in agreement, at least on the sugar front.

Sugar, remember, is a refined, processed food that is 100% carbohydrate. Fruits, vegetables, legumes, whole grains, nuts, and seeds are unprocessed, whole foods that contain complements of all the macronutrients. Maybe I'm counting my carbohydrates too soon (vegans, out of respect, don't count chickens), but perhaps Taubes has learned to make that important distinction.

There are only a few sorts of foods that are 100% anything. Sugar and other sweeteners are 100% carbohydrate; oils are 100% fat; egg whites are (essentially) 100% protein. They're all 100% bad for you. Remember my old man's dictum, *Too much of anything is no good?* It applies to foods that are too much—100%—of a single macronutrient.

Surprisingly, in the course of fact-checking this chapter, I struck up a friendly email correspondence with Gary Taubes. He seems to be a very civil guy, which makes me feel bad about attacking his work so harshly (though not quite so bad as to soften the critique). But it has become clear to me that, unlike Bourdain, he has nothing against vegans—and I almost get the feeling (I could be wrong here, admittedly, and I hate to get him in trouble with his ketogenic friends) that he would prefer to join our team if he thought he could thrive on a vegan diet. The man even has family members on the angelic side of the nutritional divide. While I don't recall any emphasis on fiber in his books, he does indeed believe that fiber is essential, and he seems to be now restricting his attack on carbohydrates to the refined sort—which brings us towards common ground. In an email to me, he acknowledged that a whole foods, vegan diet would be a much healthier diet than the "standard American fare" of processed foods.[19]

For some reason, he has convinced himself that animal fat is doing him some good, but he acknowledges that this remains unproven. I would only add that it's not for lack of trying. I think my wife's affection does me some good, but I haven't spent $29 million trying to prove it.

If I ever have the pleasure of meeting Gary Taubes in person, I'd love to introduce him to my friend, Dr. Steven Lawenda, a family doctor who works in a large medical facility in California. I'm sure Dr. Lawenda would be happy to share his story.

Like most medical students, Steve learned virtually nothing about nutrition in medical school at the University of California at Davis. After completing medical school, he began working as a family doctor while being about fifty pounds overweight himself. He feared for his own health because of a terrible family history of heart disease and diabetes. The Familial Hypercholesterolemia Foundation would have welcomed him with open arms.

He had entered the field with a desire to help people, but he found, distressingly, that even though he was practicing the standard of care, prescribing correct, up-to-date medications for the diabetes and heart conditions and hypertension and other common conditions he encountered, he rarely helped anyone improve their underlying disease process. His patients with chronic conditions weren't generally reversing their diseases; they were just adapting to taking higher doses of drugs, learning to inject themselves with insulin, and struggling, with Steve's help, to manage their symptoms.

Steve's first eight years of practice were insufficiently rewarding; his work was burning him out. It weighed on him that he was unable to help patients address the causes of their ailments. He felt like "a tour guide to disease," merely explaining to patients how to cope with their conditions as they worsened. Meanwhile, during those dispiriting eight years, his own weight ballooned to the point that he was seventy-five pounds overweight, pre-diabetic, and suffering from acid reflux, fatty liver, and sleep apnea. He and his wife, Patty, now had one young child and another on the way, and he worried about how long he would be around to enjoy, and provide for, his family.

Then one day, in the car, Patty played the audiobook of a doctor who recommended a plant-based diet. Steve assumed it was a crock of nonsense, since, after all, if the diet worked as well as the author claimed, surely some faculty instructors would have mentioned something about it in med school. The lack of attention to nutrition in medical school is, after all, a lesson in itself: *this stuff obviously can't be very important.* But, initially to humor his wife, he listened to the audiobook—and the more he listened, the more sense it started to make. He and Patty resolved to conduct an experiment: for a month, they'd eat a plant-based diet.

In that first month, he lost seventeen pounds—and so the experiment continued. Within eight months, he lost seventy-five pounds, and achieved his ideal weight. His body mass index (BMI) reached a normal 23. His blood pressure dropped considerably. So did his blood sugar levels. He thoroughly regained his health within a year, simply by eating fruits, vegetables, whole grains, legumes, and some nuts and seeds. He estimates that those food groups combined had formerly constituted about ten or twenty percent, at most, of his daily calories; now, without the meat and dairy and eggs and processed junk food and oil and sugar, they constituted one hundred percent, and suddenly he found himself a transformed man, trim and healthy, with newfound energy.

Naturally excited by what he had learned and achieved, he needed to find a way to implement it in his practice. He began discussing nutrition with all his patients, counseling them to eat a diet resembling his own. And suddenly his work as a doctor proved rewarding; after eight years of practice, he was finally actually helping his patients in visible and sometimes dramatic ways. Now he was not just managing his patients' symptoms, but often reversing their diseases. Patients who had Type 2 diabetes were able to reduce their medications, and sometimes even drop them entirely. Blood pressures were dropping significantly, and patients were able to reduce or eliminate their drugs for hypertension. Patients began losing weight. Joint pains were diminishing or disappearing. Autoimmune conditions were improving or going away entirely.

Word spread that there was a doctor in town who was achieving extraordinary results, and so Steve began a series of evening lectures at his facility that patients and colleagues and members of the community flocked to. Some of his colleagues joined him in practicing plant-based medicine. He began a fourteen-week intensive Lifestyle Medicine program that continues to this day. About forty new patients per month enroll. Of those who enroll in the program, he's found that about eighty percent make major changes in their diet, lose weight, and see their need for medications for diabetes and high blood pressure drop by approximately sixty to eighty percent.

After eight years of practice in which he rarely helped anyone reverse their diseases, Steve now does so with many patients, day after day.

My challenge to Gary Taubes would be this: if you still believe that the problem with the American diet is carbohydrate, the primary macronutrient in the foods (fruits, vegetables, whole grains, legumes) that those of us in the plant-based food movement advocate that we consume, and if people should really be turning away from plant foods and eating more animal products and fat, then please locate, anywhere in America, a Reverse Lawenda.

For those who are not familiar with the term, let me define "Reverse Lawenda." A Reverse Lawenda is a doctor who was once obese and found that he or she wasn't truly helping any of his or her patients overcome chronic health conditions. Then this doctor realized that the reason he was so fat was that he had been eating too much in the way of beans, peas, and lentils; too much brown rice, millet, buckwheat and oatmeal; too many apples and oranges and peaches and pears and berries; too many mushrooms and zucchinis and too much broccoli and asparagus. So he cut way back on those damned legumes and whole grains and fruits and vegetables, which are all lamentably high in carbohydrate, and learned instead to consume way more pork chops and roast beef and fried chicken and turkey burgers and scrambled eggs and cheese and lard, all much higher in the divine, healthy macronutrient, fat. And lo and behold, the pounds just started melting away! Before he knew it, this doctor was fit, no longer suffered from pre-diabetes and other metabolic disorders, and felt like a new person.

And so this conscientious, beef-eating doctor started incorporating the lessons of a fatty, animal-based diet into his practice. Reminding his patients of the old dictum, "A sausage a day keeps the doctor away," he counseled them to substitute pastrami and lamb chops and pork and all kinds of cheeses for those pesky fruits and vegetables and whole grains and legumes that they had mistakenly been over-consuming. And suddenly all the health metrics of his patients started improving dramatically with the addition of all these vibrantly healthy animal products. Heart disease disappeared. Blood pressure normalized. Patients were able to get off their meds. Unwanted pounds disappeared, and stayed off for good. Word spread among colleagues that it was highly effective to practice beef-and-butter-based medicine.

Surely, Gary Taubes—given that there are over one million physicians in America—surely you can find a single Reverse Lawenda?

If you can't—and of course you can't—maybe it's time you drop the nonsense of trying to convince people that deadly foods are good for them. Maybe it's time to stop advocating a diet that is—to use Anthony Bourdain's words but reverse their import—*the enemy of everything good and decent in the human spirit.* Maybe it's time to stop spending other people's not-very-hard-earned-money in the wacky hope of disproving established science.

I'll note that Taubes does, several times in *Why We Get Fat*, invoke the name of one Dr. Eric Westman, a kindred spirit in the ketogenic universe, who apparently treats his fat and sick patients by restricting "carbohydrates" severely. In a video accessible online, Dr. Westman recommends, I kid you not, sugar-free *Jell-O* with whipped cream as a way to counter sugar cravings on a carbohydrate-restricted diet.[20] Given that sugar-free *Jell-O* is a mix of aspartame, other artificial sweeteners, artificial flavors, and artificial colors, that's quite a recommendation for health!

Dr. Westman may try, but he falls far short of being a Reverse Lawenda. There are no Reverse Lawendas out there, and there never will be any, because it's not humanly possible. But there *is*, thankfully, a growing band of Lawendas. Not enough, mind you, not by a long-shot, but there are many fine doctors out there who have begun to incorporate plant-based nutrition into their practice. The *Plantrician Project* hosts annual conferences on plant-based medicine that a thousand Lawendas of the present and future attend.

If you can find one in your city or town, consider switching to her or him. They are brave souls who practice medicine the way it should be practiced.

CHAPTER FIVE: THE CURIOUS CASE OF JOANNA

This is going to be a difficult chapter to write. Nothing about marriage is ever easy, and certainly not the part where you write a chapter about your wife's health. But I try always to be a sensitive husband, so I may have to consider showing this chapter to Joanna before the book goes to print.

When she was sixteen, growing up in Lublin, Poland, Joanna was hospitalized and diagnosed with a kidney condition, chronic *glomerulonephritis* (specifically, *Mesangial proliferative glomerulonephritis*). It's a serious condition that could lead to kidney failure and dialysis.[1] For almost the next ten years, Joanna's kidney condition, and the fatigue that often accompanied it, were central concerns in her life. More than anything else, she wanted, naturally, to restore herself to vibrant health.

By her mid-twenties, Joanna had left Poland and was living in Athens, Greece. She strolled into the first health food store she had ever encountered in her life, and her eyes immediately fixed on an Ayurvedic herbal supplement from India that she saw on the shelves.[2] Strangely, an inner voice told her to buy it and take it every day for two years. She did so, and, perhaps out of desperation, she took a higher dose than recommended on the label.

Two years later, Joanna found herself in complete remission from *glomerulonephritis*. She was still in good health when I met her a few years later in Calgary, Canada. When I asked her to marry me, she again trusted her inner voice, and said yes.

That was the last time she ever trusted her inner voice.

Ask her to make a decision now, and she's a total mess.

Joanna was neither a vegan nor a vegetarian when I met her, but when we were dating, she accepted gladly my own vegan requirements (if we exclude the stuffed peppers she once baked for me that contained egg whites, as she confessed to me, with an indeterminate degree of remorse, after we had been married for about eight years), and expressed an openness to changing her diet. She had become a believer in herbs while growing up in Poland, and since she had cured her kidney condition with a supplement based on herbs, the idea of a plant-based diet had a natural appeal to her. For my part, while most of the women I had dated in my life were not vegetarian or vegan, it was hard to imagine marrying a woman who brought animal foods into the home. I was like a man willing to date out of his religion but not marry out of it. And so it was important to me that Joanna commit to at least trying to become vegetarian, if not vegan. Over the phone, one day, she did.

On my next trip to Calgary to see her, I discovered frozen *roadkill* of some sort in her freezer. I asked her what it was. She told me it was ground turkey meat. I said, "I thought you said you would try to go vegetarian?" She said she was indeed trying, and she promised to throw out the ground turkey right after my visit. That made no sense to me at all. I said, "Let's throw it out now," and dropped it unceremoniously in the garbage can, where it made quite the thud.

That dead-turkey-drop turned out to be an action that made her furious at me, as I found out many years after we were married. Probably around the same time that I found out about the egg whites in the stuffed peppers.

But Joanna did indeed become a vegetarian before we married, and in the first year or two of our marriage, she gave up the little bit of cheese she'd been eating and became a vegan. She was enjoying all kinds of new foods that I exposed her to: tofu, tempeh (fermented soybeans), seitan (a.k.a. "wheat meat," made from wheat gluten), and various meat analogues, as well as Indian food, which became her favorite ethnic cuisine. At the time, I was far less rigorous about my diet than I am now, and I enjoyed my "hot dogs" made from isolated soy proteins and all kinds of soy ice creams and vegan junk foods, and so it was easy for me to make my pitch to Joanna that she could eat a vegan diet that more or less resembled the diet she was used to, with all kinds of "meats" and "cheeses" and "ice creams," and even some new kinds of foods like tofu, so there was really no sacrifice involved.

After a few years of eating this way, Joanna developed some digestive pains, and discovered that she had an allergy to soy, so she gave up on the tofu and the meat analogues made from isolated soy proteins. That helped her feel better for a while, but some years later, she developed serious and painful joint pains.

It slowly developed into a living nightmare for both of us. It was as if all the joints in her body were inflamed, and she struggled in vain to reduce the swelling that had developed on one wrist, and the pain that emanated from joints all over her body.

Her body was breaking down before me, and she was miserable, in excruciating joint and muscle pain day and night, sometimes for weeks or months at a time. The flare-ups got worse after sun exposure; unfortunately, we lived in the hot, dry climate of the San Fernando Valley.

The bristling exchanges in our household would go something like this:

"Glen, you're supposed to be some kind of dubious, self-proclaimed health expert! Cure me!"

"*Supposed to be* is a cheap shot! I *am* a dubious, self-proclaimed health expert!"

"Then cure me!"

"Okay, okay, I'm trying."

"It looks like the vegan diet just doesn't work for me."

I didn't know what to say to that.

She discovered that her pains were reduced somewhat, but by no means eradicated, when she stopped eating bread and wheat products. We were certain that there was some sort of link there, although it didn't necessarily mean that she had celiac disease. But eliminating gluten proved to be the first positive step Joanna took toward restoring her health.

Over the years that she suffered, we went to doctors—many, many doctors. That's got to be one of the more frustrating parts of a health crisis: dealing with the conflicting opinions of the health professionals. You find yourself wondering if you should weigh their opinions according to how much they charge. One thing they all agreed upon, though, was that Joanna had some sort of autoimmune disorder; her bloodwork as evidenced by the ANA (antinuclear antibody) test demonstrated clearly that Joanna's immune system had effectively gone berserk and started to attack her own body.

The world of autoimmune diseases is, as we learned, a vague and imprecise world, a world of overlapping symptoms and blurry spectrums of diseases with different names: rheumatoid arthritis, psoriatic arthritis, celiac disease, mixed connective tissue disease, Hashimoto's disease, multiple sclerosis, lupus.

One highly unsympathetic immunologist son-of-a-bitch diagnosed Joanna with mixed connective tissue disease, and with remarkable coldness estimated that she had five years to live. (This was about eight years ago, and for the record, she's feeling fine, doc, thanks for your help.) That made for a difficult drive home, and yet you still have to pay the bill when it comes—you don't get to dismiss it on the grounds of cruelty and incompetence.

One loony rheumatologist interviewed Joanna for over an hour, asking her questions about every cold and flu she ever had in her life, and then, suspecting that Joanna suffered from celiac disease, strongly recommended that she be tested for it. The doctor explained that, unfortunately, there was only one effective way to test for celiac disease: Joanna needed to stuff herself full of gluten all day long—wheat bread and wheat pasta and barley and rye, meal after meal—for about six weeks, regardless of how sick it made her feel, in order for the test to be accurate. As extraordinary as it may sound, that was that doctor's actual medical advice, for which she argued vigorously: *Joanna needs to take this test*. It seemed to me highly questionable (to say the least) to risk making Joanna much sicker for the next six weeks, to make her suffer truly crippling pain, in order to simply do a test that would tell her whether or not to give up gluten, which she had already given up months earlier anyway.

But, partly out of curiosity, and partly to humor a clearly deranged medical professional, I asked the doctor exactly how accurate this state-of-the-art test would be, assuming Joanna complied by feasting on gluten for the next six weeks prior to undertaking it.

"Oh, about 95% accurate," the doctor replied, with a touch of pride.

So even after all that certain suffering, and a likely worsening of Joanna's underlying condition brought on by further damaging her intestinal tract lining, we still wouldn't have a result we could have complete confidence in. And, as we explained to the doctor, Joanna was going to continue avoiding gluten, regardless of the outcome of the test, because she felt better when she avoided wheat, barley, and rye. Therefore, we declined that patent insanity, along with dozens of other tests this crackpot recommended. We had to pay her, too.

Then we found a good and kind and sympathetic doctor, one of the best rheumatologists in Los Angeles, who had real respect for Joanna's determination to find some way to cure herself. He, too, interviewed Joanna about her health history (although doing so didn't take him nearly as long as it took the nutcase), and he started to piece things together. The *glomerulonephritis* that Joanna had been diagnosed with as a teenager and lived with until her late twenties was likely, he believed, a symptom of lupus. So, too, was an episode that Joanna experienced at the age of two: on a hot, sunny day, she had suffered a seizure. So, too, was a "butterfly rash" that appeared around her nose at the age of thirteen.

Perhaps, therefore, Joanna had lived with lupus all her life and we were just now discovering it. The doctor believed that lupus had now attacked her entire digestive system. She exhibited other symptoms consistent with a diagnosis of lupus: Reynaud's Syndrome, causing her fingers to briefly turn blue, was a concerning new symptom consistent with lupus, and so was the fact that her joint pain worsened in the sunshine. She had myriad symptoms that aligned with the troubling diagnosis.

Lupus is a serious disease; it can sometimes even shorten a lifespan. But it is just a word, and it is a word with a vague meaning. One person can have five symptoms, and a doctor can diagnose her with lupus; someone else can *not* have those five symptoms but have five completely different ones, and a doctor can diagnose her with lupus, too. Had Joanna gone to ten different rheumatologists, she may well have received ten different diagnoses.

It's not exactly a precise field, rheumatology.

Which isn't to say that it's worthless. It was important to learn that Joanna's immune system was attacking her own cells, and that it had probably done so, on and off, throughout her life. Something had made the condition worse recently, though. The kind and sympathetic doctor who diagnosed her with lupus had, unfortunately, nothing to offer her beyond a choice of steroids for her inflammation and pain, powerful antimalarial drugs, and chemotherapy drugs. Joanna didn't want to go down the road of damaging her body with pharmaceuticals. The doctor understood, and did not argue. He was even supportive.

Lupus can be relentless; it can attack any part of the body. Most people who suffer from lupus never overcome it. But Joanna had already overcome chronic *glomerulonephritis*. Overcoming challenging health conditions comes second nature to her. So we couldn't lose hope just because one of the finest rheumatologists in Los Angeles had nothing to offer but drugs with lists of side effects that required scrolls.

I knew, each time that Joanna announced, "The vegan diet isn't working for me," that there had to be more to it than that. Something clearly had gone wrong for her, but I knew that animal foods cause inflammation, and plant foods are usually anti-inflammatory. So it made no sense to think that her inflammatory issues could be resolved by returning to animal foods.

Still, I had to ask myself: was it just an unlucky coincidence that her health had deteriorated since she embarked on a vegan diet, or could there be something to her claim that her switch to the vegan diet was responsible for her suffering?

Unfortunately, it wasn't a coincidence, in my opinion. I think her problems were caused, or aggravated, by the fact that the particular type of vegan diet that we ate early in our marriage was not a very healthy one.

Leaky gut is a condition in which, due to increased intestinal permeability, toxins and bacteria leak from the damaged intestinal lining into the bloodstream. Sub-optimal gut health, in which harmful bacteria overwhelm the beneficial bacteria, can be one cause of leaky gut. Celiac disease or gluten sensitivity can be another.

And so it's possible that, when Joanna became a vegan and replaced some of the animal foods that she used to consume with fake meats, and particularly seitan, which is essentially pure wheat gluten, she damaged her gut lining and developed leaky gut. That doesn't necessarily mean that she has or ever had celiac disease; one study demonstrated that gliadin, a protein that is a component of gluten, "induces an increase in intestinal permeability in all individuals, regardless of whether or not they have celiac disease."[3] In addition, it may well be the case that Joanna ate more bread and other wheat products like pasta and couscous after becoming a vegan than she used to when she practiced an omnivorous diet.

Just as it's possible that Joanna always had lupus but never knew it, it's possible that she always had a degree of gluten-sensitivity, but never knew it because she had never before consumed so much gluten, nor consumed it in the processed, isolated form of seitan. And so the overconsumption of gluten—as well perhaps as the overconsumption of other high-protein meat substitutes—may have damaged her gut and brought on a resurgence of the lupus she never knew she had.

My friend Gordon, who used to argue with me about fat and coconut oil—he worried that Joanna and I weren't getting enough fat, and recommended that we consume tablespoons of coconut oil from a jar, as he did—proposed that Joanna visit an alternative doctor who, he believed, had helped him enormously with his health conditions.

Gordon and I no longer argue about fat and coconut oil because he died of sudden cardiac arrest. Nutrition is not the field to adopt if you like saying "I told you so."

But Joanna and I did, at the time, take his recommendation to see that alternative doctor, an osteopath, who recommended that Joanna do a test of her gastro-intestinal microbiome. She agreed to the test, and it showed a dramatic overgrowth of *Clostridium difficile*—affectionately known as *C. diff.* There are good intestinal bacteria and bad intestinal bacteria, and then there's *C. diff*, which even the bad bacteria don't care to associate with. *C. diff* can cause a host of problems, so while it may not have been the cause, or the sole cause, of the inflammation in Joanna's body, it certainly wasn't helping.

The likely cause of *C. diff* overgrowth is the use of antibiotics, which can result in a deficiency of beneficial gut bacteria that *C. diff* exploits. Ironically, the little bastards can be defeated only by more antibiotics (or, perhaps, a fecal transplant). Joanna defeated her *C. diff* with a fifteen-day course of *metronidazole*, and immediately focused on restoring her gut health. She took a multi-pronged approach.

First, she took a range of probiotic capsules that she selected at grocery stores. She researched and selected certain bacterial strains that she thought would be most helpful.

Second, she began drinking vegan kefirs, such as those made from coconut water. She also started drinking kombucha, a fermented tea, daily.

Third, she made sure that we both ate a lot of fermented foods, and she even began doing the fermenting of some foods herself, using high-quality cultures that she purchased. She fermented vegetables and fruits (thereby lowering their sugar content), and she fermented nut-milks into cheeses and kefirs. Every lunch and dinner we ate at home would have a component of fermented food—a little bit of vegetable kraut or pickles that Joanna made.

Fourth, she prepared meals that were mostly macrobiotic, and she found, in accordance with macrobiotic precepts, that she needed to cook all her vegetables, not eat them raw. Our greens were always blanched. In the macrobiotic tradition, we often ate pressed radishes and cucumbers, which are semi-fermented.

Fifth, Joanna made sure to eat flaxseeds in various forms; they are useful in soothing and healing the intestinal lining.

In short, the focus became gut health, and restoring her good bacteria.

At the same time, of course, Joanna continued to abstain from gluten and the processed faux meats that may have injured her gut in the first place.

And she remained a vegan.

It took her about two years of this program to slowly restore herself to good health. She has continued to enjoy good health for the last several years, and rarely experiences any of the symptoms that overtook her life for a prolonged period of time, and caused us to seek out the opinions and services of so many doctors. When we returned to see the kind, sympathetic rheumatologist, he was delighted to see how well Joanna was doing. Since he had never tried to push on her the pharmaceutical drugs that she declined, he didn't have to struggle with any cognitive dissonance to accept that she had treated her own condition without drugs. He ran another panel of blood tests, and called to tell us that there was no further sign of lupus or inflammation; all her blood results had normalized.

Throughout the ordeal of flare-ups of her lupus, Joanna had tirelessly researched autoimmune diseases and spoken with others who suffered from them, and therefore came to each of her doctor's appointments armed with knowledge and questions. You could sum up her attitude this way: *always seek medical advice before consulting your physician.*

It's fair to say that a couple of the many doctors we visited did indeed help her. In the end, it was certainly helpful to learn of, and defeat, the *C. diff* overgrowth, and it was probably of some use to Joanna to gain the perspective that she may have had lupus for most of her life.

But, mostly, she treated herself, and resolved her symptoms, with diet, herbs, and probiotics.

She *owned her health*, and didn't take a submissive attitude toward medical professionals. She refused more of their recommendations than she accepted.

That is the posture I propose to the reader.

It certainly helps, if you are determined to own your health, to have a basic understanding of the fundamentals of nutrition, so read on.

Chapter Six:
Settled Science, Part One: Nutritional Studies

For most people, most of the time, nothing will affect their health more than the food they eat. There are, of course, exceptions to this rule: people who destroy their health through lifestyle choices, especially smoking, alcohol, and drug use; people who suffer disabling accidents; people who are unlucky in their genetic inheritance and are afflicted with a disease that is a cruel, random bolt from the blue, unrelated to any factors under human control.

But that's not most people, and that's not most disease. About fifteen percent of American adults are smokers, and about ten percent have a drug or alcohol problem—and since there's a great deal of overlap, let's estimate that about twenty percent of adult Americans have a bigger health challenge than diet; they need, above all, to stop abusing drugs (be it nicotine or alcohol or meth).

We should not assume that the two issues of diet and substance abuse are completely unrelated, though. I say that because, as someone who has met countless vegans, I've yet to meet anyone on a low-fat, plant-based diet, and heroin. I have met very few vegans who smoke. An understanding of, and a concern for, human health that propels one to eat sanely is unlikely to permit its abuse by inhaled, imbibed, or injected chemicals of various sorts. It may just be the case that a society that treats food as a combination of processed chemicals whipped up in a lab and packaged smartly, with an emphasis on the addictive tastes of sugar and salt—just take a stroll down the aisles of your average grocery store and glance at the ingredients of the cereals, the crackers, the sauces, the spreads—sets itself up to be a society ravaged by drug use. In any case, the mantra of "Just Say No" clearly hasn't worked very well over the decades to stem the tide of drug use. Maybe it's time we tried, "Just Say Brown Rice and Steamed Veggies."

Obesity, Type 2 diabetes, hypertension, cardiovascular disease, cancer, and Alzheimer's—the great plagues of our time—are largely food-borne diseases. And while a healthy diet can't make you cancer-proof, it can dramatically reduce your odds of developing cancer, and it can also improve your odds of recovering from it. It's crucial to understand that if you eat human food—instead of the very different, deleterious substances that most Americans eat—you will almost certainly escape the scourges of obesity, Type 2 diabetes, hypertension, and heart disease, while dramatically improving your odds of escaping cancer and Alzheimer's.

Given that nutrition is the single most significant determinant of health outcomes, the failure of doctors to study it—which is to say, of medical schools to teach it—is shocking in the extreme. It's as if you went to law school and nobody mentioned the Constitution. It's frankly nuts.

One reason medical schools ignore nutrition may simply be that Western medicine has traditionally viewed itself as the science of treating disease, not promoting health. But another reason for this patent insanity may be even more troubling. It's that nutrition has become the domain of a war between Science and Culture, and medical schools, abdicating their responsibility to Science, are disinclined to take a stance contradicting the societal status quo. And so, by default, by their silence and inaction, medical schools have sided with Culture over Science.

Let me give you an example of what I mean by a conflict between Science and Culture. Science teaches us that human males and females are equally intelligent and equally capable of accomplishing any cognitive task, whether it be programming software, deciphering the tax code, preparing a syllabus, running an organization, or leading a nation. But that fact doesn't sit well with certain cultures and certain religious groups (you know who you are) who view females as subordinate and/or inferior to males. And so you may find, in those primitive societies, that the verifiable, objective reality that males and females are equally capable is neither taught nor acknowledged in their schools, nor embedded in their laws. It would upset the apple cart, in those backward cultures, to face the inconvenient truth of equality. Instead, the opposite of the truth is often taught, either implicitly or explicitly: that men are natural leaders, designed by divine forces to be the bosses of women. The law often acts as a cudgel to enforce the biases of the culture, with certain positions or privileges unjustly reserved for men. In America, while discrimination against women is rarely explicit today, sexist biases have of course been endemic here as well, and are rightly being systematically rooted out of our laws, our educational system, and—this seems to always be the last pillar to fall—our culture.

We've seen a similar tension play itself out in the American Bible Belt over the teaching of evolution. No serious scientist, of course, doubts that evolution is a fact, that it is an ongoing process, and that human beings evolved over millions of years as cousins to the great apes. But these are inconvenient facts if the Bible teaches you that the earth is only six thousand years old and human beings were handcrafted by the Creator in His own image. And so we have had efforts to ban the teaching of evolution in public schools, or to mandate that it be taught side-by-side with non-scientific dogma called "Intelligent Design" or something oxymoronically called "Creation Science"—in order to try to effectively establish an equivalence between, on the one hand, scientific reason and evidence, and on the other, theology. These efforts have nothing to do with Science and everything to do with Culture. Just ask a two-million-year-old hominin fossil if he thinks the earth could possibly be only six thousand years old, and you won't be surprised to learn that he'd be dumbstruck.

Now let me give you an example of settled science. Imagine if you learned that a scientific debate was going to be held in your town. Two scientists were going to argue opposing sides on this question: is cigarette smoking healthy?

Most likely you wouldn't bother to attend, since you already know the obvious answer to the question. If you did want to attend, surely it would only be for the spectacle—to satisfy the same desire for gore that brought ancient Romans to witness gladiatorial combat: to see the tobacco advocate verbally bloodied up and annihilated. Nobody, after all, can seriously believe that cigarette smoking promotes health. Making the case is preposterous. The science has been settled. We have the overwhelming evidence of thousands of scientific studies; we have longevity and disease statistics comparing smokers and non-smokers; and most of us have the personal experience of knowing smokers whose health declined in front of our eyes, or who died too young.

But we also have common sense: why in the world would inhaling the smoke of burning tobacco, with its approximately seven thousand attendant chemicals, do the body any good? How could it possibly *not* harm the lungs?

The "debate" over whether we live in a period of human-made global climate change is, likewise, an "argument" in which it's hard to take one side seriously. Virtually all serious climate scientists agree on the grim reality that human activity continues to heat up the planet. On the climate-change-denying side of the "debate" can be found just a handful of media gadflies, as well as many members of one party (you know who you are) in Congress, who in fact usually proffer the demurral that they're not scientists and so can have no opinion; oddly, they are also not economists but have strong opinions on tax cuts. Climate deniers almost always have a transparent economic incentive to commit themselves to the position that nothing untoward is happening to our planet, that we can persist in the burning of fossil fuels and prolong methane-producing animal agriculture without consequence.

The case for human-caused climate change nonetheless overwhelms any contrary skepticism: we have thermometer records going back a hundred seventy years; we have tree ring and ice core records going back thousands of years; we have statistics on rising carbon dioxide concentrations in the atmosphere (up forty percent in the last couple of centuries); we have melting glaciers; we have rising seas; we have rising global mean surface temperatures; and we have the evidence before our eyes of more energy in the atmosphere resulting in freak storms, "hundred-year floods" now recurring often, and devastating wildfires that haven't been seen before in recorded history. A thunderstorm, an event usually reserved for temperate and tropical climes, recently was detected within a few hundred miles of the North Pole. The Arctic Ocean will soon be open for shipping. Fires ravage Australia and the American West. All these phenomena confirm the predictions of scientists who have warned us for decades about the consequences of a build-up of greenhouse gases in the atmosphere.

And, again, we also have common sense: we know that if we run a car in the garage, the exhaust certainly affects the atmosphere in the garage, and makes it dangerous to breathe the air. Is it simply because of the unfathomable expanse of the earth's atmosphere that anyone could even imagine that somehow all the world's industrial and agricultural emissions would have no effect on it and our climate, would somehow dissipate harmlessly into the endless sky and the boundless oceans? But how in reality could all the billions of tons of carbon dioxide and other gases released into the atmosphere by human activities (including, most significantly, animal agriculture) *not* affect the climate? We know that greenhouse gases trap heat. And we also know that black absorbs heat, and that soot is black, and that when it lands on snow-capped glaciers it will contribute to the melting of glaciers. We know that volcano eruptions have demonstrably affected climate (with both cooling and warming effects), and yet fossil fuel emissions are a hundred times greater than volcanic discharges.[1] And that doesn't even take into account the problem of methane, a greenhouse gas that may be up to a hundred times as potent as carbon dioxide. The most significant contributor to atmospheric methane is animal agriculture. If, however, we don't stop the cycle of warming, thawing permafrost will also unleash vast quantities of methane.

Common sense confirms the avalanche of science, and whatever "controversy" remains about anthropogenic climate change can fairly be summed up as pathetic stirrings ginned up by ignoramuses or cynics with agendas.

And so it is with nutrition. The science of nutrition is clear and indisputable on the fundamental issues. We know with certainty which foods are generally healthy for human beings and which foods are not; the science is not at all muddled, as some would have you believe.

There are, to be sure, countless comparatively minor nutritional controversies—intellectually entertaining little fracases, if you will, wherein arguments with a basis in science can be made either way: whether or not coffee lowers your risk of Alzheimer's,[2] for example, or whether dark chocolate in small amounts has a protective benefit for the heart.[3] But the larger, more fundamental issues in nutrition are settled science, even if an abundance of popular literature and media mayhem contradicting the settled science seek to obscure that fact.

It is settled science that fruits and vegetables contain antioxidants that protect you from cancer and that these foods are profoundly health-promoting. It is settled science that legumes (meaning beans, peas, and lentils—let's leave the more controversial peanuts out of it) are health-promoting, and that societies that take in a good portion of their calories from legumes tend to be long-lived. It is settled science that mushrooms, especially so-called "medicinal mushrooms," offer wide-ranging health benefits, and have anti-carcinogenic properties. It is settled science that whole grains (as opposed to grains ground into flour and processed) are a healthful source of calories for most people (the exception being those with celiac disease, who need to abstain from certain gluten-containing grains). It is settled science that fiber is a required and vital nutrient (it is sometimes called a "non-nutrient" because it's not digestible; by the more general definition of nutrient as "a substance necessary for life," it's a nutrient), and that fiber is a feature of all whole plant foods. It is settled science that whole plant foods, cooked properly (not fried in oil) or sometimes eaten raw, generally have an anti-inflammatory effect on the body. It is settled science that most (not all) whole plant foods are low in fat and are usually devoid of saturated fat, and that no plant foods contain cholesterol. It is settled science that the consumption of all manner of fruits and vegetables can reduce the incidence of cancer in humans, and that those who eat more fruits and vegetables have better health outcomes. It is settled science that people who eat a plant-based diet live longer and healthier lives, with reduced risk of obesity, heart disease, and diabetes, when compared to people who eat an animal-based diet.

Likewise, it is settled science that all flesh foods and dairy are full of saturated fat and cholesterol, and that saturated fat and cholesterol team up to create atherosclerosis and cardiovascular disease. It is settled science that flesh foods and dairy are inflammatory. It is settled science that all animal foods are essentially devoid of antioxidants, although they may contain insignificant traces from the plants the animals ate. It is settled science that animal foods, much more than plant foods, are prone to bacterial contamination. It is settled science that there is no fiber in any animal food. It is settled science that an excess of protein, the likely outcome of a meat-and-dairy-based diet, serves no dietary purpose, as the human body cannot store protein. It is settled science that meat and dairy are implicated in a host of cancers. It is settled science that meat and dairy are implicated as well in heart disease, diabetes, and hypertension. It is settled science that the amount of animal food required to sustain optimal human health is precisely zero.

The "debate" between plant-based and animal-based nutrition has been resolved: one side's position—the "caveman" argument, if you will, that people need to eat meat—is so sketchy, so devoid of reason, so oblivious to towering evidence, that it cannot be taken seriously by anyone with a basic understanding of the subject. It's easy to get the false impression from media coverage of the nutrition wars that there's a serious scientific debate going on between those who advocate a meat-based diet and those who advocate a plant-based diet. In fact, it's about as serious a debate as the hypothetical debate between smoking advocates (if any such kooks linger today) and the universal anti-smoking consensus. The truth is, on the matter of whether we should be eating plants or dead animals, there's no legitimate debate at all; advocating the human consumption of meat for any alleged health benefits is scientifically preposterous.

To resolve the issue for yourself, all you really have to do is to look at flesh foods (and they are all fairly similar; flesh is flesh, whether we're talking about beef, pork, chicken, turkey, or fish) from the perspective of their macronutrient profile. They tend to be about fifty percent fat and fifty percent protein, with no carbohydrate to fuel your cells and no fiber. So what in the blazes could possibly make meat healthy? The saturated fat that we know clogs arteries? The unnecessary dietary cholesterol that helps it do so? The heme iron that's been implicated in metabolic syndrome, heart disease, and Type 2 diabetes?[4] The bacterial counts that contribute to inflammation? The lack of fiber?

Oh, the protein, you say? Yes, meat indeed contains plenty of protein: excessive, sulfuric animal protein that may well be carcinogenic.[5] Even if it were not carcinogenic, it cannot be stored, so it does the body no particular good. All the protein one needs can easily be met by eating . . . well, virtually anything. Lack of protein is not a problem that anyone who is not starving for calories has. So to eat meat for the protein is to solve a problem you do not have, and certainly will never develop if, instead of eating meat, you eat human food.

Remember: meat is not protein. Let's call out the imagined equivalence between meat and protein for what it is: a con job by the meat industry. Meat is not some purified form of protein like a powder you might find in the supplement section of your health food store—not that that's good for you, either. No, meat is the decaying muscle flesh of a dead animal; it is rife with bacteria and marbled with fat. You can't separate out the protein from the rest of the flesh with a knife, fork, scalpel, meat grinder, or magic wand. Yes, I know that your server in a restaurant may say to you, "What is your choice of protein: chicken, pork, or beef?" But, believe it or not, counterintuitive as this may be, your server doesn't know any more about nutrition than your doctor. Your server could just as accurately say, "What is your choice of saturated fat and cholesterol: chicken, pork, or beef?" It's just that experienced restaurateurs have learned that their establishments tend to fare better when their menu and their servers emphasize the protein in their entrees rather than saturated fat and cholesterol counts.

If the macronutrient profile of flesh foods isn't enough—as it should be—to convince you to avoid them, you can turn to scientific studies. And what you should do is pay attention to the pattern of these studies, the consensus that they all lead to, rather than seek to extrapolate too many conclusions from any single study.

For example, the German Cancer Research Center recently discovered new pathogens that can cause chronic inflammation in human tissues and lead to breast and colon cancer. Where do you think they found those pathogens? In apples and oranges? Nope—in meat and dairy. They named the pathogens "Bovine Milk and Meat Factors."[6]

The meat consumption habits of more than 25,000 Californian Seventh Day Adventist middle-aged men were studied for twenty years, from 1960-1980. The study found that those who ate meat daily had three times the risk of dying of heart attacks as those who did not eat meat.[7]

Studies relating diet to blood pressure are distinctly dispositive, since blood pressure is a key indicator of wellness. How, after all, could something raise your blood pressure to dangerous levels and still be good for you? The diet that leads to healthy blood pressure simply *has to be* the diet designed for humans, and the diet that leads to hypertension simply *has to be* shunned; there's no escaping that central fact of human health.

High blood pressure used to be defined as 140/90 mmHg, but that was only until Nov. 13, 2017. On that day—which I propose should become a national holiday called Hypertension Day on which friends and family gather for salt-free vegan meals, relaxation, bananas (potassium lowers blood pressure), and tickling (so does laughter)— high blood pressure got redefined by the American Heart Association and the American College of Cardiology as 130/80 mmHg, and about 35 million adults who didn't have high blood pressure the night before woke up suffering from the condition.[8] A cynic might argue that there was a pharmaceutical incentive behind the redefinition, but on the other hand, blood pressure levels between 130-139/80-89 mmHg double cardiovascular risk, so there was a case to be made for greater vigilance. In any case, we've known for a long time the most effective way for most people suffering from hypertension to lower their blood pressure. A 1983 study[9] compared the blood pressure of adult vegetarians to adult meat-eaters, with no differences in family histories regarding hypertension. The vegetarians averaged 126/77; the meat-eaters averaged 147/88. So the average vegetarian has healthy blood pressure even by today's more stringent standards, and the average meat-eater is hypertensive by any measure.

That study, along with others that confirmed its findings, should have ended the debate about meat back in 1983. Given the risks of heart attack, stroke, aneurysm, kidney failure, and dementia associated with high blood pressure, and given that we know the mechanism by which animal foods raise blood pressure (by narrowing the arteries with deposits of fat and cholesterol), the "debate" over meat should really have been ended by this finding—since confirmed many times[10]—alone.

And, when it comes to healthy blood pressure, vegans outperform even vegetarians.[11]

The evidence is likewise overwhelming for the superiority of a vegan diet for a range of other health indicators.

In 2017, the *Journal of Geriatric Cardiology* did a case study[12] of a seventy-nine-year-old man with serious coronary artery disease and shortness of breath upon mild exertion. He was put on a very specific kind of diet, and within two months, he lost eighteen pounds, his serum cholesterol fell from 201 to 137 mg/dL, his triglyceride count fell from 112 to 96 mg/dL, and he was now able to walk two miles without shortness of breath. Within a few months, his left ventricular ejection fraction—a measure of how much blood is pushed out with each heartbeat—had increased from thirty-five to fifty percent, an increase of forty-three percent, and more importantly, an increase from a heart failure level to a normal level.

Now what kind of diet do you imagine he was put on? The Paleo Diet? The Keto diet? The Atkins Diet? The Zone Diet? No, in fact, not very shockingly, his health-restoring diet "consisted of all vegetables, fruits, whole grains, potatoes, legumes, and nuts and excluded all animal-derived foods including eggs, dairy, and meat." The authors concluded, "Inflammation, which is associated with incident heart failure, may be reduced with a plant-based diet. . . . In summary, plant-based diets may be effective in preventing and treating heart failure."

"May be effective" is just standard scientific jargon that means "of course it's effective, and after we do another five thousand studies that produce the same results, we may amend that to 'may very well be effective.'" After ten thousand such studies with the same outcome, expect "may be starting to look promising."

In 2019, another such case study was reported, this time in *Frontiers in Nutrition*.[13] The subject here was a fifty-four-year-old woman suffering from obesity, Type 2 diabetes, and heart failure. She was put on a whole foods plant-based diet, and five and a half months later, she had lost fifty pounds, her diabetes had resolved (with her A1C—a measure of average blood sugar over three months' time—reduced to 5.7 without the use of pharmaceuticals), her BMI had been reduced from 45.2 to 35.1, her shortness of breath was ameliorated, and her ejection fraction improved impressively from twenty-one to fifty-five percent.

Does anybody on earth believe that she would have achieved the same results had she been put on a steak-and-eggs diet?

This is why I say that the science is settled. No scientist ever has or ever will produce disease-reversal results like this by using an animal-based diet, and everyone knows that that's true.

The *Frontiers in Nutrition* study is a favorite of mine because of two paragraphs inserted in the paper's "Background"; they read as follows (citations removed):

> *Numerous risk factors for the development and progression of HF [heart failure] are influenced by diet, including inflammation, hypertension, dysbiotic microbiome, hyperlipidemia, obesity, and diabetes. However, the medical community has traditionally focused on pharmacotherapy and devices and not on nutrition in both the primary and secondary prevention of HF.*
>
> *This focus may occur because cardiologists receive little instruction on either nutrition or nutrition counseling. In a recent survey of more than 900 cardiologists, although 95% believed that their role should include counseling patients about nutrition, 90% received minimal or no related training. This training deficit is not unique to cardiology and extends to most fields, including internal medicine and obstetrics/gynecology.*

Amen to that.

Dr. Caldwell B. Esselstyn, Jr., of the Cleveland Clinic famously worked with twenty-four patients with severe, life-threatening heart disease, and placed them on a strict, low-fat, oil-free, nut-free plant-based diet, accompanied by cholesterol-lowering medication. Eighteen of the twenty-four were compliant with the diet. Dr. Esselstyn's results with these patients, who had sustained forty-nine cardiac events between them in the eight years prior to enrolling in his study, were nothing short of remarkable. As he writes, "Among the fully compliant patients, during the twelve-year study, there was not one further clinical episode of worsening coronary artery disease after they committed themselves to keeping cholesterol within the safe range."[14]

The six non-compliant patients were not nearly so "lucky," experiencing worsening of their angina, congestive heart failure, four bypass operations, and one death.[15]

Now imagine if another doctor, with an opposing nutritional ideology, had proposed to the Cleveland Clinic that it underwrite a study in which eighteen patients suffering from advanced cardiovascular disease are put on a diet loaded with meat, eggs, and dairy. If that study happened, what do you imagine the results would be?

Undoubtedly, they would be tragic, but we can never know for sure, because the Cleveland Clinic is not clinically insane. It would never undertake the liability involved in underwriting a study whose protocols contradict all scientific knowledge and would likely lead to the expedited deaths of many or all of its participants.

That is what I mean by settled science. It's unthinkable that any researcher or medical or scientific institution would risk killing heart patients by putting them on a diet rich in saturated fats—the animal-based diet. Everyone knows the same facts that are two sides of the same coin: 1) meat and dairy contribute to heart disease; 2) a low-fat, plant-based diet can actually facilitate its reversal, as Dr. Esselstyn has proven.

Dr. Esselstyn followed up his groundbreaking twelve-year study with another study of roughly ten times as many patients suffering from cardiovascular disease.[16] This time, 198 heart patients, forty-four of whom had already experienced heart attacks, were put on a diet that eliminated all animal products and allowed no added or "free" oils, or processed foods that contained oils. The diet was comprised of whole grains, legumes, vegetables, and fruits. Nuts and avocados were ruled out because of their fat content; sugary foods and fruit juices were likewise banned. Participants received education in plant-based nutrition as well as plant-based recipes. Exercise was "encouraged but not required."[17]

Of the 198 patients, 177, or 89%, adhered to the terms of the diet for a mean of 3.7 years. Only one of the 177 experienced a cardiac event (a stroke).

104 of 112 of the compliant patients who reported angina at the start of the study ("baseline") found the condition improved or completely resolved.

Of the twenty-one non-compliant patients, thirteen (sixty-two percent) experienced adverse events: two sudden cardiac deaths, one heart transplant, two strokes, four angioplasties with stent placements, three coronary artery bypass surgeries, and one endarterectomy (surgery to remove plaque) for peripheral arterial disease.

The non-compliant minority of the patients actually served the interests of the study (however perversely) by demonstrating how seriously sick the collective body of the cohort was, and how dramatically and radically different the outcomes of the non-compliant would prove to be from the outcomes of the compliant.

Dr. Esselstyn's findings improved upon the already impressive results achieved in similar nutrition and lifestyle studies conducted on larger numbers of heart patients by Dr. Dean Ornish. In his Multi-Center Lifestyle Demonstration Project, for example, Dr. Ornish proved that he could help heart patients improve cardiac function, lower cholesterol, lose weight, increase exercise capacity, and avoid the need for revascularization of their arteries (via vascular bypass or angioplasty) by following a low-fat, plant-based diet.[18] Dr. Ornish's results have been impressive, yet not as remarkable as Dr. Esselstyn's, in my view, and that could be attributed to the fact that the Ornish diet has traditionally included "non-fat" dairy, egg whites, and fish oil supplementation. All of those non-vegan items, including the fish oil supplementation, strike me as inimical to the rest of the Ornish protocol.

The touted benefits of fish oil have proven to be minimal at best. Dr. Howard LeWine, a practicing internist and Chief Medical Editor of Harvard Health Publishing (affiliated with the Harvard Medical School), sums up a November 2018 study in the *New England Journal of Medicine* by saying that "omega-3 fatty acid supplements did nothing to reduce heart attacks, strokes, or deaths from heart disease in middle-age men and women without any known risk factors for heart disease. Earlier research reported in the same journal in 2013 also reported no benefit in people with risk factors for heart disease."[19] He then goes on to strongly advise against fish oil supplementation— unless it's recommended by your doctor! (You can't make this shit up.)

Just as all magicians are duty-bound to never reveal the secrets to their sorcery, all doctors are duty-bound to feed the narrative that all doctors must be obeyed.

I would argue that no study has offered convincing evidence that fish oil is more devoutly to be desired than snake oil.

Whatever insignificant, marginal benefit there may be to fish oil has been demonstrated only in people who eat badly, not in people who eat a low-fat, plant-based diet. If a study found a tiny benefit of fish oil to the lung function of smokers, would the advice be to keep smoking and take fish oil, or to stop smoking and not need it? Until they do a study in which they find a benefit to fish oil for people on a low-fat, plant-based diet, I'm not interested. And you won't find a mackerel in the world worried that that study will ever happen.

Dr. Ornish is a medical pioneer who has helped improve and extend countless lives, and has added greatly to our understanding of the benefits of plant-based nutrition, particularly in reversing heart disease, but for whatever reason, he has never embraced the full implications of his own work by promoting a purely vegan diet. Just consider this interesting quote:

> There is a study by M.E. Levine in *Cell Metabolism*[20] that found that animal protein is harmful, independent of the whole fat-vs-carbs issue. This may be mediated in part through changes in trimethylamine-N-oxide (TMAO) levels, which Stanley Hazen[21] at the Cleveland Clinic is working on, and other mechanisms that we don't fully understand. People who eat a lot of animal protein have a 75% increase in premature death from all causes, a fivefold increased risk for premature death from diabetes, and a 400% increase in death from the major forms of cancer (prostate, breast, and colon cancer).[22]

Those words were spoken by Dr. Dean Ornish.

How can Dr. Ornish reconcile his understanding of the dangers of animal protein with his incorporation of egg whites (which are 100 percent animal protein) and "non-fat" dairy in his protocol? There's no good answer to that question, but I suspect that Dr. Ornish just didn't want his diet to look too "extreme"—perhaps in order to get Medicare to reimburse his program for reversing heart disease. In sum, to give Dr. Ornish his due: he has made a giant contribution to our understanding of the benefits of a plant-based diet; all the same, it's fair to ask whether, when confronted with the full implications of his own scientific work as it relates to an antagonistic culture, the man made some compromises that ran contrary to his own science. It's also fair to ask whether, perhaps for institutional or economic reasons, he felt he had no choice.

Ornish's fundamental recommendations to eliminate meat have been confirmed by any number of individual studies, as well as meta-analyses of multiple studies, all of which have associated meat intake with cardiovascular disease, diabetes, and all-cause mortality.[23]

To take a recent example (published in the *British Medical Journal* in 2019), an analysis using data from the renowned Nurses' Health Study, a study of 53,553 women and 27,916 men without cardiovascular disease or cancer at baseline, found that an increase in red meat consumption over eight years of the study was associated with a higher mortality risk in the next eight years; specifically, an increase of just half a serving per day increased mortality risk by ten percent.[24] Keep in mind that those eating a mere half a serving less of red meat were not necessarily replacing it with sweet potatoes or beans; they could have been replacing it with chicken or fish or *Oreos*. That is why the results, while significant, are less than dramatic.

The Oxford Vegetarian Study[25] was a prospective cohort study that involved 6,000 vegetarians and 5,000 non-vegetarians in the U.K. recruited in the first half of the 1980s and followed up for the next twelve years. All-cause death rates were lower in the non-meat-eaters than the meat-eaters, as were death rates specifically for heart disease and cancer. The lowest and healthiest cholesterol levels were recorded by the vegans, followed by the vegetarians and then the fish-eaters. Mortality from heart disease was directly related to intake of total animal fat, saturated animal fat, and dietary cholesterol. (And here's a more surprising, admittedly minor, but interesting fact: non-meat-eaters had half the risk of requiring an emergency appendectomy.) Body mass index was lower for non-meat-eaters than meat-eaters across all age groups and both men and women.

The importance of dietary fiber intake in preventing cardiovascular disease was established in a powerful study published in the *Journal of the American Medical Association* (JAMA) in 1996.[26] Dr. Eric Rimm, working with Dr. Walter Willett and others, measured the dietary fiber intake of no less than 43,757 U.S. male health care professionals (considered an ideal cohort for responsible participation in self-reporting health studies) who were between the ages of forty and seventy-five and free of diagnosed cardiovascular disease and diabetes. They reported how much fiber they ate and from what sources—you can imagine how annoying this must have been—and were followed up over the next six years. The research team determined how many suffered heart attacks (734 cases) and investigated the relationship between dietary fiber and heart attack risk. Conclusion? Unsurprisingly, fiber reduced risk. A mere ten extra grams of fiber reduced risk by nineteen percent. That's about the amount of fiber in two apples or two pears. If the fiber came specifically from cereal grains, it reduced risk by twenty-nine percent. Their conclusion, stated in the modest language of scientific research: "Our results suggest an inverse association between fiber intake and MI [myocardial infarction, or heart attack]."

Now how did the fiber reduce heart attack risk? One likely possibility is something well known to be true: fiber binds with cholesterol in the digestive system and escorts it out of your body before it's absorbed in your bloodstream. Therefore, it reduces the build-up of cholesterol, a known contributor to heart disease, in your artery walls.

But here's another possibility as well: someone who eats an extra apple and an extra pear per day might be likely to be eating a little less of foods that are bad for the heart. In other words, it may not have been just the fiber that was helping reduce the risk; it may have been the chance that—assuming that the extra-fiber-eaters weren't eating more food by weight per day than everyone else, a fairly safe assumption—the healthier eaters were having an apple and a pear instead of, say, French fries and a sausage. And so the extra-fiber-eaters were likely also the less-saturated-fat eaters, even though that particular fact wasn't measured in the study.

The same cascading ambiguity regarding causality is at play in many, if not most, nutritional studies; take, for example, the endless scientific literature[27] demonstrating a link between higher serum cholesterol count and heart disease risk. But is the cholesterol the cause of the cardiac risk or simply a marker of the risk? Let's examine this.

First, we need to ask: does the cholesterol actively do something to bring on heart disease? The answer is yes: it builds up in the walls of our arteries, making them atherosclerotic, raising blood pressure and slowing down or potentially blocking blood flow to the heart.

Then we need to ask: could cholesterol be serving as a marker of heart disease risk in ways unrelated to its own role in contributing to the disease? The answer is also yes: since those who have higher serum cholesterol are likely eating more animal (cholesterol-rich) foods, they are likely to be ingesting more saturated fat and causing more inflammation in their body. And those who eat more animal foods are likely to be eating less fiber. So, if you reduce your cholesterol count by taking statins without changing your diet, the saturated fat and inflammation, coupled with the fiber deficit, attendant to your diet may still kill you. So cholesterol is, in sum, not only a contributing factor in heart disease but a marker of the degree of unnatural eating that is wreaking havoc on the bloodstreams of human beings, who are designed by nature to be herbivores, as we shall see.

The Academy of Nutrition and Dietetics (AND; formerly the American Dietetic Association) is far and away America's leading organization of nutritionists, representing over 100,000 of them, and it is in fact the organization whose credentialing agency, the Commission on Dietetic Registration, has certified them as "registered dietitian nutritionists (RDNs)." You can't call yourself a dietitian (although in some states you can call yourself a nutritionist) without earning your credentials under the umbrella of the AND. Traditionally, one can't expect much in the way of honest science-based policy from this group. Michele Simon's 2013 report, *"Are America's Nutrition Professionals in the Pocket of Big Food?"*[28] answered its title with a resounding yes, detailing the organization's extraordinarily transparent corruption. Among the organization's most loyal sponsors are the National Cattlemen's Beef Association, ConAgra, General Mills, Kellogg, the National Dairy Council, Coca-Cola, and Pepsico. These corporations sponsor "continuing education" seminars facilitated by AND. As Simon pointed out, a nutritionist attendee of, for example, a Coca-Cola Company Beverage Institute for Health and Wellness seminar would have learned that "aspartame is completely safe, including for children over one year," that there's no link between sugar and children's behavior, and that the use of low-calorie sweeteners may serve as an "index of healthier diets," as "Diet soda consumers had better diets!"[29]

One could go on about the corruption of the organization, but Michele Simon already did that job admirably and definitively in her report. What is of more note today is a surprising and exceptional position paper of the Academy published in its own journal in Dec., 2016.

Entitled "*Position of the Academy of Nutrition and Dietetics: Vegetarian Diets,*"[30] the paper evaluates health risks, one-by-one, to the American population, citing significant and well-known prior studies, as they relate to a plant-based diet. For example, it concludes (in accordance with those many and varied earlier studies) that plant-based diets are associated with a lower body mass index, with vegans achieving the best scores. It also concludes that plant-based diets mitigate the risk of cardiovascular disease by improving not one, but many CVD risk factors: abdominal fat, blood pressure, blood glucose, and cholesterol profile. Moreover, plant-based diets decrease inflammation. Vegans, the paper points out, eat the most fiber and the least fat and saturated fat, and have the healthiest body weights and blood pressure. The plant-based diet even confers benefits on children—benefits that may well stay with them into adulthood: "Vegetarian children and teens are at lower risk than their nonvegetarian peers for overweight and obesity. Children and adolescents with BMI values in the normal range are more likely to also be within the normal range as adults, resulting in significant disease risk reduction." The paper cites two studies demonstrating that vegans are seventy-seven percent and sixty-two percent, respectively, less likely than meat-eaters to develop Type 2 diabetes. And that's not all: the paper summarizes the findings of several studies that demonstrate reduced risks of various cancers in vegetarians and vegans.

Now let's take a step back for a moment. Here's an organization, the Academy of Nutrition and Dietetics, that is notoriously venal, that traditionally can be counted on to advance the interests of such contributors as the National Cattlemen's Beef Association. And yet somehow, miraculously, the mountain of scientific evidence has built up to a point at which even this crummy, mercenary arm of the nation's nutrition industry publishes in its own journal a position paper that cites the overwhelming evidence supporting plant-based diets, evidence that for the most part favors vegan over vegetarian diets. Citing an array of significant studies, it supports the notion that plant-based eating can help you maintain a healthy body weight and healthy blood pressure, avoid diabetes, avoid cardiovascular disease, decrease inflammation, and avoid cancer. Holy cow! If you eat this way, you're dramatically reducing your risk of all the modern Western health plagues! It's better than any pill Big Pharma will ever come up with, has no associated costs, and there are no side effects! It's the best new thing since streaming movies! So surely the Academy must conclude this impressive report with a degree of enthusiasm that it has just stumbled upon the nutritional Holy Grail and must go on to forcefully recommend the plant-based diet to everyone?

Not a chance.

Its report concludes modestly that, "It is the position of the Academy of Nutrition and Dietetics that appropriately planned vegetarian, including vegan, diets are healthful, nutritionally adequate, and may provide health benefits for the prevention and treatment of certain diseases. These diets are appropriate for all stages of the life cycle, including pregnancy, lactation, infancy, childhood, adolescence, older adulthood, and for athletes. Plant-based diets are more environmentally sustainable than diets rich in animal products because they use fewer natural resources and are associated with much less environmental damage."

Wouldn't you say that's underselling a diet that, as the position paper has just demonstrated, dramatically reduces the risk of virtually all the major health epidemics confronting the country: obesity, hypertension, cardiovascular disease, diabetes, and cancer? A diet that can effectively solve our national health crisis (not to mention the environmental crisis), and all we're advised is that, if "appropriately planned" (sounds like hard work), it is "nutritionally adequate" (talk about damning with faint praise) and "may" (the word often used in science to mean "will") provide health benefits.

So does a plant-based diet have to be more "appropriately planned" than an omnivorous diet?

No. In fact, there's more planning involved when you eat flesh foods. Far more. That's because there's so much you have to be prepared for. You have to plan how to prepare the meat—which is, after all, part of an animal carcass rife with bacteria—in such a way that it doesn't infect your knives, other kitchen implements, cutting boards, countertops, and your own hands with *E. coli* or salmonella or campylobacter. You have to plan economically as well by saving a lot of money for medical expenses, or else you may need to plan to declare bankruptcy when the medical bills pile up. You have to plan your work schedule around a lot of doctor visits. You have to plan on doing a lot of clothes shopping because your size keeps increasing. And, at a younger age, you need to prepare your will.

On a plant-based diet, the only thing you have to plan for is a long and healthy life, retirement, and a higher probability of taking vacations. And vacations do indeed have to be planned, so I'll give the Academy that.

Instead of the plant-based diet that the *Journal of the Academy* touted in the body of its 2016 position paper, here's the diet (in italics) that the Academy actually endorses for women on their website,[31] with my comments below each recommendation:

At least three ounce equivalents of whole grains such as whole-grain bread, whole-wheat cereal flakes, whole-wheat pasta, brown rice or oats.

Now why would the Academy suggest such small servings (a measly three ounces) of healthy foods—especially the brown rice or oats, which are not flour-based? Is that based on any science? Of course not.

In fact, you can feel free to eat oats all day long. Go ahead, really, eat as much oatmeal as much as you want, three meals a day if you so choose, until you're full, throw some fruit on top of it, and you'll be eating a healthier diet than the Academy could ever dream of, and certainly a healthier diet than most Americans eat today. Three ounces? You could eat three pounds of oatmeal a day and I wouldn't worry about you. (Not three pounds of bread, though! There's a difference between a whole grain and a flour product.)

Three servings of low-fat or fat-free dairy products including milk, yogurt or cheese; or calcium-fortified plant-based alternatives.

While only three *ounces* of healthy whole grains were suggested, three *servings* of unhealthy dairy are recommended. Or, yes, three servings of much healthier plant-based alternatives. But there's no equivalence between cow's milk and plant milk, and in fact no similarity at all beyond the word "milk." The Academy is creating a food category premised on linguistics. Cow's milk will make you fat, clog your arteries, help bring on osteoporosis, and increase your risk of many types of cancer. Plant milk is fine, but you don't need it to get enough calcium, nor do you need to ensure that your plant milk is calcium-fortified. Leafy greens, all kinds of vegetables, nuts and seeds, and legumes are powerhouses of calcium. Drinking cow's milk will not give you strong bones; that's a lie.[32] Studies have shown that those who take in the most calcium from dairy actually suffer the most bone fractures.[33] In one study, each additional daily glass of milk in a boy's teenage years was associated with a nine percent greater risk of hip fracture as an adult.[34] The best strategy for protecting your bones is to do a lot of exercise and eat a plant-based diet rather than a diet of excess protein—and especially not sulfuric animal protein, high in the problematic amino acid methionine. You should eat zero servings of dairy products; you can have some plant milk if you so desire, but you certainly don't need to.

Five to five-and-a-half ounce equivalents of protein such as lean meat, poultry, seafood, eggs, beans, lentils, tofu, nuts and seeds.

Boy, that sounds very specific! They know exactly how much protein you need: somewhere between five ounces and five and a half ounces of certain foods. They must have done a lot of studies to prove that! Of course, they make it sound like these foods are pure protein, but all of them, except the beans and lentils, actually come with a lot of fat.

And, by the way, what the hell is "lean meat"? You hear the term a lot and it's never defined. I'll tell you what "lean meat" is: an oxymoron that gives dietitians deniability. It gives them their out. "Oh, you ate meat as advised and you still got a heart attack? Yeah, but I told you to eat LEAN meat! Did you check to make sure your meat was lean? Did you tear it apart, examine every shred, and measure the percentage of fat marbled within it? No? Well, sorry, but you got what's coming to you, pal."

"Lean meat" is like "clean coal"—an industry's p.r. claim with the single drawback of being an out-an-out fantasy. "Lean meat" doesn't exist. If you want to eat something lean, eat a potato. Eat a mango. Eat a portabella mushroom. Here's a helpful hint: if you have to "trim the fat" off a food, it ain't lean.

The Academy, with its "five-and-a-half-ounces of protein" recommendation, does its best to promote the dangerous myth that meat equates to protein, that they are one and the same. Meat, poultry, seafood, and eggs (unless we're speaking only of egg whites—the Academy doesn't bother saying) are, let's not forget, rich not only in protein but in saturated fat and cholesterol, as well. And all protein is not equal: the animal-based protein will be more sulfuric than the plant-based protein, and so more problematic for your kidneys and bones.

Plant protein is superior, period. A 2014 study published in *Cell Metabolism*[35] analyzed over 3,000 individuals aged fifty to sixty-five over eighteen years, and broke them down into those eating a high protein, moderate protein, or low protein diet. It found that those on the high protein diet had a seventy-four percent increased risk of all-cause mortality, and were four times as likely to die of cancer as those on the low-protein diet. Importantly, though, the source of the protein was key: the plant-based protein didn't have the death-promoting effect. "When we controlled for the effect of plant-based protein," the authors wrote, "there was no change in the association between protein intake and mortality, indicating that high levels of animal proteins promote mortality and not that plant-based proteins have a protective effect."

The authors concluded, "In agreement with other epidemiological and animal studies . . . our findings suggest that a diet in which plant-based nutrients represent the majority of the food intake is likely to maximize health benefits in all age groups."

Plant protein has also been found to be better for your kidneys than animal protein. If you're not a regular reader of the *American Journal of Kidney Disease*, you might have missed an article published in 2016 entitled, "The Associations of Plant Protein Intake with All-Cause Mortality in CKD [Chronic Kidney Disease]."[36] Using data from a study of nearly 15,000 participants, the authors concluded, "A plant protein–rich diet is also associated with decreased production of uremic toxins . . . implicated in CKD progression, cardiovascular disease, and mortality in kidney disease patients. Since these uremic toxins accumulate in more advanced CKD, a diet high in plant sources might be more beneficial in preventing or managing advanced CKD." The authors of the study speculate that the reason for the kidney-protective effect of plant proteins may be that they reduce the phosphorus burden on kidneys in comparison to animal proteins.

But remember I spoke earlier of the cascading ambiguity of nutritional studies, the difficulty of isolating cause and effect? Well, the authors of the kidney study own up to it: "Despite plentiful evidence from observational research on the benefit of plant protein in decreasing cancer, cardiovascular mortality, blood pressure and diabetes, caution is needed in interpreting these results. Whether the results are related to the plant protein itself or to the higher polyunsaturated fatty acid and lower saturated fatty acid or increased fiber levels associated with more plant-based diets is difficult to establish without intervention trials that increase solely plant protein."

In other words, the kidney protection associated with plant protein may be due to the nature of plant protein itself, or it may have to do with the fact that plant protein comes attached to healthier fats than does animal protein, or it may be that plant protein, unlike animal protein, comes attached to fiber. Or it may be all three.

But, remember, you don't have to concern yourself with protein at all. It's a myth. It's poppycock. Just eat food. Protein, remember, is omnipresent in food. So don't worry yourself about some imaginary "protein group," into which the Academy, like the USDA with its latest "Food Plate" or (formerly) "Food Pyramid" nonsense, lumps together a very diverse group consisting of human foods (beans, lentils, tofu, nuts, and seeds) as well as foods highly appropriate for carnivorous animals ("lean" meat, poultry, seafood, and eggs). You should eat legumes frequently (aim for at least two servings a day); nuts, seeds, and tofu—because of their fat content—more sparingly; and animal foods not at all.

Returning now to the nutritional recommendations of the Academy:

Two cups of fruits—fresh, frozen or canned without added sugar.

Okay, I won't argue with that, since it would represent an improvement to the diets of most Americans. But here's my bias: fresh is best, and organic is even better. And I, for one, don't worry about how many "cups" of fruit I eat; call me nutty, but I don't measure fruits in cups before I eat them. I might in a given day eat an apple, a couple of bananas, a lot of blueberries and strawberries, a pear, and maybe a papaya or a mango—I guess that's a lot more than two cups. Is there some science telling us to limit ourselves to two cups? No, there is not. But there's a lot of science telling us that Americans don't eat enough fruit and vegetables. Fruits are packed with antioxidants and fiber, your best protection package against cancer. You don't have to go through life counting how many you've had, and concerning yourself with some upper limit. Just eat a lot of fruit.

Two-and-a-half cups of colorful vegetables—fresh, frozen or canned without added salt.

Wow, there's that remarkable specificity again! These scientists really must know what they're talking about! Have two-and-a-half cups—not three, heaven forbid—of colorful vegetables. The specificity is there to make it sound like there's some science involved, when in fact there is none. I guarantee you that the members of whatever godforsaken committee was cobbled together to concoct this remarkably precise recommendation pulled it straight out of two-and-a-half of their asses. What would happen if you had three cups, or even four, of colorful vegetables? Would your skin start turning green, or maybe orange? The truth is, there's no upper limit, within reason, on your vegetable intake. The more, the merrier. Eat until you're full. Nobody in human history ever got fat or diabetic on steamed broccoli or asparagus. Again, organic is even better. And eaten steamed or sautéed in water or vegetable broth is ideal. Don't make your vegetables unhealthy by adding oil.

The reason for the unnecessary upper limit placed on vegetables, fruits, and whole grains is to leave room for the entirely unnecessary meat and dairy that the diet advises, ignoring the limitless scientific evidence contrary to this advice.

As an aside, why does the Academy recommend this diet specifically for women? What's that about? Do women need to eat differently than men? Other than the fact that menstruating women may need to be concerned about their iron levels, the answer is no. A larger person has higher caloric needs than a smaller person, but of course some women are larger than some men, so that's a matter of size, not sex. Sex-specific diets represent just a little added dose of confusion from professional nutritional imposters.

Given the overwhelming scientific evidence against the consumption of meat, why is it that nutritional studies generally don't conclude with a full-throated endorsement of the vegan diet? Let's consider the outlook of Dr. Rimm, Professor of Epidemiology and Nutrition and Director of the Program in Cardiovascular Epidemiology at the Harvard T.H. Chan School of Public Health, and Professor of Medicine at the Harvard Medical School, who was the lead researcher in the fiber study cited above. In an interview, Dr. Rimm was quoted as follows: "But avoiding it [trans-fats] if at all possible is ideal. We can't tell people to stop eating all meat and all dairy products. Well, we could tell people to become vegetarians. If we were truly basing this only on science, we would, but it is a bit extreme."[37]

There you go. The man said it aloud. It comes back to Science versus Culture. All the science—and you might be forgiven for imagining that a scientist like Dr. Rimm would be committed to the principles of science—points to the superiority of the plant-based diet. But when Dr. Rimm, whose job is precisely to research the health effects of diet, studies any data on the correlation between diet and disease, his analysis is framed by the cultural assumption that people must of course eat meat and dairy, and that any advice to do otherwise would be unthinkable, no matter where the evidence points. He considers it too "extreme" to strictly follow the dietary path the scientific evidence suggests, and makes sure that any conclusion he reaches and advice he gives comports with his view of what is culturally acceptable. He is a scientist who has sided against Science, in deference to the authority of Culture.

Dr. Walter Willett is about as well-known, celebrated, and mainstream an epidemiologist and nutrition researcher as you can find; he was the long-time director of the Nurses' Health Study, and worked with Dr. Rimm on the fiber study. A dietary truth slipped out of his lips when he was interviewed by Gina Kolata of The New York Times in 1990: "If you step back and look at the data, the optimum amount of red meat you eat should be zero."[38] But in his own book, *Eat, Drink, and Be Healthy*, he doesn't promote a zero-meat diet. Instead, he writes, with the kind of moderation my father would have admired, "Eat more good fats (these mostly come from plants) and fewer bad fats (these mostly come from meats and dairy foods)."[39] And he writes, "Choose healthy sources of protein, limit your consumption of red meat, and don't eat processed meat." What does "limit your consumption of red meat" mean? Once a month? Once a week? Once a day? Why not limit it to the "zero" that he admitted was the optimum intake of red meat?

Because he just doesn't think that that's possible, and he wants his book to sell. He's taking the side of Culture.

Remember that FH Foundation I mentioned earlier? The organization dedicated to helping people suffering from "familial hypercholesterolemia?" Well, since they want to help people like my family, they offer diet tips on their website. And, credit where credit is due, some of their advice happens to be right on the money: "*WHAT TO AVOID: Strive to bring your fat intake to a minimum. The most harmful types of fat are saturated fat and trans fat, which are found in foods from animal sources, such as meat and dairy products, as well as packed snacks, fast food, and baked goods (biscuits, cakes, etc).*"

This is followed by even better advice: *"WHAT TO EAT: Fiber! Fiber is found in plant foods such as fruits, vegetables, whole grains, nuts, seeds and legumes. Research indicates that eating more than 25 grams of fiber per day can reduce risk of heart disease. As a rule of thumb, think plants (not animals): fruits, vegetables, grains, and beans. MORE! Barley, oatmeal, sunflower seeds, almonds, soy, tofu, edamame, chickpeas, black beans, kidney beans, lentils, Brussels sprouts, carrots, apples, bananas, pears, oranges, grapefruit, prunes, blackberries."*[40]

Fantastic. So far, so good. Eat plants, not animals, and include legumes and whole plant foods. Nothing wrong with more barley, oatmeal, beans, lentils, fruits and vegetables. I couldn't agree more.

If they stopped right there, they'd actually be giving helpful advice. But they can't stop right there because of the Culture they serve. And so they go on, with mind-bogglingly foolish and contradictory advice:

Limit intake of cheese. Just one ounce of cheese (one inch cube) has roughly six grams of saturated fat. Try a low-fat cheese or use a cheese slicer to slice a couple of slivers of a flavorful cheese to top apple slices or a few whole grain crackers.

Eat leaner cuts of beef and pork, such as eye of round and pork tenderloin, and trim as much visible fat as possible before cooking. Reduce portions to 3 ounces, about the size of a deck of cards, and supplement your plate with a variety of colorful vegetables and some whole grains. . . .

In casseroles, soups and stew, cut the amount of animal protein in half and substitute beans (drain and rinse first, if using canned beans) for the remaining amount of meat.

Remove skin from chicken and other poultry before eating.

Fish is a great source of healthy omega-3 fats. The American Heart Association recommends eating 3.5 ounces of fish (especially oily, omega-3 rich fish) at least twice a week. Note: Tilefish, shark, swordfish, and king mackerel have high mercury content and should be eaten only occasionally.

Include a meatless meal at least once a week. Some people are trying "Meatless Monday", but you can choose the day of the week that works best for you.

Yes, they suggest boldly embarking on a diet that includes one meatless meal per week. Presumably, that's one out of twenty-one. That's simply the best they expect you can do. And, heck, you can even choose your own day of the week! Don't feel in any way restricted—it absolutely does not have to be Monday! Maybe for breakfast, on Tuesdays, you can have an English muffin. That should make up for the other twenty meat-based meals a week. Oh, and make sure to eat your chicken without the skin—that should remove the cholesterol and saturated fat!

And so, first they tell you to "think plants (not animals)," then they go on to advise you to eat more animal foods daily than a hungry lion in the wild would be able to chow down on a dare.

It's pretty much a sure thing that I would have been diagnosed with FH, given my family history and my cholesterol levels before I got my diet right. And certainly my bloodwork would never have improved (as it did when I went vegan, and further when I gave up oil) had I followed the screwy and self-contradictory dietary guidelines on the foundation's website, believing that I was on the beeline to health by removing the skin from my chicken.

I don't know who wrote the FH Foundation's extraordinary list of dietary recommendations, but after a good start, each successive one is so suffused with nutritional ignorance that it's all but certain that medical professionals were involved. The one about the lean cut of pork tenderloin is a particular favorite of mine, and you can be sure it's redounded to the economic benefit of untold legions of cardiologists attending to sufferers of "familial hypercholesterolemia."

This is the stunning level of stupidity and cognitive dissonance you encounter when Science capitulates to Culture.

Having presented you in this chapter with a small sampling of the voluminous body of scientific literature that establishes the superiority of the plant-based diet, let me now confess that I don't place a high level of trust in most nutritional studies. The exception would be the two studies undertaken by Dr. Esselstyn, whose results, if extrapolated to the larger cohorts of such studies as the Adventist Health Study or the Nurses' Health Study, would blow them out of the water.

Why don't I put great stock in most nutritional studies? One reason—the lesser reason—is the conflicts of interest that taint many such studies. Marion Nestle has written about the corruption attendant to industry-funded research in her book *Food Politics*.[41] The egg industry, to name just one tricky food industry, has often succeeded in underwriting research that obfuscated the plain fact that eggs are cholesterol factories.[42] Jeff Nelson, a vegan activist, online journalist, and founder of the *VegSource* website, has taken even advocates of plant-based nutrition to task for touting the benefits of nuts while relying on studies that were funded by the nut industry.[43] (I have tried to filter out any ethically compromised studies in any sources I cite in this volume.)

More importantly, even entirely well-intentioned and ethical nutritional research studies may leave much to be desired because they are often self-reporting studies of large populations eating whatever they want to eat, and quite possibly reporting their food intake inaccurately or incompletely. Take, for example, the Adventist Health Study that found a threefold higher risk of fatal cardiac ischemia for meat-eaters than vegetarians. That's certainly significant evidence that fits into the overall body of evidence establishing the danger to your heart from eating meat. But it doesn't tell you a lot because the researchers could not control the diets of their respective cohorts. Were the vegetarians eating a lot of cream cheese, for example? Were they drinking a lot of soda pop? It's possible, after all, that some of the meat-eaters in the study might have been consuming more fruits and vegetables and less dairy than some of the vegetarians, and so those particular meat-eaters might have had diets that were in many ways superior, from a health standpoint, to the diets of some of the vegetarians.

That prevalence of myriad confounding factors infects most nutritional studies. That could be why the Adventist Health Study demonstrated that eliminating meat from your diet reduces your risk of fatal heart disease by only two-thirds.

Had the comparison been, instead, between the meat-eaters and those following the whole-food, oil-free, vegan dietary regime into which Dr. Esselstyn enrolls his heart patients, we wouldn't be looking at a ratio of 3:1 in relative heart disease risk. It would be closer, I can only guess, to 3,000:1. And we might not be able to express it in ratio form at all, because those on the Esselstyn diet might not have suffered any fatal heart attacks at all, and you can't create a ratio when one of the numbers is zero.

When you see a study, such as the Oxford Vegetarian Study, that shows the best outcomes for vegans, the second best for vegetarians, and the worst for meat-eaters, that may be significant, but it's also vague. "Vegan" is a word that describes what people don't eat: animal foods. "Vegetarian" also describes what people don't eat: flesh foods and eggs. Neither word describes what people *do* eat. And it's perfectly possible—indeed it may be the rule, rather than the exception—that people often eat very unhealthy vegetarian and vegan diets.

That's why the Esselstyn studies tower above the others: his subjects were instructed to eat healthfully, and were taught how. The Esselstyn studies, in other words, are studies in which one group (the overwhelming majority, those who stayed true to his plan) ate healthfully, and another group (the non-compliant minority) did not. And even had there been no non-compliant participants—as I'm sure Dr. Esselstyn would have preferred—in his study, the validity of his work would still be unimpeachable, as the contrasting "cohort" could simply be viewed as the American population writ large, or any population of heart patients writ large, because we already have plenty of data on how well they fare on the standard American diet; we also have data on how poorly the study participants themselves fared before they learned to eat correctly.

Neither I nor anyone else in the plant-based food movement seeks to make the case that robust and abundant health is the likely outcome of a diet of vegan junk food: vegan ice creams, donuts, cookies, cupcakes, waffles, potato chips, oily salad dressings, pretzels, and beer, or of highly processed vegan meat substitutes: faux-meat sausages and other fake meats made from isolated soy protein, coconut oil, wheat gluten, and (usually) long lists of ingredients. We make the case only for a whole-foods, low-fat, plant-based diet. Studies that involve cohorts of "vegetarians" or "vegans" are not particularly meaningful; the fact that those studies overwhelmingly show "vegetarians" and "vegans" outperforming omnivores in a wide range of health metrics only hints at the remarkable potential benefits of a truly healthy diet: a low-fat, whole foods, vegan diet. When I read pablum in the popular press about the supposed health benefits of the meat-laden Caveman Diet, I dearly wish that some of the original cavemen had actually adhered to the Esselstyn program.

They might still be around today to call out the bullshit.

While I was writing this book, a truly pathetic salvo came forth from some desperate advocates of flesh consumption—pathetic, at least, from a scientific standpoint, although it was probably effective from a p.r. standpoint. Popularly called "The Red Meat Papers," this nonsense was published by the *Annals of Internal Medicine*, formerly considered a respectable scientific journal, on Oct. 1, 2019.[44] The report's shocking finding was to endorse continuing current levels of red meat consumption. Naturally, this made headlines in all sorts of publications and broadcasts across the country and around the world, undoubtedly resulting in millions of consumers throwing up their hands once again and feeling confirmed in their belief that science just hasn't been able to determine a healthy way to eat.

So upon what new research, you might ask, did this study base its endorsement of red meat consumption? Well, there was no new research at all; it was a "meta-analysis" of existing research. The authors put together a panel of fourteen members, not all of whom had health science backgrounds, and asked them to review nutritional research using certain metrics, designed for the analysis of pharmaceutical drugs, that place a higher value on randomized controlled trials, which are the gold standard of pharmaceutical trials but are generally inappropriate for nutritional studies. It's unethical, after all, to randomly assign one cohort to eat meat, since we know it's harmful, while assigning another cohort to eat healthfully; furthermore, it's hardly practical to assign trial participants diets to follow for periods of years. For that reason, most nutritional research takes the form of observational studies in which people report what they've been eating. Therefore, the panel gave a "weak" grade to all the evidence it reviewed, while acknowledging that that evidence showed that red meat consumption is associated with increased risks of heart disease, stroke, cancer, and all-cause mortality. It then weighed that "weak" evidence against a more "critically important" factor in its grading system: the proposition that people do not have a "willingness to change unprocessed red or processed meat consumption."

In the study's own words, which should have been enough to discredit it from consideration for publication in a scientific journal: ". . . the panel believed that for the majority of individuals, the desirable effects (a potential lowered risk for cancer and cardiometabolic outcomes) associated with reducing meat consumption probably do not outweigh the undesirable effects (impact on quality of life, burden of modifying cultural and personal meal preparation and eating habits)."

So a study that made headlines internationally as if it offered some exciting new research contradicting the scientific consensus against red meat consumption was in fact no more than the result of applying a preposterous methodology to the existing evidence—a methodology that assigned relatively fewer points to all the evidence that red meat consumption leads to heart attacks and cancer, and relatively more points to the authors' assumptions that people really enjoy their sausages and don't want to give them up.

You can make the case for cigarette smoking and even heroin use with a methodology like that.

If you're surprised to find highly opinionated language about the "burden of modifying cultural and personal meal preparation" in a journal once believed to concern itself with science, well, it's just more evidence that, in the ongoing tussle between Science and Culture, Culture keeps winning. Even scientific journals appear willing to abandon the fortress of Science to flock to the winning side.

The study's august panel, by the way, voted 11-3 for these recommendations; there were three dissenters who favored a tougher stance against meat, but this was a case of *majority rules*. The science of nutrition, it turns out, is a democracy.

When you hear about "scientific" studies that contradict the broad consensus against flesh and dairy consumption, this is the quality of "research" you can expect to find.

Have I cherry-picked studies to omit other studies, more persuasive than "The Red Meat Papers," that show a benefit to eating animal foods? There are very few such studies, and they tend to be tainted either by corrupt intent (paid for by a dairy interest, for example) or by flawed study design. The animal food that is most often reported in the popular press to have health benefits is fish; we often hear that it's been found to be good for the heart. But studies that show a benefit to fish consumption for the heart, like those in a meta-analysis published in the *American Journal of Medicine* in September 2014,[45] demonstrate that benefit only in comparison to people eating the standard American diet without fish (or with less fish). So that study proves only that fish is less bad for you than cheeseburgers or steak. It does not prove that fish is better for you than lentils, brown rice, and asparagus. It has no relevance at all to those of us eating the natural, human diet.

All nutritional studies that do not involve a cohort eating a truly low-fat, plant-based diet are simply studies that seek to compare and contrast between people eating badly. It's like doing studies of two groups of blindfolded drivers and trying to determine whether antilock brakes or airbags provide them with greater safety.

It's a little hard to take many of these studies seriously. I would humbly suggest, if you want to get real results, take the blindfolds off.

The blindfolds in this case are the blindfolds of culture. If you take them off and examine the science, it all points to the inescapable conclusion that we should be eating plants, not animals.

The American health crisis will not end until we do. Medicare-for-All, in the event that it ever happens, won't make a lick of difference to American's health. The only thing that will is changing the food we eat.

CHAPTER SEVEN: SETTLED SCIENCE, PART TWO: COMPARATIVE ANATOMY

If, beyond all the scientific studies that point to the health advantages of a plant-based diet, more proof were needed of the appropriateness and superiority of plant nutrition for human beings, the science of comparative anatomy clinches the case.

Scientists examine, compare, and contrast the anatomical structures of all mammalian carnivores, omnivores, and herbivores. That way they can determine where humans fit into the mix, since we seem to have misplaced the instinct ingrained in all other mammals to know what to eat. And, to make matters worse, unlike all other mammals, we have to contend with advertising. Our defining characteristic, after all—what truly makes us human and separates us from all other creatures—is a limitless fog of dietary confusion all our own.

What better way to end that confusion than by comparing and contrasting ourselves to other mammals? (I acknowledge my debt here to Dr. Milton Mills, an urgent care physician in the Washington, D.C., area, who has argued this case forcefully.)[1]

Scientists therefore examine such characteristics as the configuration and motion of the jaw, the structure of the dentition, the presence or absence of enzymes in the saliva, the acidity and capacity of the stomach, the length and features of the intestines, the presence or absence of claws, and many other characteristics. And in every case—every single one, bar none—humans align with the herbivores, never the omnivores or the carnivores. It's not even a contest.

Carnivores and omnivores have facial muscles that allow for a wide oral gape to seize, dismember, and swallow prey. Humans and other herbivores do not.

Carnivores and omnivores have greatly elongated canine teeth for stabbing and shredding prey. Humans and other herbivores do not.

Let it be noted, however, that humans have managed to develop the most elaborate language skills of any mammal, allowing us to label certain remarkably small and unimpressive human teeth "canines" so as to add a unique linguistic flair to our own species-defining fog of confusion, and to give obtuse talking points to the most tedious members of the species.

Carnivores, most of whom hunt at night, have night vision many times keener than humans. Carnivores and omnivores have claws well-adapted to seizing prey. Humans have fingers well-adapted to the piano, which, when played at night by these same humans, generally requires lighting.

Carnivores, needing to conserve their energy, instinctively target diseased or weak prey. Humans and other herbivores are attracted to beautiful, healthy plants.

As creatures of the hunt, carnivores run many times faster than we do.

Carnivores and omnivores do not chew their food; humans and other herbivores do. Our jaw joints allow for the side-to-side motion needed to chew plant foods. The bite force of carnivores and omnivores is many times that of humans and other herbivores.

Carnivores and omnivores do not have carbohydrate-digesting enzymes in their saliva; humans and other herbivores do. The amylase in human saliva is designed to digest starches and break them down into sugars, and helps make potatoes taste delicious by giving them added sweetness.

Carnivores as a rule make their kills infrequently, often only once a week. Then they gorge themselves, swallowing huge chunks of meat that can pass through their wide esophagi and land in their huge stomachs, where the meat is dissolved by very acidic stomach acid, usually while the animals rest after their hunt. With food in the stomach, the stomach acid of carnivores and omnivores has a pH of 1 or less. Humans and other herbivores cannot swallow huge chunks of meat (most human choking deaths involve meat), have narrow and muscular esophagi, relatively small stomachs, and stomach acid that has a very moderate pH of 4-5 with food in the stomach.

Given their hunt-kill-gorge-rest lifestyle, carnivores can go for long periods without eating. I get a headache if I skip lunch.

Carnivores and omnivores have short intestines to facilitate the exit of putrefying dead animal remains from the body as quickly as possible. Humans and other herbivores have long small intestines (required for the processing of cellulose), about ten times our body length (defined, for the purpose of comparison, as head to tail bone), that perform the task of absorbing nutrients. Only fibrous foods (plant foods) have the bulk required to travel that distance efficiently.

Carnivores and omnivores do not develop heart disease from a diet rich in saturated fat and cholesterol. Humans do.

Carnivores have short gestation periods. Humans and other large herbivores have long gestation periods. Carnivores tend to have litters; humans and other large herbivores usually have single births. Carnivore babies are born at a very early stage so as not to burden the pregnant female for long by keeping her from hunting.

Carnivores tend to not live as long as herbivores. Just ask any dog why we've come up with the phrase "dog years." The majority of humans, though, apparently unappreciative of the greater longevity that is our birthright as herbivores, manage to shorten their lifespan by convincing themselves, on the basis of no scientific evidence whatsoever, that they are omnivores.

* * *

To summarize this chapter and the last, we've looked at the macronutrient profiles of plant vs. flesh foods, which alone should convince us that we should be eating plants, not dead animals; we've sampled some of the scientific studies underlying the settled science that humans who eat plants primarily or exclusively are likely to enjoy better health than meat-eaters; and we've looked at the case presented by an analysis of comparative anatomy, which leads us to the inescapable conclusion that humans have evolved as herbivores.

All of which brings us, finally, to common sense. We are primates. Look in the mirror. Do you look more like a chimpanzee or a tiger? Doesn't it follow that our diet should be the diet of a primate? We evolved from arboreal animals. In the canopy of trees, the most abundant food is fruit, not roast beef, pork, or cheddar cheese.

All our fellow Hominidae (or Great Apes) eat a diet that is 95 percent or more plants. Orangutans eat a diet that is up to 90 percent fruit, supplemented by leaves, shoots, bark, and yes, insects and bird eggs. Gorillas may consume up to forty pounds of plants per day—fruits, leaves, stems, shoots, roots, and flowers—while about 2 or 3 percent of their diet consists of insects. And then there are the chimps—our closest relatives, and, alas, a special case. I regret that, in the interest of objectivity, I am duty-bound to inform the reader fully about the dietary behavior of our cousins the chimps.

Chimps, which have far more impressive canine teeth (perhaps evolved as a form of defense) than humans, eat a diet that's about 95 percent plants. They are big-time fig-lovers: figs can make up about half of the chimp diet. Of course, they eat other fruits, too, as well as nuts and seeds, flowers, bark, and leaves. Famously, Dr. Jane Goodall discovered that chimps also use sticks as tools to fish for termites. We can't be sure if they really, truly like to eat termites—which certainly seems improbable to me—or if, as I would contend, they were just trying to impress the wildly supportive Dr. Goodall. In any case, termites and ants comprise only a small part of the chimp's diet, just 2 or 3 percent. From my perspective, the real inconvenient truth is that once in a while—about nine days a year,[2] on average —chimps have meat days. I will have to appeal to the reader to be liberal-minded about this unfortunate fact.

Here's what happens, and I'm not going to sugar-coat it. In the canopy, male chimps will surround a monkey—red colobus monkeys being a particular delicacy—trap it, and seize it. They'll slam it against the branches of the tree and break its neck; then they'll rip apart its living flesh and give out pieces of that flesh to female chimps—in exchange for sex.[3]

We can all agree that that's appalling behavior. I'm not going to try to justify it. But to be fair, they're not doing it for nutritional reasons; they're doing it to get laid.

When I was single, I did far worse.

Okay, allow me now to anticipate the objection the reader may raise after considering the diet of our primate cousins. *Hold on!* I can hear you saying. Since the other great apes are omnivores, not herbivores, shouldn't we live as omnivores, too? Didn't the case for a vegan diet just go up in smoke?

To which I say, politely: *give me a break.* Yes, our ape cousins are behaviorally omnivores, but their diets are all overwhelmingly centered around plants. They're not having bacon-and-eggs for breakfast, cheesesteaks for lunch, and fried chicken for dinner. There's no dairy in their diet. (And—not to overlook vegan sins—they also don't add oil or sugar to their food.) Most of the few percent of their diet that is not fruit or nuts or seeds or leaves or flowers is living insects. And, yes, deplorably, in the case of chimps, there's the occasional romantic monkey tartare dinner.

If you want to have a 97 percent plant, 3 percent termite diet, go ahead, knock yourself out. You'll be doing far, far better than most Americans. As a bonus, you may find work with a pest control company.

And if, say, on nine days of the year, you succumb to a desire to share a slab of flesh food with an individual for whom you harbor romantic interest, I judge you not. I hope it works for you. Do first make sure that your enamored isn't a vegan, though, or you'll blow the whole thing.

I see no reason for the human diet to be even 3 percent animal-based, whether insect or fish, but I would be positively giddy if most Americans adopted a 3 percent animal-food, 97 percent whole-plant-foods diet. The general population would get so much healthier that we could stop arguing about health insurance, making cable news watchable again. Currently, according to the USDA,[4] Americans get about 30 percent of their calories from animal foods, about 25 percent from grains, about 20 percent from plant-based oils and fats, about 15 percent from sugar and other sweeteners, about 8 percent from fruits and vegetables combined, and a couple of percent from nuts. These lamentable numbers may be even worse than they seem because the grains are not all whole grains, but rather include flour products like white bread, pizza crust, and chocolate cake. The vegetables not only include, but positively feature, French fries.

Consider that we humans share about 98 percent of our DNA with our cousins, the chimpanzees. Consider that they are probably the second most intelligent creatures on the planet, after (most) humans. Consider that, like the best of us, they can recognize themselves in a mirror. Consider that their dinner plans can be as devious as ours. Consider that chimpanzees have the same number of teeth as humans, but far more impressive canine teeth than we do, teeth that are far more suitable than ours for biting into flesh. Then consider that, despite this fact, they eat a diet that is 95 percent whole fruits and vegetables, while we Americans get about 8 percent of our calories from fruits and vegetables. Chimpanzees are not plagued by obesity and diabetes. Clearly, they know what they're doing when they eat, and just as clearly, we proud humans do not. We have the comparative advantages that we can cook and digest whole grains and legumes, but these are advantages that we don't exploit sufficiently or correctly. Between whole grains, legumes, fruits, fungi, and vegetables (especially including calorie-dense starchy vegetables such as potatoes and sweet potatoes), we need to attain at least 95 percent of our calories, with the remaining few percent, I'd suggest, reserved for nuts and seeds, rather than termites (which never go over well at a dinner party). Instead, many Americans get literally less than 10 percent of their calories from healthy sources.

And then we argue ad nauseam about who should pay for our health insurance. Chimpanzees eat correctly and don't even bother with health insurance. They're saving a fortune.

The diets of our ape cousins should serve as a giant, screaming clue to humanity to tell us what we should be eating—although I can imagine an objection from Creationists. And so to Creationists I would say this: if you believe that we were designed by God in Her image, then all we can say with certainty, and all that it is important for you to understand, is that God must be a vegan. Because all the scientific evidence tells us that humans were designed to eat plants. And, after all, it's pretty hard to picture Her grilling hot dogs, much less toiling in a slaughterhouse. If You were God, would You want to deal with caging animals, pumping them up with antibiotics, slaughtering them, slicing them up, refrigerating them, and making sure You cook them above 145 degrees Fahrenheit? Surely You would have better things to do.

Perhaps, dear reader, you recognize the validity of the arguments made here but you are one of those folks who can't seem to imagine giving up animal foods entirely and going vegan. Maybe it's because you have a mental image of vegans and always thought of them as "other," and you'd just hate to join our team. Or maybe it's because you so dearly love the taste of salmon or some other flesh food. Perhaps the problem is your living situation—the perceived resistance of those with whom you share your life, the difficulty of proposing a whole new style of eating that might sound radical to him/her/them. Could you therefore just become "vegan-ish," you wonder? Would that be good enough? Would your health be badly compromised if you ate, for example, one serving of salmon per week, or per month?

The short answer is probably not. No study has ever compared the health outcomes of one cohort of folks on a low-fat, whole-foods vegan diet with another cohort of folks on a low-fat, whole-foods, plant-based diet supplemented by one serving of salmon per week. I'll wager that that study will never be done. (We have few enough studies in which any cohort at all is actually on a healthy diet.) First of all, it's expensive to conduct nutritional research, and nobody's going to pony up for a study that targets a hairsplitting dietary distinction. Moreover, there are limitations to the sensitivity of nutritional research.

We know, for example, that potato chips are unhealthy, but no researcher ever has or ever will do a study of the effect of eating three potato chips a week. So all we can do is extrapolate. It's inarguable that potato chips are terribly salty and fatty and devoid of nutritional value. But the effect of three potato chips per week? Probably just a tiny bit bad for you. Maybe in a way that isn't even measurable.

Similarly, one serving of salmon per week? Probably just a tiny bit bad for you.

So if you are transitioning from the Standard American Diet to a low-fat, whole-foods plant-based diet supplemented by one serving of salmon per week, or for that matter three potato chips a week, you will be taking a great leap forward. There's a good chance that, if you already suffer diet-related chronic health problems, you will find those issues improved or resolved over time. Or, if you're commencing this new way of eating in good health, you will be more likely to sustain that good health.

From a health perspective, the key is dietary pattern. If you're getting your fuel—the bulk of your calories—from healthy sources (potatoes, sweet potatoes, beans, rice, corn, oats, and other whole "starchy" foods), supplemented by fruits and non-starchy vegetables and mushrooms, that's the key to health. That's the single most salient dietary factor affecting your well-being. A few weekly potato chips or a single serving of salmon, however unnecessary and unhelpful, would be unlikely to undo all the good you will do for yourself by eating right most of the time.

The risk, of course, is that three potato chips per week will turn into a dozen, then two dozen, then the whole bag. And one serving of salmon per week will turn into three or five. So my advice would be to aim high and go whole-foods vegan.

Nonetheless, I know that many people prefer to change their diet more gradually, and that's fine.

And you may just find, if you embark on a fish-once-a-week-style plant-based diet, that you wake up one day a vegan. You'll realize that some weeks or months went by without your prized flesh food and you didn't miss it. If the occasional serving of fish now makes the transition easier for you, so be it.

Finally, you may ask, if you go the route of a healthy, whole-foods, plant-based diet, supplemented by flesh foods once a week, would you still be welcomed to the side of the angels? Would you get into Vegan Heaven?

I've got to confess here that it's not really up to me. But if it were, I'd certainly let you in as a guest.

CHAPTER EIGHT:
HOW TO EAT WELL
AND STICK AROUND

If you are making a transformational change in your diet, from eating the way most Americans eat—a high-fat, animal-foods-based diet—to eating the way your body was meant to be fueled, this chapter is designed to help guide you. Whether your primary objective is weight loss on one hand, or health and longevity (both of which, of course, are related to weight) on the other, the rules remain basically the same.

Let's start by repeating the fundamentals: the natural human diet consists of whole plant foods. We classify these as fruits, vegetables, fungi (mushrooms, often lumped together with vegetables), whole grains, legumes, nuts, seeds, herbs and spices.

In order to feel full when we eat, we need to get the bulk of our calories from the category of foods that are sometimes described as "complex carbohydrates" and sometimes called "starches": potatoes, sweet potatoes, beans, corn, rice, and other whole grains like millet, barley, rye, buckwheat, and oats. You'd struggle to get enough calories if you tried to live off just non-starchy vegetables (think salad greens and steamed broccoli) and fruit. When you give up unhealthy but filling flesh foods, you should naturally gravitate to healthy starches in order to feel satisfied.

Potatoes, an ideal starchy vegetable, are not fattening; that's a myth. There are about 163 calories in one medium-sized potato. There's actually less than one calorie per gram of potato. Now, don't be fooled when people make the mistake of calling potatoes "carbohydrates." Potatoes are whole foods that contain, besides carbohydrates, protein and a smidgen of fat. Consider that there are four calories in a gram of carbohydrate. So how can there be less than one calorie in a gram of potato (often derided as a "carb")? Answer: most of the weight of a potato is calorie-free fiber and water.

There are more varieties of potatoes than you can count, and they are all healthy, non-fattening forms of fuel. The only thing that can make a potato fattening is the butter or sour cream or other fatty topping that people are accustomed to spoiling it with.

Most people need to eat about four pounds of food per day to feel satisfied. If you ate four pounds of potatoes per day (without putting any topping on them), you'd ingest about 1600 calories per day. For virtually everyone, a 1600-calorie-per-day diet would be a very successful weight-loss diet.

If you ate four pounds of celery per day, you'd be taking in only a little over 300 calories per day, and the weight loss would be much greater, although your mood would likely be foul.

If you ate, instead, four pounds of nuts per day, you'd be on a 12,000-calorie-per-day diet, and you'd pack on the pounds.

So if you had to choose a food item around which to base a four-pounds-of-food-a-day monotrophic diet (in which you eat only one type of food), the potato would be as good a choice as any, since you'd get plenty of calories and you'd feel full as you lost weight. Oatmeal would be another good choice: there are about 150 calories in a bowl of oatmeal, so you could eat ten or eleven bowls of oatmeal per day to get the same caloric intake you'd achieve by eating four pounds of potatoes. The celery diet would result in rapid weight loss but you'd likely feel very hungry, and the nut-only diet would lead to obesity in short order. The magician Penn Jillette lost over a hundred pounds recently by adopting a (mostly) vegan diet, and he jump-started the diet with a couple of weeks of eating nothing but potatoes.[1] Andrew Taylor of Melbourne, Australia, earned some media attention in 2016 by reducing his weight from 334 to 220 pounds in a year by eating nothing but potatoes (including sweet potatoes; he also added a bit of soymilk for preparing mashed potatoes); he ate them baked, boiled, or mashed.

The man estimated that he achieved this weight loss while actually eating eight to nine pounds per day of potatoes![2] His cholesterol, blood pressure, and blood sugar improved, and he even states that the diet helped him overcome clinical depression. Now that he's lost the weight and restored his health, he eats a more diverse whole foods, vegan diet, but, perhaps from a sense of abiding gratitude, still centers it around potatoes.

Of course, there's no reason anyone has to go on a monotrophic diet. But once you understand roughly how many calories are in a pound of different types of food, you understand the key to weight loss.

My good friend Chef AJ, an amazing chef who has graced this volume with more than seventy-five delicious, distinctive, brand-new recipes, is a vegan lecturer, personality, weight-loss expert, and author. In her best-selling book *The Secrets to Ultimate Weight Loss* (which I was proud to co-author), AJ explains calorie density as well as anyone. The foods she places on the healthy, slimming, left side of what she calls "the red line" are vegetables, whole grains, legumes, and fruits (except for the rare fatty fruit such as coconut or avocado). On the fattening, right side of the red line you'll find all animal foods (flesh foods, eggs, dairy), oil, fatty fruits, nuts, seeds, and sugar, as well as bread and other flour products. As AJ puts it, "Eating the delicious bounty of whole natural foods to the left of the red line curbs overeating, eliminates cravings, and results in satiety, the end of hunger. And if you consistently eat to the left of the red line, you will reach satiety sooner, and in a more healthful manner and on far fewer calories."[3]

I choose to eat some foods on the more caloric, right side of the red line: nuts, seeds, avocado, and olives, along with bread and other vegan flour products. If I were trying to lose weight, though, I would cut down on those foods or cut them out entirely. Good health is my primary objective, not weight loss.

Whether or not you choose to occasionally stray, as I do, to the more calorically dense side of the red line by eating nuts, seeds, avocado, olives, and bread, what is crucial to good health is abstention from the most salient causes of inflammation and disease: animal products, oil, and sugar.

For many of you, the prospect of going vegan may be daunting. The social pressure alone that militates against healthy eating should not be underestimated, and I don't dismiss it lightly, although I, for one, never let it affect me. I always swatted it away with less focus or attention than I'd give to gnats. When I know that what I'm doing is right, I don't have any concern for what others think. I guess I didn't get that gene.

I understand that for most people who have been eating a standard American diet, it may seem unthinkable to give up animal products. It may be hard to imagine life without grilled burgers, Thanksgiving turkey shared with family, or pepperoni pizza shared with friends or co-workers. It may be harder still to imagine eating differently from family members in your own home who show no interest in joining you on your journey to health.

Well, if you care about your health and the environment, you need to not only imagine it but to do it. With the planet melting, and animal agriculture the single leading cause of climate change—and with a pandemic brought on by purveyors of animal foods (this time in China; the next time it could be here)—the time has come for all of us to eat human food. There's no reason to fear standing apart from the unhealthy majority; eventually, they'll come to see you as a good example. If the majority of people persist in the folly of basing their diet around animal products, eating flesh (as the average American does) more frequently than do nature's obligate carnivores—well, that's their problem, and also, unfortunately, the planet's problem, but we can at least feel good about doing the right thing for ourselves and our environment.

So if your friends at a July 4th barbecue give you a grilling for not wanting a steak, so be it. Take it good-naturedly. Bring an oil-free potato salad and grill some corn. If your relatives act concerned that you're not having any turkey at Thanksgiving, tell them that the holiday is actually about gratitude, and you're grateful to live in a world with an abundance of healthy and delicious plant foods so that you don't need to eat a turkey bred to a grotesque size, debeaked, and fattened in a horribly crowded shed where it likely spent its short, miserable life breathing in pathogens and ammonia before being slaughtered.

That ought to shut them up.

Bring your own delicious vegan dish to the gathering. There are plenty of Thanksgiving-themed vegan foods—sweet potatoes, cranberry sauce, and pumpkin pie spring to mind. You can even make a vegan stuffing—just don't let Aunt Sylvia stuff it into a dead bird.

Standing apart from the unhealthy majority by avoiding flesh foods, dairy, and eggs should not be a source of embarrassment, but a point of pride. As your friends and family watch you thrive on a diet of human food, you'll find that over time, instead of mocking you, they'll start to ask you sincere questions about how you do it.

Building your diet around whole grains, legumes, fruits, fungi, vegetables, nuts, and seeds is actually the easy part. The hard part is avoiding oil. Restaurants cook with it, as do most people at home. We've been brainwashed into thinking that it's the natural liquid in which to cook food. And, because it's cheap and tastes good to folks accustomed to a fatty diet, it gets added to all manner of processed foods. In grocery stores, it's hard to find, for example, a pasta sauce made without olive oil.

Don't kid yourself that olive oil, or any other oil, is some magically healthy substance. All oils are inherently processed foods, and 100 percent fat. None is a health food. Although oil does not contain cholesterol, it will, if you consume it, induce your liver to produce more cholesterol. And so a fatty vegan diet of fried and oily foods, even though it contains zero cholesterol, can result in high serum cholesterol and heart disease.

An aside here to the many people I've met who have joined the vegan cause as an expression of their concern for animal rights or the environment, but who care not at all about consuming oil or vegan junk food, and are often themselves overweight or obese or diabetic as a result: my friends, if you care so much about animals and the environment, then you should want all people to go vegan. And others will be much more likely to adopt a vegan diet if they see that you are fit and healthy. So, whether you give a damn about your own health or not, there's no good excuse for a self-indulgent, overly sweet and fatty version of the vegan diet. Commit to your own health so that you'll have a longer, more energetic life in which to advocate for animals and the environment.

Okay, so what do you do if you're committed to a healthy, low-fat diet without oil and you want to make for yourself a quick pasta with tomato sauce, but all the jars of tomato sauce in your grocery store contain olive oil?

Here's your choice. Either, at best, you make your own tomato sauce using tomato paste, or chopped or diced fresh or canned tomatoes; or, at worst, you resign yourself to using a commercial tomato sauce that contains oil, but you look for a jar that has less fat—say, one gram of fat per serving, rather than four grams of fat. All the fat is likely going to be coming from the oil, so the sauce with one gram of fat is going to have 75 percent less oil than the sauce with four grams of fat.

Again, zero oil is the goal. Even a small quantity of oil represents a small injury to the endothelial cells lining your blood vessels that keep them open and elastic. Joanna and I never cook with oil at home. We try to avoid it in restaurants, but that's very difficult to do. And we manage to virtually always avoid it in packaged foods, but on the rare occasion that we can't, we choose the product with less fat. Mostly, though, we don't buy packaged foods; we buy produce and whole grains and create our meals without the need to open many jars and boxes.

When you sauté vegetables, you have many better choices than oil. You can sauté in water, in vegetable broth, in soy sauce, in aquafaba (the brine from legumes, such as the water from a can of garbanzo beans), in any other oil-free vegan sauce, or in wine. And, of course, you can steam or roast your vegetables.

Your ticket to health begins with your trip to the grocery store. If most of your shopping cart isn't filled up with fresh (or frozen) produce, your priorities are off. Beans and other legumes, whether packaged or obtained from bulk bins, also belong in your shopping cart, along with whole grains.

Most packaged foods will require your attention to the nutrition label, so let's take a look at that.

First, you need to read the list of ingredients, which are listed in descending order by weight. Think of a long list of ingredients as a warning sign that a product is overly processed and not worth your consideration. Steer clear of animal products such as whey or cream or gelatin. Steer clear of margarine and oil. Steer clear of artificial colorings and preservatives. Steer clear of isolated soy protein, wheat gluten, and other forms of isolated proteins.

Within the nutritional information, train yourself to focus on what matters most: the grams of saturated fat and sugar per serving. Saturated fat and sugar are the deadly sins of the American diet—along with cholesterol, of course, but as long as you limit yourself to vegan foods, the cholesterol count will always be zero. Ideally, you want to purchase only items free of oil and sugar or other sweeteners (corn syrup, agave, honey, molasses, etc.). But just as it can be hard to find a tomato sauce that's oil-free, it can be hard to find a cold cereal, for example, that's free of sweeteners. So in cases in which you can't avoid a sweetener, I recommend a limit of five grams of sugar per serving.

In grocery stores, I'll occasionally buy, for example, a favorite cold cereal that's sweetened with organic pear juice concentrate and barley malt extract, both of which I take on faith are preferable to cane sugar—but, more importantly, in this particular cold cereal, there are only five grams of sugar to a serving. The other ingredients are whole oat flour, brown rice flour, whole millet, oat bran, and sea salt—so, as cold cereals go, this is about as healthy as it gets. I naturally skip over plenty of other brands in the aisle that have ten or more grams of sugar (usually cane sugar) to a serving.

Over my cold cereal, I'll usually pour unsweetened soymilk or almond milk, whose packaging informs me that they contain zero grams of saturated fat. Occasionally I'll use hemp milk, with one gram of saturated fat per serving. My strong advice would be to avoid coconut milk, which will have about four grams of saturated fat to a serving. And avoid any plant milk made with oil; you can find plenty of plant milks made without it. And then I'll top the cold cereal with a lot of organic berries. I think of the cereal as simply an excuse for eating the berries.

In grocery stores, I'll also occasionally buy vegan burgers, but never any that contain any type of oil. Nor do I buy vegan burgers made from isolated soy protein or wheat gluten. Here's the ingredient list of my favorite: brown rice, sunflower seeds, pinto beans, rice syrup, onion, paprika, garlic, sea salt, black pepper. Because of the sunflower seeds, it's got a pretty fair amount of fat: fourteen grams of fat in one burger (with about 50 percent of its 250 calories coming from fat), and 1.5 grams of saturated fat. It has just one gram of sugar, nine grams of protein, and seven grams of fiber.

Now that's fattier than most of the foods I eat, since my overall diet is in the range of 10 to 15 percent of calories as fat. But I figure that it's healthy fat from sunflower seeds, and so for lunch I might have the burger on whole wheat bread, alongside a salad, and perhaps with some steamed vegetables on the side. Those other, non-fatty foods (bread, salad, vegetables) will reduce the percentage of fat in the meal. The 1.5 grams of saturated fat in the burger is about as high as I care to go; I rarely eat anything with two grams or more of saturated fat to a serving. And of course I will limit myself to one burger. If I'm still feeling hungry, then I need to fill myself up with more salad or more vegetables or potatoes—not a second burger, which would turn my lunch into a fat extravaganza (not by the standards of Burger King, of course, nor even by the standards of American society, but by the more relevant standards of *Homo sapiens*).

It's essential to go easy on fatty fruits. I never eat more than half an avocado per day. (There are about three grams of saturated fat in an avocado.) I rarely touch coconut. For reasons that surpass my understanding, coconut was designed by nature as the cheeseburger of fruits, wildly high in saturated fat.

If you are salt-sensitive or have high blood pressure, you'll want to choose foods that are low in sodium. I personally don't concern myself much with sodium, since my blood pressure is fine, but I might check any given packaged food to make sure that the sodium content in milligrams per serving does not exceed by much the number of calories per serving.

On the right side of the nutritional label, you'll find a column that says "% Daily Value." Ignore this, since it's meaningless. For example, one hamburger would provide you with twelve grams of saturated fat, which will be labeled as 60 percent of your Daily Value; that means that the Daily Value of saturated fat is apparently a mind-blowing and heart-stopping twenty grams per day. (That's about 1000 percent of my daily intake.) A hamburger will also provide you with 100 mg of cholesterol, or 33 percent of your Daily Value of cholesterol. That makes it sound like you need dietary cholesterol and so should eat a couple more burgers per day. Of course, as almost no one will dispute, the optimal amount of dietary cholesterol is zero. There's no good definition for "Daily Value," but the closest thing would be "Daily Average of the Overweight Population Eating the Fatty Western Diet." So why does the "% Daily Value" column even exist? Undoubtedly because the animal agriculture industry lobbied the FDA for a confusing metric that would make cholesterol and saturated fat appear to be required nutrients.

Your tax dollars at work.

If you are transitioning from the standard American diet to a low-fat, plant-based diet, you would be well-advised to give yourself a transition week in which you eat very simply. During that week, eat meals that would do a monk proud. Whether you emulate Penn Jillette and eat nothing but potatoes for a week or two, or eat simple meals like oatmeal or buckwheat cereal, or steamed vegetables with brown rice, you will achieve the same end: rid yourself of the taste for fatty foods, and overcome any addiction you may have to sugar or salt. You will also, if you are trying to lose weight, jump-start your diet.

Allow me here to interrupt my nutritional advice to share with you a traumatic incident from my otherwise very pleasant childhood. This was really the only thing that ever went wrong, and the memory is painful.

On some special occasion, when I was three years old, my parents took my sister and me out to breakfast. This was a rare treat, and because it turned into a disaster, I have never gone out to breakfast since.

We went either to a diner or perhaps to one of the world's first IHOPs—an institution that had just been founded, adding some architectural pizzazz to the suburbs—and I remember that I ordered directly from the grown-up menu (I had learned to read earlier that morning for the occasion). Because of its antioxidant value, I ordered the blueberry pancakes.

When our food arrived, I took command of the syrup dispenser, which must have been about the size of my head, and with rare skill and a carefulness that belied my age, I poured for myself on the side of my plate just a thimbleful of maple syrup that would serve the purpose of enhancing slightly—while not overwhelming—the flavor of the delicious pancakes.

At that point, for reasons that are lost to history, a very nice man and his evil wife—total friggin' strangers—approached our table and began to speak with my parents. Probably they wanted to compliment them on their adorable, polite, and well-behaved children.

The evil woman looked down at my pancakes and said, "Little boy, that's not enough syrup! Your pancakes will be too dry!" And the woman took it upon herself—without asking my permission!—to grab the syrup dispenser and drown my delicious pancakes in a sea of mediocre maple syrup!

Well, I was a good boy and had taken a vow to behave maturely in public. But this was an outrage that defied my best intentions. I began to scream and cry like nobody's business. The very nice man scolded his evil wife, and ordered for me a new batch of pancakes. But the damage was done. Our special family occasion was ruined. I make sure to eat breakfast at home now.

The next day, that very nice man divorced his evil wife.

I knew very well, at the age of three, that sugar—even in the form of maple syrup—was a treacherous substance that required delicate handling and restraint. I didn't want to become insensitive to the taste of sweetness, so I knew to use very little of the syrup and to savor the sweetness, not become numb to it. And I wanted to be able to taste and celebrate the healthiest part of the meal—the blueberries. I also didn't want to get fat.

It's a true story, and one that contains an important lesson. (Okay, I made up the part about the divorce, but it comforts me.) Substances that add sweetness and fattiness to our diet are to be used sparingly, if at all. Otherwise you will lose your taste for the delicious food whose flavor you are seeking to enhance, not to overwhelm.

And so, if you must use maple syrup, use just a drop. And do not—as some people apparently do—put sugar in your oatmeal, for Chrissake. That would be counterproductive. It's breakfast, not dessert. You may have heard the platitude, "Life is short. Eat dessert first." The flip side is more to the point: eat dessert first, and life may turn out to be way too short.

The insidious thing about adding sugar to your oatmeal, beyond turning a healthy meal into an unhealthy one, is that it will affect your sensibilities of taste. Will you then need to put a sweetener in your tea? Will you prefer a plant milk sweetened with cane sugar? Will you gravitate toward sweet salad dressings and sauces? Will you start craving desserts as soon as you wake up?

In a memorable passage in his book *Presto!*, Penn Jillette describes the glorious, shocking sweetness of a simple ear of corn that he eats after two weeks of eating nothing but potatoes.[4] The corn tasted almost like candy; it had a sweetness he'd never encountered before simply because he had cleaned his palate with his diet of potatoes. Well, the opposite happens to you if you unwisely put sugar on your oatmeal; you dumb down your taste buds. You become increasingly insensitive to sweetness.

The taste for fat rivals the addiction to sugar as a source of ruin to human health. And so, during your transition week, stay clear of nuts, nut butters, seeds, avocados, olives, coconut, and of course anything containing oil. Avoid fatty sauces. Make sure, for example, not to put on your salads any dressing that contains any fat. If you need a dressing on your salad, squeeze a lemon, or drizzle some vinegar. Eat pure, low-fat foods: brown rice, steamed veggies, legumes, and fruit.

After a week of clean eating, your taste buds should adjust to the point that you'll recoil from the mere thought of adding sugar to your oatmeal. But feel free to add fruit to your oatmeal; your newly clean palate will really appreciate the natural sweetness.

And now, if you choose to allow yourself some fatty foods, use them sparingly. For example, if you want have a slice of whole wheat bread with sesame tahini, use very little tahini. Spread a teaspoonful on the bread. You'll find that, after eating like a monk for a week, your taste buds will have adjusted, and just that little bit of tahini will suffice. Stay in the habit of minimizing your use of fatty foods. Your healthiest source of fat will be flax seeds, rich in Omega-3's. When Joanna and I make smoothies, we make sure to add flax seeds.

Think of a healthy diet as containing two components: fuel, plus fortification.[5] (I use the term "fortification" in the sense of defense against disease, not in the sense of the artificial enrichment of foods with vitamins and minerals.) Choosing healthy fuel, from which you'll obtain most of your calories, is of paramount importance, since it's going to replace the unhealthy reliance on animal foods as a source of energy. That's why you'll need to base your diet around rice (in its countless varieties), corn (sweet corn is usually the only type available), potatoes (in their countless varieties), sweet potatoes (in several varieties cultivated domestically), beans (in their countless varieties), lentils (brown, black, green, yellow), millet, buckwheat, and other whole grains.

These ideal fuel foods, while all terrifically health-promoting, do not boast the same degree of nutritional density as the foods that will provide you with your greatest fortification against disease: leafy greens, non-starchy vegetables, mushrooms, (non-fatty) fruit, and herbs and spices. These are the foods that are your best defense against cancer and other diseases. These are the foods that you can eat in great abundance, if you choose, because they are not calorically dense; they are, in Chef AJ's imagery, way to the left of the red line. (The fruits live somewhat closer to the red line than the vegetables.)

When I eat cold cereal, for example, the cereal is my fuel; the blueberries and strawberries that I put on top are my fortification. When I eat oatmeal with fruit, the oats are my fuel; the berries and banana and pear and cinnamon are my fortification. When I eat a meal of rice and beans with shiitake mushrooms and steamed greens, the rice and beans are my fuel; the shiitakes and steamed greens are my fortification.

Alliums, such as garlic, onion, leeks, and chives, have a vital role to play in your fortification. So do spices such as cinnamon, turmeric, and ginger. They reign as perhaps the most nutritionally dense foods, providing an extraordinary array of health benefits per calorie.

Getting your fuel right is key to maintaining a healthy weight, healthy blood pressure, and healthy blood sugar levels. Providing fortification to your cells is your best strategy for staving off cancer and other diseases.

There's nothing boring about eating this way. In fact, it's begun to seem that every meal that Joanna and I sit down to (she's the chef in the family) differs from every meal we've ever had before. One night we might have black rice with maitake mushrooms, chick peas, blanched greens, steamed cauliflower, and steamed Japanese sweet potatoes in a tahini sauce; the next night we might have baked red potatoes, black beans, blanched greens, and steamed broccoli in a miso/ginger sauce; the next night we might have red lentils, purple sweet potatoes, blanched greens, and steamed asparagus in a mushroom sauce. You'll note some similarities: blanched greens in all the meals, legumes in all the meals, some form of potatoes or rice (or both) in all the meals, and some kind of sauce. But a steamed Japanese sweet potato tastes nothing like a baked red potato; chick peas taste nothing like black beans or red lentils; the steamed vegetables change; the blanched greens may change; the sauce changes; the herbs and spices change. And with the abundant variety of legumes and potatoes and rice and vegetables, no two meals ever taste alike, even if they have building blocks from the same family.

One other thing Joanna adds to all our meals: a spoonful of fermented (kim-chi style) vegetables. And we use a few different types.

Strive for at least two servings per day of legumes, an important source of the essential amino acid lysine.

For more ideas about how to keep plant-based eating healthy, delicious, and varied, just turn to the recipe section of this book. There's nobody with better ideas than Chef AJ!

Okay, by now you should have the basics: 1) base your diet around whole plant foods, ideally avoiding animal foods entirely; 2) understand that you'll need to get most of your calories—your fuel—from whole grains, starchy vegetables, and legumes; 3) eat an abundance of fortification foods: greens, other non-starchy vegetables, mushrooms, fruit, herbs, and spices; 4) add an element of fermented foods; 5) to the extent that you use packaged foods, read the nutrition labels and seek to avoid or at least minimize sugar and oil, and keep the saturated fat to a minimum.

So far, so good. But should you take any supplements?

A widespread consensus exists among the leaders of the vegan movement that it's wise to supplement with Vitamin B12. I try to remember to pop a B12 tablet a few times a week. There have been weeks that I have forgotten, and I have not fallen down. So while I don't worry about it much, I naturally join the consensus in recommending Vitamin B12 supplementation, since it's otherwise lacking in a vegan diet (except for certain fortified foods, such as some plant milks and nutritional yeast).

There's also a growing consensus among the leaders of the movement that no other supplementation beyond Vitamin B12 is necessary or desirable. Here I personally take a slightly different tack. I take two other forms of supplements: probiotic capsules (which I open up and spill into apple sauce or a drink), and liquid chlorophyll. I simply see no risk to this supplementation, and I believe I feel the benefits of the chlorophyll. I don't feel strongly enough about it to make a wholesale, blanket recommendation regarding supplementation to the reader, but the subject of supplementation deserves at least a mention, and I wouldn't be honest if I claimed not to consume any supplements beyond the widely recommended Vitamin B12.

I also believe that it's important to distinguish between vitamin supplements and herbal supplements. The science is fairly conclusive that multi-vitamins, for example, are unnecessary at best, harmful at worst. I think of herbal supplements, on the other hand, as tiny servings of food in pill form. If you open up a pill of olive leaf extract, for example, you've got, well, crushed olive leaves. Arguably, that's food. It seems to me more reasonable to consume pills containing herbs and plant extracts than those containing isolated vitamins and enzymes. All of the above get labeled as "supplements," but I see a significant difference, and Joanna and I turn to herbs and plant extracts as resources to help combat illnesses. Joanna found, for example, that black currant extract helped her enormously with her joint pains.

Joanna's experience with her autoimmune condition has impressed upon me the need to maintain a healthy gut, and that's why we supplement with probiotics; it's also why we eat fermented vegetables and drink vegan kefirs (often made with coconut water). And even though we eat blanched greens almost every day, I believe the liquid chlorophyll aids in the production of nitric oxide, and so I think it's well worth adding a few drops to a cup of water every day. I haven't found a downside, and the upside seems considerable.

Let's not forget sleep and exercise, of course. Most people don't get enough of either. Sleep deprivation will boost your production of cortisol, increasing your appetite—particularly for sweet and refined snack foods in the middle of the night. One reason exercise is good for you is that it will help you sleep. And proper nutrition helps enable both exercise and sleep. So there's a virtuous circle here that we all need to try to establish for ourselves, and we need to be wary of the risk that sleep deprivation can throw the whole thing off.

Throughout my thirties, I suffered from a bad case of insomnia. I overcame it by learning to focus on a purposefully created strain in my eyes. Sleep, after all, is all about the eyes—we need to have them closed when we sleep, and rapid eye movement (REM) sleep is vital to the brain, making sleep particularly useful to those who have fallen for the Caveman Diet nonsense.

How do you create strain in your eyes? Hold your head straight. Now try to roll your eyes upward so you can see the ceiling. Feel that strain? Now close your eyes, and keep that strain going, as if you're still trying to see the ceiling through your closed eyelids. Then, as you go to sleep, focus on that strain. Don't let your thoughts wander to other matters; let the eye strain be your mantra, your center of focus. Next thing you know it's the morning, and you don't know how it happened.

At least it works for me.

You now have in this short chapter what few doctors will give you: the recipe for health. A low-fat, plant-based (preferably vegan) diet, free (or as free as possible) of oils, in which your fuel comes from healthy starches (starchy vegetables, whole grains, and legumes) and your fortification comes from fruits, vegetables, mushrooms, some nuts and seeds, herbs and spices, and some fermented foods. It's a diet that needs to be supplemented only with Vitamin B12, probiotics, and (optionally) liquid chlorophyll.

Knowing that you're eating all the right things should help you sleep well, which in turn will help you eat right.

And it's eating right—not relying on the doctor, but eating right—that will give you your best shot at sticking around.

CHAPTER NINE: PUBLIC POLICY

Health matters more than health insurance.

That's a statement that's hard to disagree with, isn't it? Surely, if given a choice between, on the one hand, perfect health unaccompanied by health insurance, or, on the other, a Cadillac health insurance plan with which to offset the costs of a terminal diagnosis, we'd all opt for escaping the bad news.

And yet, to listen to politicians debate their respective "healthcare plans," ranting and raving like nothing could be more important, you'd think that health itself is an irrelevant commodity. You'd think that the only things that matter are getting our premiums and deductibles down, and making sure that everyone enjoys the blessings of the financial product called "health insurance."

That's what it is, after all: a financial product. As with other forms of insurance, being insured can save you money (if you're unlucky enough to have claims that are high, and lucky enough to get them paid) or it can cost you money (if premiums exceed covered claims). Given the fact that health insurance companies make significant profits, it's fair to say that, writ large, health insurance (like car insurance or home insurance) costs Americans more than it saves them. Health insurance has cost me a fortune for most years that I've had to pay for it, since I almost never go to the doctor. That's not to say that it doesn't serve a vital purpose, or that I would prefer to be without health insurance; it's just a matter of keeping this financial product in perspective. While health insurance is not completely irrelevant to health outcomes, it ranks way down the list of factors affecting our health.

When an employer pays the cost of health insurance, its employees incur the unseen cost of reduced salary; naturally, employee salaries would be higher if employers didn't need to cover at least a share of their health insurance costs. Even if we were to move to the system of Medicare-for-All, we would, of course, all still incur a cost, though it wouldn't be in the form of monthly premiums to a private insurance company, or in the form of reduced salaries, or in the form of doctor bills. It would take, instead, the form of higher taxes, higher federal deficits, or, quite likely, both.

Medical care doesn't suddenly become free when the government accepts financial responsibility for it. All of us have to pay the government's costs. But when medical care appears to be free, and a visit to the doctor doesn't increase one's personal cost, it's a good bet that people will avail themselves of more of it, potentially driving up our collective costs.

On the flip side, there would also be cost-containing aspects to a Medicare-for-All system, by cutting out the profit margin of insurance companies, and (as could be achieved even now, without Medicare-for-All) by driving down pharmaceutical pricing with more robust federal negotiating.

Only one thing remains certain: nothing we can ever do as a society will ever stop health insurance from being the single most excruciatingly boring subject ever conceived by the human mind. It is therefore extraordinary that it remains such a constant distraction from more pressing health concerns.

Americans are, simply put, the sickest and fattest population ever to walk Planet Earth, and yet collectively we seem capable of discussing only one thing remotely related to that unfortunate fact: who should pay for the attendant costs of our health care. You never hear politicians utter a word about confronting the diseases their constituents eat their way into—not a word about reducing obesity and Type 2 diabetes and heart disease. No, they opine only about who should pay for the doctor visits.

Here's a wild proposal: how about we focus instead on no longer reigning as the sickest and fattest population ever to exist? That would save our economy a fortune, since being the unhealthiest non-starving population in human history is costing us 18 percent of our Gross Domestic Product, or about three and a half trillion dollars a year.

Given that we are, for now, a nation so terribly fat and sick, Medicare-for-All could prove more expensive than its advocates estimate. Remember my mother's doctor who thought there was cholesterol in carrots? Well, I was outraged to discover that she sent my asymptomatic mother, at the age of ninety, for an annual preventive mammogram. Hell, *Medicare will pay for it*, so why not? I never felt more guilty than when I made the mistake of calling 911 when my father, in his late eighties, and suffering from Parkinson's disease and related dementia, passed out from orthostatic hypotension. A fire truck and ambulance showed up; he was taken to the hospital, where he was kept for a week and where the doctors conducted every test they could think of on a frail, dying old man who didn't know what was happening but knew he resented being there. The doctors failed, naturally, to stabilize his blood pressure. Their sole achievement was giving him a urinary tract infection from the catheter. And they billed the taxpayer $70,000 for their services, because, hell, *Medicare will pay for it.*

Medicare-for-All is an idea that embraces values I support: inclusion, equality, community. But there's a real risk that, should it ever come to pass, and wind up draining the national budget, it could ultimately prove a setback for progressive goals. I'll remind my fellow progressives that money wasted on preposterous over-testing (I am of course not referring to coronavirus testing, of which we currently need far more) and the often unnecessary medical interventions that follow is money that is not available for education, the environment, and infrastructure. It's money stolen from the young and bestowed upon the medical industrial complex. Feeding the medical industrial complex shouldn't be considered a progressive goal.

Whether Medicare-for-All is a good idea or not, we shortchange ourselves by making it our focus. We need to focus on eating ourselves into health instead of testing ourselves to death.

Changing our health insurance model will surely not affect in the slightest our status as the world's sickest and fattest population. President Obama's signature achievement, the Affordable Care Act, expanded the ranks of the insured by some fifteen million people. The

113

Affordable Care Act, to its credit, ended the obscenity of pre-existing conditions excluding people from obtaining health insurance. But how effective has Obamacare truly been, in health metrics? Well, the adult obesity rate in America stood at a mind-boggling 35.7 percent when Obama took office in 2009.[1] Eight years later, after President Obama had presumably provided fifteen million people with greater access to medical care, the adult obesity rate stood at 39.8 percent.[2] When you start at a stratospheric level of obesity, and you still manage a ten percent increase over eight years—hey, hats off to Obamacare. Call me a skeptic, but I never would have believed it possible for Americans to get still fatter and sicker.

Have I taken a cheap shot at Obamacare? Is it unfair to expect a health insurance reform to reduce obesity? Perhaps the answer to both questions is yes. But Obamacare was sold not just as a financial reform; it was sold as a way to save lives and improve our collective health. And there have indeed been some cases of people who have spoken out with gratitude to say that their lives were saved by the greater access to healthcare that they received under Obamacare. By ending the injustice of coverage denied because of preexisting conditions, the program certainly helped many. It helped many more save on cost.

But heart disease and cancer deaths increased after the passage of Obamacare,[3] while life expectancy in the U.S. has been on a shameful decline for the last three years.[4] The nation's most significant health metrics have simply not improved since President Obama presumably helped send fifteen million more Americans to the doctor.

And, clearly, going to the doctor does not pass muster as a strategy for fighting obesity. This isn't surprising, since a 2012 study found that more than half of primary care doctors are themselves overweight or obese.[5] You see, the fact that the medical community has not studied nutrition has not served them well, either.

Do those with health insurance enjoy greater access to medical care than those who lack insurance? It's pretty certain that they do, but it's far more certain that "enjoy" is the wrong word. Besides, it's not like there was zero access to medical care for those fifteen million people before they got covered, and then easy and free access afterwards. If you need to pay monthly premiums, then you are out-of-pocket a certain amount of money that might otherwise be available to you for medical expenses. So when you factor in the cost of insurance as one cost of medical care, and then you look at how many dollars are left available to fund your actual use of medical care, the advantage of having health insurance can be seen as more gray than black-and-white.

I think of a fellow I knew in Los Angeles, a legal immigrant from the Czech Republic, who was in his mid-twenties and worked in a retail store, undoubtedly for not much more than minimum wage. I asked him if he had health insurance. He said no. He told me that a health insurance agent had offered him a subsidized plan through "Obamacare" (specifically the Covered California Health Exchange), but he had opted not to get it. I asked him how much it would have cost. He chuckled; the cost, after the subsidy, had come to exactly one dollar per month.

"Are you crazy?" I said. "You can get health insurance for one dollar a month and you're not doing it? You're out of your mind!"

"No, it's not worth it," he said. And he explained that, in order to obtain the insurance, he would have to upload his immigration records to the Covered California Health Exchange. He had become a U.S. citizen, so he had nothing to hide, but he didn't like the thought of sharing his private records with an agency that could get hacked. He said there was a clinic near his apartment where he could always get treatment, without health insurance, for a flat twenty bucks. In a normal year, he said, he would go there maybe once with a flu and they'd take care of him.

"Okay, but what if you got into a car accident and faced really high costs?" I asked.

"They'd still have to take care of me in the hospital," he said. "And I don't have any assets. What can they take from me?"

"Still," I said, "it's only a dollar a month!"

"Unless my business succeeds," he said. He was an entrepreneurial fellow, and he was referring to a business he had started selling goods online and at flea markets. While it was unlikely that he would earn much money at it, if he did succeed and earned enough that his income doubled to about $48,000 per year, then he'd be obligated to pay back his subsidy, and suddenly he might owe, say, $4000 for the health insurance that he'd been promised for $12 per year. Earning one dollar too much could cost him thousands. That's because Obamacare subsidies, which are not phased in gradually, are maddeningly tied to your next year's earnings, not your previous year's earnings. Here's a shocker: many people don't know their next year's earnings. And there was no way that this healthy young man, struggling to get by, wanted to pay $4000 for health insurance, when he found that his usual medical costs were $20 per year.

I could see his point. While most of us would have gladly accepted the deal he was offered, health insurance just wasn't worth, for my Czech friend, the buck it would cost.

While all Americans should, of course, have equal access to medical care, we shouldn't lose sight of the fact that medical care is not an unmitigated good. Visits to the doctor are not without risks. Hard as it may be to believe, medical care ranks as the third leading common cause of death in America. (I am not including as a common cause of death what we all hope will be a short-lived pandemic.)

They call it iatrogenic death—death by healthcare. It can be caused by botched surgery, by hospital-acquired infections, incorrect prescriptions, adverse effects of drugs, or other medical errors. Dr. Sanjay Gupta, in a 2012 N.Y. Times op-ed entitled "More Treatment, More Mistakes,"[6] estimated iatrogenic deaths in America at 200,000; I have seen estimates that are considerably higher, but since Dr. Gupta is a well-respected and mainstream medical reporter (as well as a neurosurgeon), let's accept his number.

It's impossible to give a truly accurate accounting of iatrogenic deaths since causes of death involve ambiguities. If a person is prescribed a medication that causes drowsiness, and then dies as a result of falling asleep at the wheel, that's not going to be considered an iatrogenic death, though arguably it should be. If psychiatric patients react violently to psychotropic drugs they've been prescribed, and kill themselves and/or others, those deaths won't be recorded as iatrogenic deaths, though perhaps they should be. And certainly not all drug interactions that lead to death will be discovered. An FDA "learning module" put it this way:

. . . studies estimate that 6.7 percent of hospitalized patients have a serious adverse drug reaction with a fatality rate of 0.32 percent. If these estimates are correct, then there are more than 2,216,000 serious ADRs [adverse drug reactions] in hospitalized patients, causing over 106,000 deaths annually. If true, then ADRs are the 4th leading cause of death—ahead of pulmonary disease, diabetes, AIDS, pneumonia, accidents, and automobile deaths.[7]

Since the opioid crisis exploded in the last decade, about 50,000 Americans have died annually of opioid overdoses; about 40 percent of these deaths stem from prescription opioids.[8] These are not recorded as iatrogenic deaths.

But who is more to blame for the opioid crisis than doctors and pharmaceutical companies? In 2017, even after years of a full-blown crisis, Ohio physicians wrote 63.5 opioid prescriptions for every 100 persons—and that was a considerable decrease from writing more than one prescription per person in 2010![9] Opioid overdose deaths in Ohio increased by some 1100 percent between 1999 and 2017.

While street, non-prescription opioid overdoses cannot be attributed directly to doctors and pharmaceutical companies, I would argue that, since it was the medical industry that introduced this genie into our midst, it should take responsibility for all the ugly consequences to which it has led. Street pushers didn't deal in fentanyl until our respected family physicians blazed the trail.

And yet the leading politicians from one of our political parties (you know who you are) can disagree about only one thing on the subject of health care: the best way to get more Americans to see more doctors at little or no out-of-pocket cost, while enjoying richer drug benefits.

Who knows how many people they might kill with their good intentions?

Here's what we never hear from politicians: calls to pull the medical licenses from these doctors who have been dispensing opioid prescriptions like candy.

Again, medical care is not an unmitigated good. No public policy on health care can be considered rational if it doesn't recognize that indisputable fact—what Al Gore, who oh-so-shyly went vegan in 2013, would call an "inconvenient truth."

We ought not to be struggling for new ways to send more people to more doctors at some redistributed cost. We ought to be seeking new ways to make more people healthier so they have less need to see doctors and can even learn to avoid them—as I do, at all cost.

The government has played a leading role in making us the fattest and sickest population in human history, so it ought to play a role in remedying the situation it has helped create.

Here's how the government has made us so sick.

First, we spend twenty billion taxpayer dollars a year on farm subsidies. Those subsidies go overwhelmingly to animal agriculture, artificially reducing the cost of dairy and meat. We therefore collectively subsidize the generation of heart disease, stroke, hypertension, diabetes, Alzheimer's, cancer, obesity, and climate change.

Second, governments at all levels purchase and serve meat and dairy products in schools, prisons, public hospitals, and other public institutions, and to our military personnel all over the world. This is yet another way in which we collectively subsidize animal agriculture and accelerate the climate crisis.

Third, federal nutritional guidelines have been placed under the jurisdiction of the Department of Agriculture, which naturally does the bidding of animal agriculture in promoting disinformation about health.

Fourth, our government has allowed "food deserts" to be created in our inner cities and on our Native American reservations, making it difficult for those who live there to purchase fresh produce.

Here's a simple program for reducing the deficit, helping our economy, and dramatically improving America's health:

1) End all farm subsidies immediately. This will save $20 billion per year. (This figure does not include many additional billions in state water subsidies, nor the untold billions in "externalities"—the costs animal agriculture imposes on society to clean up its messes. If

you think these externalities are not significant, consider that the many *trillions* spent to cope with the effects of the coronavirus pandemic are, when you get right down to it, an international animal agriculture externality.) Plus, by significantly increasing the cost of animal foods, ending farm subsidies will result in their reduced consumption and therefore the greatest contribution to America's health that we've seen since the polio vaccine.

2) Stop serving animal foods in all public institutions, including schools, prisons, hospitals, and the military. Why should we serve to our children and our soldiers foods that science knows to be unhealthy?

3) Place nutritional guidelines under the jurisdiction of an agency that answers only to science, such as the Office of the Surgeon General. Then appoint someone who understands the science of nutrition—someone like Dr. Neal Barnard—to be Surgeon General of the United States.

4) Since private concerns have failed to bring fresh produce to food deserts across this country, the government needs to step in. Let's stop arguing about socialized medicine and instead let's have a dose of socialized distribution (state-run produce markets, if nothing else works) of human food. Of course, human food means grains and legumes and produce, not meat and dairy.

5) Make the industry that is the leading cause of climate change— animal agriculture—pay for at least a fraction of the damage it has caused to the environment by instituting a slaughterhouse tax, a fisheries tax, and a dairy and egg tax. If we were to impose a tax of $5 on each chicken and turkey slaughtered, $100 on each pig or cow slaughtered, $10 on each egg-laying chicken, a mere dollar on each fish killed on commercial farms, and a dollar for each gallon of milk produced, that would in total generate about $350 billion dollars annually.[10] There could be further taxes on other animals used for food, such as sheep, and there could be a tax on wild-caught fish and a tariff on imported animal foods. These would be taxes that you, the consumer, wouldn't have to pay; you could escape even their indirect costs simply by shunning animal foods. Since not everyone will do so, the taxes would raise hundreds of

billions to help pay for the environmental destruction animal agriculture causes. Plus, of course, we'd be saving $20 billion in farm subsidies. Starting from our (pre-pandemic) trillion-dollar deficit, we could go a long way toward balancing the budget just with taxes on animal foods and an end to farm subsidies.

But the improvement to the country's bottom line wouldn't stop there. All these policies would result, of course, in a more honest pricing of animal foods that accounts for their real cost of production and their real cost in environmental degradation. And so the new, much higher, and more honest price for flesh foods, dairy, and eggs would give consumers sticker shock, and diminish consumption of those foods markedly. This in turn would dramatically reduce obesity, diabetes, heart disease, and other ailments, and save us untold billions in healthcare costs.

Simply raising the price of animal foods, in other words, would do far more for our health than Obamacare or any other mere health insurance proposal ever could.

That's the good news.

The bad news will not surprise you. The bad news is that these proposals are not politically feasible today. Not even close.

There would be few votes in Congress for ending farm subsidies, and certainly none for a slaughterhouse tax. And don't expect Congress to ban animal foods from schools, hospitals, or our armed forces any time soon.

So these elegant and painless—indeed, pain-reducing—ways to balance the budget remain, for the moment at least, just a vegan's fevered political pipe dream.

More realistically, what could be accomplished now?

First, it wouldn't hurt for these kinds of proposals to at least enter the political dialogue; I remember a time, not so long ago, when gay marriage was a political pipe dream. Second, if we can't end farm subsidies outright, we may be able to at least reduce them as part of a deficit-reduction package. Third, if we can't ban animal foods from public institutions, we can at least advocate for making healthy plant-based options always available to students, hospital patients, prisoners, and soldiers. Fourth, it should be feasible to remove the issuance of nutritional guidelines from the inherently conflicted Department of Agriculture. Fifth, it shouldn't be beyond our political imagination to find a way to put an end to food deserts in this country. We should be able to make it at least as easy to buy apples and broccoli in every neighborhood across the land as it is to buy cheeseburgers, fries, chips, and milkshakes.

Most importantly, though, we can all take our own health into our own hands.

If we shop for the right foods, we can, with our own dollars, support the production of organic human food, and deal a body blow to animal agriculture. Let's capitalize upon the fact that food production answers to demand. That means that agricultural decisions to grow one sort of food or another ultimately rest in our collective hands as consumers. We can change the agricultural landscape and help save the planet by boosting demand for human food, and reducing demand for factory-farmed roadkill.

We can inform our elected representatives that a constituency exists that cares more about health than health insurance, and wants them to cut farm subsidies and make sure that healthy plant-based options are available to all school students, all prison inmates, all hospital patients, and our military wherever they may serve.

We can stop looking to doctors to save us from ourselves. Instead, we can save ourselves, quite simply, by eating human food. And then, as we get healthier, we can tell our doctors all about it. Some of them may even be interested.

There's nothing extreme about eating a diet consisting of whole plant food. I've been doing it for a long time, and it's not hard at all. Nothing could be less risky.

On the other hand, there's something terribly extreme and risky about supporting animal agriculture by consuming its products and allowing Australia and the American West and the Amazon to continue to burn, and the glaciers to melt, largely as a result of our taste for flesh.

And the Covid-19 pandemic should remind humanity of the terrible price we pay when humans are put in contact with crowded populations of animals—the inevitable consequence of raising them for food. We would not be suffering a pandemic today if people around the world did not make the mistake of eating dead animals. This pandemic arose from a wet market in Wuhan, China. The next one could just as easily arise from an industrial chicken "farm"—a warehouse of battery cages—in Arkansas, or a pig "farm"—a warehouse of crates—in North Carolina. Should we risk another pandemic, and then another, because flesh is just so darned tasty?

You would think that humanity could do better than such chicken "farms" and pig "farms," but you've got to hand it to the p.r. guy who decided to call torturing animals "farming."

Jane Goodall had this to say about the pandemic: "We have brought this on ourselves because of our absolute disrespect for animals and the environment. Our disrespect for wild animals and our disrespect for farmed animals has created this situation where disease can spill over to infect human beings. . . . Scientists warn that to avoid future crises, we must drastically change our diets and move to plant-rich foods."

"If we do not do things differently," Jane Goodall added, "we are finished. We can't go on very much longer like this."[11]

We are a profoundly confused species. Humanity has misunderstood our relationship to food from the very beginning. The original sin wasn't eating an apple. It was eating a dead animal.

We don't have much time to get it right.

Here's the truth, my friends: we've got only one realistic shot at turning around both our health crisis and our environmental crisis. We need to eat human food.

I know what my mother would say.

What's taking us so long?

Easy, Delicious, and Healthy
RECIPES

by
CHEF AJ

Chef AJ has a celebrated and distinctive knack for making food as tasty as it is healthy. All recipes are free of sugar, oil, flour, gluten, and salt.

The recipe section belongs to Chef AJ, and I turn over the narration to her . . .

GM

A Word From Chef AJ

I'm Chef AJ and I have followed a plant-exclusive diet for over 43 years. I was thrilled when Glen asked me to create the recipes for this book because I believe its title, "Own Your Health" says it all. You really can control much of your health destiny by your daily lifestyle choices, and it starts with the food.

The recipes in this book are not only free of all animal products (meat, fish, fowl, eggs, and dairy products), but are also free of chemicals like sugar, oil, and salt that fool the satiety mechanisms in your brain and can cause you to overeat. (If you'd like more information on this phenomenon, we highly recommend reading *The Pleasure Trap* by Dr. Doug Lisle and Dr. Alan Goldhamer.)

In addition, all of the recipes are gluten-free and nut-free and low in fat. We like to call this way of eating *UNPROCESSED*, which is the title of our first book together. We prefer to use only whole plants that are found in nature. While it's true that we offer the option of using a few convenience items like canned salt-free beans, when we do recommend foods that have labels, they generally contain only the one ingredient listed on the label.

You will find here not only over 75 delicious recipes created by me, but 35 delicious recipes from my friends, many of whom have blogs and *YouTube* channels and practice the same style of eating. Feel free to tweak any of these recipes to your liking and make them your own. When you use fresh, whole natural ingredients, the possibilities are endless.

In these recipes, I use a few ingredients that you may be unfamiliar with and may not see in your local grocery store but are available online. I use them for their distinctive flavors. Here are the products that may be new to you.

Jackfruit: Ripe jackfruit is one of the most delectable fresh fruits you will ever taste. It actually tastes like *Juicy Fruit* gum. It is sometimes found in the refrigerated section of many grocery stores, but the jackfruit that I call for in my savory recipes in this book is the young jackfruit, which is unripe and can be found in cans and boxes. I prefer the boxed varieties as they don't contain salt and have a meaty texture. I encourage you to try jackfruit if you can.

Salt-free mustard: Growing up, I always disliked mustard. Whether it was the yellow ballpark mustard or the French varieties made with white wine, I never cared for the taste. And then I found a mild stone ground mustard from the company *Westbrae,* which makes a variety without salt; it's not as pungent as, say, a *Grey Poupon*. Whatever mustard you decide to use in these recipes, make sure you like the taste of it before adding it.

Vanilla powder: Vanilla is one of the most expensive spices in the world, second only to saffron, and the powder is even more expensive than the extract. But once you've used it, you realize that it's more potent than vanilla extract, especially in recipes like the Desert Date Shake or the ones in which you really want that deep vanilla flavor. Vanilla powder is simply ground vanilla beans. You can find instructions online on how to make your own vanilla powder, but I find it's easier just to buy it. While it's expensive, a little (½-1 teaspoon) goes a long way. If you are going to use vanilla extract, I recommend you get a pure one rather than an imitation. Many vanilla extracts contain glycerin and/or alcohol, whereas you can get vanilla powder simply made from the whole bean. To substitute vanilla extract for vanilla powder, you would use 1 teaspoon of vanilla extract for each ½ teaspoon of vanilla powder.

I would encourage you, if you can, to try the vanilla powder and see if it does make a difference. Make sure that you get a brand that contains only vanilla beans, as some contain sugars and fillers.

Balsamic vinegar: Quite a few of these recipes call for balsamic vinegar. I recommend a specific brand that I love called *California Balsamic* (www.californiabalsamic.com), but you can use any brand or any flavor you like. Please keep in mind that vinegars vary widely in their taste, quality, and most importantly, their acidity. Most vinegar has 6% acidity, which is why it tastes so sour. Some people, like my husband, actually enjoy this tartness, and if you are one of these people then feel free to use vinegar that has not been reduced. Reduced balsamic vinegar has about 4% acidity. As opposed to the 6% acidity vinegar, which is thin and watery, the reduced vinegars are thick and syrupy. They all taste so much sweeter, with the sweetness coming from the grapes. Many people enjoy the taste of the reduced vinegars better, and when you have a sauce or dressing that you truly enjoy, it makes it easier to eat larger quantities of salads and vegetables. The thickness of the reduced balsamic vinegars coats the salad greens and the vegetables better, whereas the traditional vinegars are watery and just sink to the bottom of the bowl.

It is possible to make your own balsamic reduction. You simply take 2 cups of a balsamic vinegar, white or dark, bring it to a boil, reduce the heat and simmer until it becomes one cup of liquid. This is not only time-consuming, but you really don't save any money and you don't have the wide variety of flavors available to you.

The companies that make the flavored or infused vinegars do so in large batches, and this allows the spices and seasonings to incorporate easily. Because most home cooks don't make large batches or have the proper equipment, I find that the spices never get mixed in fully. To me, it's worth a few extra pennies to buy these delicious, quality vinegars, and I keep a wide assortment of my favorite flavors. Because they are so flavorful, a little truly does go a long way, and I can get away with using only 1 to 4 tablespoons in many recipes.

Whichever brand of vinegar that you buy, make sure that it is free of any added sugar, oil, or salt. If you get a chance, it's great to go to a store where you can taste all the flavors. You often find such opportunities at farmers markets, festivals, and conferences. While there are many fine reputable companies making specialty vinegars, I have specifically promoted *California Balsamic* in my recipes simply because all of their reduced balsamic vinegars are SOS (sugar, oil, and salt) free and so far it seems to be the company with the greatest variety of savory flavors like Curry, Dill Mustard, Ruby Red Onion, Gilroy Garlic, Blazin' Habanero, Sweet Heat and Teriyaki, that I can use in place of sauces in entrees and side dishes.

And as always, remember to EAT YOUR GREENS!

Love & Kale,
Chef AJ

APPETIZERS

"FRIED" ARTICHOKE HEARTS

You don't have to give up the taste of your favorite fried foods when you use wholesome ingredients and an air fryer.

INGREDIENTS:

1 12-ounce bag frozen artichoke hearts, defrosted
¼ cup gluten free oats
¼ cup nutritional yeast
1½ teaspoons *Benson's Table Tasty* (or your favorite salt-free seasoning)
1 teaspoon SMOKED paprika
⅛ teaspoon chipotle powder

PREPARATION:

Defrost the artichokes and squeeze out any excess liquid. Place all ingredients except for the artichoke hearts in a high-powered blender and blend until smooth. Pour into a bowl. Dredge the artichokes in the "breading" and place on an air fryer tray. Air fry at 400 degrees F for 20 minutes.

CHEF'S NOTE:

These are delicious served with your favorite oil-free marinara sauce. You can also use mushrooms, hearts of palm, or steamed cauliflower florets in place of the artichoke hearts.

HOT SPINACH ARTICHOKE DIP

This is a staple hot appetizer dish served at many restaurants and is made from cheese, butter, and cream. Not mine. Mine is made from actual food!

INGREDIENTS:

12 ounces of cauliflower (approx. 4 cups), steamed
2 Tablespoons lemon juice
4 Tablespoons nutritional yeast
¼ cup cloves roasted garlic
1 12-ounce bag frozen artichoke hearts, defrosted
2 cups finely chopped spinach, or more to taste

PREPARATION:

First, steam the cauliflower and roast the garlic. The absolute quickest and easiest way to roast garlic is to place the peeled cloves in an air fryer at 370 degrees F for ten minutes (or a little longer if you prefer them well-done). Place all ingredients except for the spinach in a high-powered blender and blend until smooth and creamy. Stir in the spinach by hand. If you prefer, you can also finely chop the artichoke hearts and stir them in by hand. Microwave until hot. Serve as a dip with your favorite veggies such as bell pepper or with baked tortilla chips.

PEPPERONI MUSHROOMS

You would swear you are eating pepperoni!

INGREDIENTS:

Sliced cremini or white mushrooms
Pepperoni seasoning

PREPARATION:

Wet the mushrooms and drain excess water. Sprinkle with pepperoni seasoning. Air fry at 400 degrees F for 20 minutes. Pepperoni seasoning is available at www.LocalSpicery.com. Or use my friend Kathy Hester's seasoning recipe below. Kathy Hester can be found at *PlantBasedInstantPot.com*.

KATHY HESTER'S SALT-FREE PEPPERONI SEASONING

It's amazing what a little spice blend can do to your meals.

INGREDIENTS:

3 Tablespoons smoked paprika
2 Tablespoons granulated garlic
1 Tablespoon basil
½ Tablespoon fennel seeds (or 1 teaspoon ground fennel)
1 teaspoon oregano
½ teaspoon onion powder
½ teaspoon black pepper (or less, to taste)
¼ teaspoons mustard powder or ⅛ teaspoon whole mustard seeds

PREPARATION:

Add all the ingredients to your small blender or spice grinder and blend until smooth. Store in an air-tight container for up to 6 months or more. The flavor may be less bright over time, but the spice will not go bad.

CHEF'S NOTE:

Try some sprinkled on a potato, over streamed veggies, or anywhere else you could use a burst of flavor! Like yours extra spicy? Add ½ to 1 teaspoon red pepper flakes or cayenne powder.

TOASTED EVERYTHING BAGELS

For those who do not eat gluten or flour, your prayers have been answered!

INGREDIENTS:

Yukon Gold potatoes
Everything Bagel Seasoning

PREPARATION:

Steam potatoes and chill for several hours or overnight. I cook them in an *Instant Pot* pressure cooker in a basket for 5 minutes and immediately release the pressure. Then refrigerate them. After they are refrigerated for at least several hours or overnight, slice them in half and make a round hole in the center using an apple corer. Place the seasoning in a small bowl and dredge the cut side of the potato in the seasoning until fully covered with spices. Place them face up on a tray and air fry or bake at 400 degrees F for 20-30 minutes.

CHEF'S NOTE:

To make these look exactly like bagels, choose potatoes that are nicely rounded and the size of a bagel. Salt-free *Everything Bagel Seasoning* made by *Spice Hunter* is available at many grocery stores and *Amazon*.

Salads

CHRISTMAS KALE SALAD

The finely chopped red bell pepper looks like little Christmas lights on the greens. You could also add pomegranate arils for a festive, delicious, and nutritious touch. Don't let the name fool you. You can enjoy this all year round.

INGREDIENTS:

8 ounces baby kale or arugula
1 large red (or yellow or orange) bell pepper (or a combination), finely chopped
(approx. 1 cup)
Lemon Poppy Seed Dressing, to taste (see recipe page 179)

PREPARATION:

Place the greens in a bowl. Finely chop the red bell pepper and add to the greens. Massage the salad with the lemon poppy seed dressing.

CHEF'S NOTE:

Pomegranate arils are a delicious addition to this salad. I don't recommend green peppers in any of my recipes as they are unripe and not as delicious and can give many people GI distress.

F.A.R.M. FRESH SALAD

F.A.R.M. is an acronym for Fennel, Apple, Raisin, and Mint. And this salad tastes as fresh as it sounds. This is a great dish to bring to your Fourth of July BBQ or any potluck because it can withstand being out of the fridge for a bit.

INGREDIENTS:

2 bulbs of fennel, shaved or very thinly sliced
2 cups of apples, diced (I prefer Envy or Gala)
1 cup golden raisins
1 cup fresh mint, chopped (about ¾ ounce)
4 Tablespoons *Simply Lemon California Balsamic* vinegar

PREPARATION:

Thinly slice the fennel bulbs and dice the apples. Place in a bowl along with the raisins and mint. Drizzle the vinegar over the top and mix well. Serve chilled.

CHEF'S NOTE:

Add 1 cup of pomegranate arils when in season. If you don't have the lemon vinegar, you can use lemon juice. Use Meyer lemons, if you can, as they are sweeter. Or you can use 4 Tablespoons of the Lemonade Dressing (see recipe page 178).

SWEET POTATO AND WILD RICE SALAD

This was inspired by a wonderful recipe in the annual *Forks Over Knives Meal Planner*. I love serving this over a large plate of mixed salad greens.

INGREDIENTS:

1 pound wild rice, cooked and chilled
4 cups orange sweet potato flesh, chilled
2 very large sweet apples (Envy or other sweet apple preferred)
1½ cups chopped scallions (approx. 6 scallions)

PREPARATION:

Cook wild rice according to the directions on the package. I simply place the rice in an *Instant Pot* pressure cooker with 4 cups of water and push the multigrain button. Chill. Cook the sweet potatoes however you prefer. Peel and chill. Dice the sweet potatoes and apples and mix with the wild rice and scallions. Pour Sweet and Smoky Dressing (see recipe page 184) over the salad. Chill.

Soups

CHILLED CANTALOUPE GINGERED SOUP

This is a refreshing summer soup and also makes a great aperitif when served in a pretty glass.

INGREDIENTS:

1 cantaloupe
2 peeled oranges
1 cup unsweetened plant-based yogurt
2 Tablespoons peach balsamic vinegar
fresh ginger, to taste (I use a one-inch piece)
fresh purple grapes, cut in half
fresh mint for garnish

PREPARATION:

Place all ingredients in a high-powered blender and blend until smooth and creamy. Pour into a pretty bowl and garnish with grape halves and fresh mint.

CHEF'S NOTE:

You can buy unsweetened yogurt at many stores or make your own. Soy, almond, and oat-based yogurts will have less fat, and less saturated fat, than coconut-based.

CREAMY CAULIFLOWER BISQUE

This is a variation of the Broccoli Bisque adapted from and inspired by Mary McDougall. One day I was making it at *TrueNorth Health Center* in Santa Rosa and all they had was unsweetened vanilla almond milk, and believe it or not, it was delicious! Putting the sweet potatoes and head of cauliflower in whole saves prep time. The green leaves of the cauliflower are healthy and delicious.

INGREDIENTS:

1 head whole cauliflower, about 2 pounds
2 pounds Hannah yams (white sweet potatoes)
6 cups no-sodium vegetable broth or water
1 large sweet onion
8 cloves garlic
2 Tablespoons dried dill
2 Tablespoons *Benson's Table Tasty* (or your favorite salt-free seasoning)
1 Tablespoon SMOKED paprika (different than regular paprika)
¼ teaspoon chipotle powder
4 Tablespoons *Westbrae* salt-free stone ground mustard
4 Tablespoons nutritional yeast (optional)
3 cups unsweetened non-dairy milk (depending on desired thickness)

PREPARATION:

Place all ingredients except for the non-dairy milk, mustard, and nutritional yeast, if using, in an *Instant Pot* pressure cooker and cook on high pressure for 12 minutes. Release pressure and add the non-dairy milk, mustard, and nutritional yeast (if using). Purée the soup with an immersion blender right in the pot or carefully in a blender until smooth.

CHEF'S NOTE:

I like to garnish the dish with fresh arugula and serve over brown, black or wild rice. You can substitute broccoli or asparagus for the cauliflower and use Japanese or orange sweet potatoes if you can't find the Hannah yams, but do try to find them as they make this soup extra creamy and spectacular. They are often called white Sweet Potatoes or Jersey Yams. You can also use frozen vegetables as well. This soup freezes very well.

CREAMY LEEK SOUP

Leeks can be very dirty and difficult to clean. Many stores offer pre-washed leeks, enabling you to make this thick and creamy soup in virtually no time.

INGREDIENTS:

4 cups water
16 ounces leeks
12 ounces broccoli
12 ounces cauliflower
16 ounces zucchini
12 ounces butternut squash
16 cloves garlic
½ cup rolled oats

PREPARATION:

Place all ingredients in an *Instant Pot* pressure cooker. Cook on high pressure for 6 minutes. Release the pressure and puree the soup right in the pot using an immersion blender. Add any seasonings you desire.

CREAMY TORTILLA SOUP

INGREDIENTS:

1 large red onion, peeled and left whole
4 cloves garlic
2 14.5-ounce cans *Muir Glen* fire-roasted tomatoes, salt-free
2 cups water
1½ teaspoons mild salt-free chili powder
1½ teaspoons SMOKED paprika
1½ teaspoons oregano
½ teaspoon chipotle powder
6 small corn tortillas (oil-free and salt-free, made from just corn or corn and lime)

PREPARATION:

Place all ingredients in an *Instant Pot* pressure cooker and cook on high pressure for 10 minutes. Release pressure and blend with an immersion blender until smooth. Garnish with chopped scallions and baked tortilla strips if desired. Serve with lime wedges to squeeze on top.

GARLIC LOVERS ALL-VEGGIE SOUP

I created this recipe during a cold winter when I was a guest chef working at the *TrueNorth Health Center*. I thought I was coming down with a cold, but by having this soup every day for breakfast it never manifested. With ½ cup of garlic cloves, you will also make yourself vampire proof! You can make this soup a hearty meal by serving over rice or adding beans or potatoes.

INGREDIENTS:

8 cups of water
1 10-ounce bag Cruciferous Crunch (or 10 cups of finely shredded vegetables like Brussels sprouts, cabbage and kale)
2 14.5-ounce cans *Muir Glen* salt-free fire roasted tomatoes
1 10-ounce bag sliced mushrooms (approx. 3 cups)
1 10-ounce bag chopped onion (approx. 3 cups)
½ cup peeled garlic cloves finely chopped
4 cups chopped zucchini (you can also use spiralized zucchini as zucchini noodles, aka "zoodles")

PREPARATION:

Place all ingredients in an *Instant Pot* pressure cooker and cook on high pressure for 5 minutes. Enjoy as is or add your favorite starch (like cooked rice, beans, or potatoes) for a heartier meal.

CHEF'S NOTE:

Trader Joe's sells a wonderful blend of cruciferous vegetables called *Cruciferous Crunch*. Many other stores like *Costco* and *Kroger* sell their own shredded cruciferous veggie blend. If you can't find it, you can easily make your own.

ENTREES

BAKED DOUBLE MASHED POTATO STRATA

Believe it or not, I actually like to serve this at Thanksgiving. You can make it ahead of time; it makes a lot and everyone loves it!

INGREDIENTS:

4 pounds Yukon Gold potatoes
¼ - ½ cup unsweetened plant milk
¼ cup nutritional yeast
1 teaspoon *Benson's Table Tasty* (or your favorite salt-free seasoning)
½ teaspoon garlic powder
4 pounds Hannah yams
1 recipe of the Best Damn BBQ Sauce Ever! (see recipe page 170)

PREPARATION:

Preheat oven to 400 degrees F. Place the Yukon Gold potatoes in an *Instant Pot* pressure cooker filled with water up to the rack and cook on high pressure for 12 minutes. Let the pressure come down naturally. Drain the potatoes, then add the plant milk and seasonings and mash with a potato masher until well combined.

Roast the Hannah yams. I generally roast them at 400 F. for 60 minutes. Peel and mash with a potato masher. In a casserole dish, evenly spread the mashed Yukon Gold potatoes. Cover with half of the BBQ sauce. Carefully spread the mashed Hannah yams on top of the BBQ sauce and cover with the remaining sauce. Bake uncovered for 45 minutes at 400 F. Let rest for 10 minutes and slice.

CHEF'S NOTE:

If you can't find Hannah yams, use Japanese sweet potatoes.

BBQ JACKFRUIT

An exotic and satisfying meal.

INGREDIENTS:

1 red onion, chopped
6 cloves garlic, finely chopped
1 7-ounce box unseasoned jackfruit
¼ cup BBQ sauce or more to taste (see recipe page 170)

PREPARATION:

Dry sauté the onion until nicely browned, adding water a tablespoon at a time if necessary. Add the garlic and sauté for another minute or two. Add the jackfruit and cook until warmed through. Add the BBQ sauce and cook until warm.

CHEF'S NOTE:

If you can't find jackfruit, use small roasted cauliflower florets instead. Serve over your favorite grain. If you don't want to make the BBQ sauce, simply use *California Balsamic Hickory Smoke Vinegar* instead.

COMFORT STEW

This simple dish of potatoes, cabbage, and onions is pure comfort! Thank you to Anne West for inspiring this spectacular and easy-to-prepare recipe. When she brought it to a potluck, I ate three servings. It's a two-part recipe because the first part requires the preparation of the slow-cooked onions, which are so delicious that you might want to make extra to add to other dishes! I tweaked this recipe a bit to include more vinegar and figured out how to make it quickly in the *Instant Pot* once the onions are prepared. This dish will make a cabbage lover out of you yet!

INGREDIENTS:

2 cups onions (red, white, yellow, and/or sweet)
2 pounds red or gold potatoes, cut into large cubes
1 large head of cabbage
1 Tablespoon fresh garlic, finely chopped
2 teaspoons mustard seeds
¼ cup white balsamic vinegar (a good quality, reduced brand like *California Balsamic* preferred)

PREPARATION:

First, prepare the onions by peeling and slicing them. Place in crock pot and cover. Cook on a low setting for 24 hours and they will turn into caramelized onions! Once ready, drain the liquid and set aside. Place the cabbage, potatoes, garlic, and mustard seed in the *Instant Pot* pressure cooker along with the liquid from the cooked onions. Cook on high pressure for 10 minutes. Release the pressure and pour into a large bowl and stir in the caramelized onions and vinegar!

CHEF'S NOTE:

This dish is delicious as is or served over a whole grain like brown rice.

CRISPY MASHED POTATO STEAKS

A great use for any roasted garlic mashed potatoes.

INGREDIENTS:

Large serving of roasted garlic mashed potatoes (see recipe page 228)—or your favorite leftover mashed potatoes.

PREPARATION:

Place the roasted garlic mashed potatoes in a silicone loaf pan. Let the pan sit overnight in the refrigerator. Invert loaf pan on a cutting board and cut into ½" thick slices. Place slices on a nonstick silicone baking mat and bake at 400 degrees F for about 45 minutes. Flip the slices halfway through.

CHEF'S NOTE:

Enjoy with your favorite gravy: Groovy Mushroom Gravy (see recipe page 176) or Caramelized Onion Gravy (see recipe page 171).

CURRY IN A HURRY

Here is what you do when you need curry in a hurry. Using a bag of frozen organic rice and a bag of broccoli, I can make this quick and satisfying meal in the microwave in 7 minutes flat.

INGREDIENTS:

2 cups cooked rice
12 ounces of steamed broccoli (chopped finely after steaming)
¼ cup golden raisins
¼ cup chopped scallions (the green part)
¼ - ½ teaspoon dry turmeric
3 Tablespoons *California Balsamic Curry Vinegar* (or 3 Tablespoons reduced white balsamic vinegar plus ½ teaspoon curry powder)

PREPARATION:

Mix all ingredients together and enjoy!

DIY POKE BOWLS

While I prefer to avoid restaurants, when I must go to one, I look for a Poke Bowl restaurant. But why pay $10 for a bowl when you can make a more plentiful and more delicious one at home for the fraction of the cost?

INGREDIENTS:

Cooked grain of your choice (brown rice, white rice, millet, quinoa, corn, wild rice or a combination of whole grains)

Very thinly sliced fruit, herbs, and vegetables of your choice (such as kale, cucumbers, red onions, scallions, fresh ginger, cherry tomatoes, jalapeno peppers, cilantro, carrots, purple cabbage, mango, grapes, or pineapple)

Dressing of your choice (I simply use a variety of the savory flavors of reduced balsamic vinegar like Curry, Teriyaki or Gilroy Garlic from *California Balsamic*)

PREPARATION:

Cook your grain according to your preferred method or simply microwave frozen, organic rice. Any color of rice will work well, as will millet. Add your favorite toppings in any amount and your favorite sauce.

CHEF'S NOTE:

The secret to a spectacular Poke Bowl is a good mandoline for slicing the vegetables. Be sure to always be safe and use a mandoline glove.

DOUBLE POTATO PANINI PIZZA

It's worth it to get a panini press even if you use it only to make this recipe!

INGREDIENTS:

Roasted garlic mashed potatoes (see recipe page 166)
Steamed baby Brussels sprouts
16-ounce bag frozen hash brown potatoes, defrosted

PREPARATION:

Prepare mashed potatoes and steam Brussels sprouts. Preheat a panini press. When it's ready, pour the bag of hash browns evenly and carefully over the press. Cook for 30 minutes or until crisp and remove from the press. Carefully spread the mashed potatoes over the crust. Press the Brussels sprouts in the mashed potatoes. Drizzle with your favorite reduced balsamic vinegar.

CHEF'S NOTE:

My favorite vinegar for this dish is the *California Balsamic Hickory Smoke.*

INSTANT DINNER

They say that necessity is the mother of invention. One day after coming home from a trip, this was all I had in my fridge. I just threw it all in the *Instant Pot* and was it delicious! I served it with a bit of fresh Pico de Gallo on top. The texture will be halfway between a stew and a soup—call it a *stewp*. Eat your stewp with a spork.

INGREDIENTS:

4 cups water
2 Hannah yams
½ red onion
2 pounds of veggies (carrots, cauliflower, zucchini, broccoli)

PREPARATION:

Place all ingredients in an *Instant Pot* pressure cooker and cook on high pressure for 12 minutes. Release the pressure and blend right in the *Instant Pot* with an immersion blender. Add any seasonings you desire.

CHEF'S NOTE:
If you can't find Hannah yams, use Japanese sweet potatoes.

PINEAPPLE UNFRIED RICE

No need for take-out when you can quickly make a much healthier version of take-in at home.

INGREDIENTS:

1 large sweet onion, chopped
6 peeled garlic cloves, finely chopped
1 thumb size knob of fresh ginger, finely chopped
1 thumb size knob of fresh turmeric, finely chopped
4 ounces of shredded carrots (approx. 2 cups)
4 ounces of shredded purple cabbage (approx. 2½ cups)
1 20-ounce can of pineapple chunks, in its own juice, drained and liquid reserved
6 cups cooked brown rice
½ cup *California Balsamic Teriyaki Vinegar* (or vinegar of your choice)
fresh cilantro, optional

PREPARATION:

Dry sauté the onion until nicely browned, adding water or the unsweetened pineapple juice if needed. Add the garlic, ginger and turmeric and sauté for another minute or two. Add the cabbage and carrots and cook until soft. Add the rice and pineapple and cook until heated through. If the dish appears dry or needs more liquid, add the remaining pineapple juice. Stir in the vinegar. Add fresh cilantro if desired.

CHEF'S NOTE:

Try cooked quinoa in place of the rice.

RAINBOW CONFETTI GAZPACHO RICE

I created this recipe while I was a presenter on the Holistic Holiday at Sea cruise. They actually had a daily gazpacho bar and all I did was add rice to make it a hearty and satisfying starch-based meal.

INGREDIENTS:

Cooked rice
Finely chopped vegetables such as tomatoes, red cabbage, red, yellow and orange bell peppers, green or red onions, cucumbers
Finely chopped herbs such as basil or cilantro (or a flavored balsamic vinegar)

PREPARATION:

Mix all ingredients together in the proportions that you enjoy. Setting up a Gazpacho Bar is fun for the whole family! Guests love it as well.

CHEF'S NOTE:

I like to use the flavored vinegars in either Basil or Cilantro from *California Balsamic* rather than fresh herbs. This could be a side dish, as well as an entrée.

RED NO-LENTIL CHILI

Here is a lentil-free version of one of my most popular recipes from *The Secrets to Ultimate Weight-Loss.*

INGREDIENTS:

4 cups water
⅓ cup dry millet
16 ounces riced cauliflower
1 14.5-ounce can of *Muir Glen* salt-free fire roasted tomatoes
1 red bell pepper
6 Deglet Noor dates
2 Tablespoons apple cider vinegar
5 ounces chopped red onion (approx. 1 cup)
4 cloves garlic, peeled
1 teaspoon dried parsley
1 teaspoon SMOKED paprika
¾ teaspoon salt-free chili powder
¾ teaspoon oregano
¼ teaspoon chipotle powder
⅛ teaspoon crushed red pepper flakes

PREPARATION:

Place 4 cups of water in an *Instant Pot* pressure cooker. In a high-powered blender, blend the tomatoes, bell pepper, dates, tomato paste, and apple cider vinegar. Add the puree to the *Instant Pot* along with the remaining ingredients. Cook on high pressure for 10 minutes. Release the pressure immediately when it's done cooking.

CHEF'S NOTE:

I love to serve this over brown rice sprinkled with chopped scallions and Enlightened Faux Parmesan. (That recipe is in *The Secrets to Ultimate Weight Loss* but all you have to do is blend three ingredients: 1 cup of gluten-free oats, 1 cup of nutritional yeast, and 1 Tablespoon of *Benson's Table Tasty* or your favorite salt-free seasoning.)

SAVE THE CHICKEN CURRY

If you can't find (or don't like) jackfruit, you can leave it out or substitute sliced mushrooms for a meaty texture.

INGREDIENTS:

2 cups chopped sweet onion (about 8 ounces)
4-6 cloves peeled garlic, finely chopped
½ inch piece ginger, chopped
12 ounces broccoli, lightly steamed
4 cups fresh spinach
1 cooked Russet potato, cubed
1 14.5-ounce can *Muir Glen* salt-free fire roasted tomatoes
1 7-ounce box of unseasoned jackfruit
½ cup *California Balsamic Curry Vinega*r (or ½ cup reduced white balsamic vinegar plus 1 teaspoon curry powder)

PREPARATION:

Lightly steam the broccoli. Water or dry sauté (depending on your pan) the onion until translucent. (Add water a tablespoon at a time as necessary if you dry sauté.) Then add ginger and garlic and sauté a minute or two longer. Add tomatoes, potato, jackfruit, and broccoli and cook until heated through. Stir in spinach just until it wilts. Remove from heat and stir in vinegar. Serve over your favorite grain.

ZOODLES ARRABIATA

The perfect dish for those who like it hot!

<u>INGREDIENTS:</u>

1 15-ounce can salt-free fire roasted tomatoes
8 cloves garlic, minced
1 sweet onion, diced
1 12-ounce bag frozen artichoke hearts, defrosted and cut in half
1 pound zucchini, spiralized into "zoodles"
½ cup (more or less, to taste) fresh chopped basil
1 teaspoon *Benson's Table Tasty* (or your favorite salt-free seasoning)
1 teaspoon SMOKED paprika
½ teaspoon crushed red pepper flakes (more or less, to taste)

<u>PREPARATION:</u>

Drain the can of tomatoes, and reserve the liquid. You will be using that liquid to sauté your onion. Preheat your pan and dice your onion. When pan is ready add the onion and dry sauté at first, adding the tomato liquid when necessary so the onions won't stick. Cook onion until golden brown. Add the chopped garlic and cook 1-2 minutes longer. Add the artichokes, the spices, the tomatoes and the zoodles. Garnish with fresh chopped basil and Enlightened Faux Parmesan, if desired. (See Chef's Note to Red No-Lentil Chili, page 154.)

ZOODLES POMODORA

This is a quick, easy meal and especially satisfying with an added starch like cannellini beans.

INGREDIENTS:

1 sweet onion, diced
8 cloves of garlic
1 pound of zucchini spiralized into "zoodles"
1 pound of cherry tomatoes, cut in half
3 ounces sundried tomatoes, about ¾ of a cup
Fresh chopped basil

PREPARATION:

Preheat pan. Dice onion and place in pan. Begin to dry sauté. If the onion begins to stick, add water a few tablespoons at a time. Cook until nicely browned. Add the minced garlic and cook another 1-2 minutes. Add the cherry tomatoes and sun-dried tomatoes. Cook just until soft. Then add the zoodles and cook until desired tenderness is reached.

CHEF'S NOTE:

You can also make this with spiralized sweet potatoes or butternut squash which you can often find fresh in the produce section or in the freezer.

Side Dishes

ASPARAGUS WITH HOLLANDAISE SAUCE

Hollandaise is sauce is one of the five mother sauces in French cuisine. Traditional hollandaise sauce is very high in fat and made from egg yolks and melted butter. Now you can make this decadent sauce virtually fat-free without sacrificing flavor.

INGREDIENTS:

Asparagus, in desired amount
8 ounces cooked Yukon Gold potatoes (approximately 1 cup)
8 ounces unsweetened non-dairy milk
4 Tablespoons lemon juice
1 teaspoon mustard powder
¼ teaspoon garlic powder
¼ teaspoon onion powder
⅛ teaspoon turmeric.

PREPARATION:

Cook asparagus according to your preferred method (steam, roast, or grill). Place all other ingredients in a high-powered blender and blend until smooth and creamy. With a high-powered blender you can actually heat it up by running the blender for a few minutes. Pour over the cooked asparagus. Refrigerate any unused portion.

CHEF'S NOTE:

Also delicious over steamed broccoli!

CREAMY DILL MUSTARD POTATO SALAD

Steamed cauliflower becomes so creamy that it actually takes the place of high fat mayo. The fennel gives it a unique flavor.

INGREDIENTS:

1½ pounds baby red potatoes
12 ounces cauliflower
1 cup finely chopped red onion
1 cup finely chopped fennel
½ cup *California Balsamic Garden Dill Mustard Seed Vinegar* (or ½ cup reduced white balsamic vinegar plus 2 Tablespoons dried dill)

PREPARATION:

Steam potatoes, chill, and cut into fourths. Steam cauliflower and chill. Mix the finely chopped red onion and fennel in a large bowl with the chilled potatoes. In a blender, blend the chilled cauliflower and *Garden Dill Mustard Seed Balsamic* until smooth. Pour over the potato mixture and mix well. Serve over greens like arugula and sprinkle with dill.

CREAMY RAINBOW COLESLAW

This is literally the best coleslaw I have ever tasted AND I DON'T EVEN LIKE COLESLAW! It's so good that the first time I made it I ate the whole thing!

INGREDIENTS:

SLAW
6 cups finely shredded white cabbage
6 cups finely shredded purple cabbage
6 cups grated carrots
1 cup chopped scallions (green part preferred)
1 cup golden raisins

DRESSING:

24 ounces cauliflower, steamed, then chilled
½ cup *Island Pineapple Balsamic Vinegar* from *California Balsamic* (or ¼ cup reduced while balsamic vinegar plus ¼ cup unsweetened pineapple juice)

PREPARATION:

Place the cauliflower and balsamic vinegar in a high-powered blender and blend until smooth and creamy. Pour over slaw and mix well. Chill well before serving.

CHEF'S NOTE:

For an interesting kick, add one very thinly sliced jalapeno pepper to the slaw.

HOLIDAY SWEET POTATO STACKS

These are as pretty as they are delicious. Almost as much fun to make as they are to eat.

INGREDIENTS:

½ cup of each of 2 or 3 varieties of mashed sweet potatoes in at least 2 different colors. (I like to use Hannah yams and Garnet yams.)
½ cup of your favorite cranberry sauce (try the Cherry, Peary Cranberry Sauce on page 173)

PREPARATION:

Preheat oven to 400 degrees F. Wash and poke the sweet potatoes and roast for an hour until very soft. Peel while still warm and mash until smooth. Separate them by color.

ASSEMBLY:

Using the *Stackable Gourmet*, or a can that has been hollowed out, make stacks by layering the mashed sweet potatoes with the cranberry sauce and repeat the layers, ending with the cranberry sauce on top. For a beautiful, colorful presentation, serve on a white plate with the Christmas Kale Salad (see recipe page 133).

KALE HASH

This is delicious with any of the BBQ sauce recipes in this book or even with ketchup.

INGREDIENTS:

1 large sweet onion, chopped
6 cloves of garlic, finely chopped, cubed
6 cups of Yukon Gold potatoes
1 10-ounce bag kale (approx. 12 cups), shredded
1 Tablespoon SMOKED paprika
Benson's Table Tasty (or your favorite salt-free seasoning), to taste

PREPARATION:

Steam potatoes, cool, chill, and cut into cubes. Dry sauté the onion until nicely browned, adding water a tablespoon at a time if necessary. Add the garlic and sauté for another minute or two. Add the potatoes and dry seasonings and cook until nicely browned. If they stick to the pan, add water a tablespoon at a time. Add the shredded kale and cooked briefly until *al dente*.

CHEF'S NOTE:

You can use cooked and cooled sweet potatoes for a delicious variation or add a 3-ounce bag of sundried tomatoes.

MEDITERRANEAN KALE

Inspired by the daily breakfast of Cooking Instructor and Certified Health Coach, Sharon McRae, all of these ingredients are easily found at *Trader Joe's*, but if you don't have one near you, you can find them at your local store too! Reminiscent of pizza, kale never tasted so good!

INGREDIENTS:

2 10-ounce bags kale (approx. 24 cups)
1 12-ounce bag frozen artichoke hearts
1 3-ounce bag salt-free sun-dried tomatoes (approx. ¾ cup)
1 ounce fresh peeled garlic cloves, finely chopped (approx. ¼ cup)
1 cup water
1 cup fresh basil, cut into long thin strips

PREPARATION:

Finely chop the kale and artichoke hearts. Place all ingredients except for the fresh basil into an *Instant Pot* pressure cooker. Set on high pressure for zero minutes. It will take several minutes to achieve desired pressure, and once it reaches that level, it's fully cooked. Release pressure immediately and stir in the fresh basil. Drizzle with a good quality reduced balsamic vinegar or Enlightened Faux Parmesan if desired. (See Chef's Note to Red No-Lentil Chili, page 154.)

NUTRIENT-RICH MASHED POTATOES

The stealth approach, hiding veggies in familiar dishes, is a great way to get family members to eat more vegetables.

INGREDIENTS:

4 pounds Yukon Gold potatoes
1½ pounds of parsnips
1½ pounds of cauliflower
1 cup unsweetened non-dairy milk
½ cup nutritional yeast
1 Tablespoon *Benson's Table Tasty* (or your favorite salt-free seasoning)
1 Tablespoon dried parsley flakes
1 teaspoon garlic powder

PREPARATION:

Place a basket or the rack that comes with your pressure cooker in the pot and fill it with water just up to the basket or the rack. Place the potatoes, parsnips, and cauliflower in an *Instant Pot* pressure cooker and cook on high pressure for 12 minutes. When the unit beeps, wait about another 12 minutes to release the pressure. Drain the water from the basket or insert, add the remaining ingredients and mash the potatoes right in the pot using a potato masher.

ROASTED GARLIC MASHED POTATOES

When you roast garlic, it becomes very mellow and is a great addition to almost any dish. You may find that you don't need any additional seasonings. If you have an air fryer, you can roast the cloves in minutes.

INGREDIENTS:

4 pounds Yukon Gold potatoes
2 cups water
1 cup peeled garlic cloves (or fewer, to taste)
1 pound bag frozen corn (optional), fire roasted preferred

PREPARATION:

Roast the garlic by placing the peeled cloves in an air fryer at 370 degrees F for ten minutes (or longer if you like them more well-done). Combine water and potatoes in an *Instant Pot* pressure cooker. Cook on high pressure for 10 minutes. Let come down to pressure naturally. Mash by hand with a potato masher in the potato water. Add the roasted garlic cloves and mash again. Stir in frozen corn if desired.

CHEF'S NOTE:

Try this with your favorite gravy.

ZUCCHINI SAUTÉ

It's amazing how 4 simple ingredients can be so delicious. Purple and green are my favorite colors, so to me it's as pretty as it is delicious.

INGREDIENTS:

Large sweet onion, chopped
4 cups diced zucchini
6 garlic cloves, peeled and finely chopped
8 ounces shredded purple cabbage (approx. 5 cups)

PREPARATION:

Dry sauté the onion until nicely browned, adding water a tablespoon at a time if necessary. Add the garlic and sauté another minute or two. Add the zucchini and cook until softened to your preference. Add the cabbage and cover and steam for a few minutes until cabbage is soft.

CHEF'S NOTE:

This is great as a side dish on its own or over mashed potatoes or over your favorite grain such as millet, quinoa, or rice. I like to finish it with a bit of reduced balsamic vinegar.

Dressings & Sauces

APPLE FIG MUSTARD DRESSING

Fig balsamic is one of the more common flavors of balsamic vinegar that is available in most grocery stores. If you can't find fig vinegar then use a regular good quality (preferably reduced) balsamic vinegar and throw in a dried fig or two.

INGREDIENTS:

1 large Envy Apple (about 10 ounces after removing the core)
¼ cup *Westbrae* salt-free stone ground mustard
¼ cup Fig Balsamic Vinegar

PREPARATION:

Place all ingredients in a high-powered blender and blend until smooth. Refrigerate any unused portion.

BALSAMIC TAHINI-DILL DRESSING

A delightful variation on the Original Sensational Tahini-Dill Dressing.

INGREDIENTS:

4 Tablespoons balsamic vinegar
¼ cup tahini
⅓ cup lemon juice (add zest if using fresh)
¾ cup water
¾ ounce of pitted dates (approximately 1 Medjool or 3 Deglet Noor)
1 Tablespoon dried dill

PREPARATION:

Place all ingredients in a blender and blend until smooth.

CHEF'S NOTE:

Use a good quality reduced balsamic vinegar with 4% acidity.

BEST DAMN BBQ SAUCE EVER!

Slightly sweet, slightly smoky—you may never buy bottled sauce again!

INGREDIENTS:

1 14-ounce bag frozen fire roasted peppers and onions, defrosted
1 14.5-ounce can of *Muir Glen Fire Roasted Salt–Free Tomatoes*
1 3-ounce bag oil-free sun-dried tomatoes (approx. ¾ cup)
½ cup *California Balsamic Hickory Smoke Vinegar* (or 6 Tablespoons *Napa Valley Naturals Grand Reserve* + 2 Tablespoons Apple Cider Vinegar)
1 Tablespoon SMOKED paprika (different than regular paprika)
1 teaspoon cumin
1 teaspoon garlic powder
1 teaspoon onion powder
½ teaspoon mustard powder
¼ teaspoon chipotle powder

PREPARATION:

Place all ingredients in a high-powered blender and blend until smooth.

CHEF'S NOTE:

If you can't find the fire roasted peppers and onions or don't have a *Trader Joe's* nearby, you can just roast some onion and bell pepper.

CARAMELIZED ONION GRAVY

Many gravy recipes have a long list of ingredients and take a while to prepare. This is one of the most delicious gravies you've ever had. The fact that it contains only 2 simple, healthy ingredients will blow your mind!

INGREDIENTS:

1 12-ounce bag cauliflower, steamed and drained
3 large onions

PREPARATION:

Peel and slice onions about ¼" thick. Place as many as will fit in your crock pot and cover. Turn it onto the low setting and wait 24 hours for the magic to occur. You don't need to add ANYTHING, not even water!

24 hours later, steam the cauliflower until soft and drain. Place the cooked cauliflower in a high-powered blender and blend until smooth. Add as many of the cooked onions as you desire to get the right flavor and texture. I usually add about ⅔ of them, reserving the rest of the onions as a topping for bean burgers.

CHEF'S NOTE:

Any unused onions can be frozen. If you would like to give this gravy a holiday flavor, add a pinch, or more, of a spice like rosemary, Herbs de Provence or poultry seasoning. I like to use a variety of onions like red, white, yellow, and sweet. These are a delicious accompaniment to everything and they can even be frozen. They are especially good over baked or mashed potatoes.

CHEATER'S BAREFOOT DRESSING

The original Barefoot Dressing from our last book, *The Secrets To Ultimate Weight Loss*, is delicious but this is a quicker version and makes a smaller amount.

INGREDIENTS:

½ cup reduced balsamic vinegar (with 4% acidity)
¼ cup lime juice
¼ cup unsweetened applesauce
¼ cup *Westbrae* salt-free stone ground mustard
2 cloves peeled garlic
½ teaspoon chia seeds

PREPARATION:

Place all ingredients in a high-powered blender and blend until smooth. Refrigerate any unused portion.

CHERRY, PEARY CRANBERRY SAUCE

A new twist on an old favorite.

INGREDIENTS:

1 cup of roasted pear halves (this is the yield from 1 25-ounce jar of pears in their own juice) or approximately 2½ cups of pears if using fresh or canned
1 large navel orange, peeled, plus the zest
8 ounces frozen cherries defrosted (approx. 1½ cups)
12 ounces unsweetened fresh cranberries
½ inch piece fresh ginger (or more, to taste)
2 Tablespoons chia seeds

PREPARATION:

Roast the pear halves until golden brown on a *Crisp Ease* tray, piece of parchment paper, *Silpat*, or other non-stick silicone baking mat. This will take about 35-45 minutes in an oven preheated to 400 degrees F. Zest the oranges and then peel. Place all ingredients in a food processor fitted with the "S" blade and process until a uniform texture is reached. Do not liquefy.

EASY BBQ SAUCE

Most BBQ sauces are very high in sugar. Here the sweetness comes just from the grapes in the vinegar. I always have both ingredients on hand to make a quick dip for my air fries in no time.

INGREDIENTS:

2 Tablespoon tomato paste
2 Tablespoons *California Balsamic Smoked Hickory Vinegar* (or more, to taste)

PREPARATION:

Mix both ingredients together. Refrigerate any unused sauce.

FRESCO SAUCE

When I was speaking in Chicago for their *Vegfest,* I stayed with Julie Marie Christensen, the creator of *The Protective Diet* (www.protective-diet.com), and we came up with this recipe together. You can use this zesty sauce as a dip for baked tortilla chips, as a salad dressing, or as a flavorful sauce for your burritos or veggie/grain bowls.

INGREDIENTS:

1 cup unsweetened pineapple
1 cup cucumber
1 lime, juiced, plus zest
1 clove peeled garlic
1 Tablespoon cilantro
½ of a small jalapeño, optional (more or less, to taste)

PREPARATION:

Place all ingredients except for the cilantro in a high-powered blender and blend until smooth. Add cilantro and pulse until finely chopped. Refrigerate any unused portion.

CHEF'S NOTE:

This sauce can be a base for a green gazpacho by adding finely chopped veggies like cucumber, carrots, and red bell pepper.

GROOVY MUSHROOM GRAVY

Cauliflower makes everything smooth and creamy. It's a great way to sneak in more veggies.

INGREDIENTS:

10 ounces of onions (approx. 3 cups)
10 ounces of sliced mushrooms (approx. 3 cups)
½ cup of garlic cloves, roasted
12 ounces of cauliflower, steamed

PREPARATION:

Steam the cauliflower and set aside. Dry sauté the onion until browned, adding water a tablespoon at a time if needed. Add the mushrooms and cook until all the water is evaporated. Carefully place all of the ingredients in a high-powered blender and blend until smooth.

CHEF'S NOTE:

If you would like the gravy thinner, add a small amount of unsweetened non-dairy milk to the blender. Feel free to add spices like *Benson's Table Tasty* or up to a teaspoon of poultry seasoning for a holiday flavor.

"HONEY" MUSTARD DIP

The bestselling brand of honey mustard dressing contains these ingredients: Water, Soybean Oil, Vinegar, Sugar, Honey, Dijon Mustard (Water, Mustard Seed, Vinegar, Salt, White Wine, Citric Acid, Tartaric Acid, Fruit Pectin, Sugar, Spice), Modified Cornstarch, Contains Less Than 2% Of Salt, Egg Yolks, Mustard Seed, Natural Flavor, Sorbic Acid And Calcium Disodium Edta (To Protect Flavor), Dried Onions, Spice, Beta Carotene (Color). It also contains 5 grams of fat, including 1 gram of saturated fat per serving. Not to mention all the sodium and cholesterol. Compare it to mine, made of only 3 healthy ingredients!

INGREDIENTS:

12 ounces of cauliflower, steamed and chilled
4 ounces of pitted dates
½ cup of *Westbrae* salt-free stone ground mustard

PREPARATION:

Steam cauliflower and then chill. Place in high-powered blender with remaining ingredients and blend until smooth.

CHEF'S NOTE:

Use as a delicious dip, dressing, or spread. For a fun presentation, hollow out a red bell pepper and fill with the dip.

LEMONADE DRESSING

One day, when preparing the Lemon Poppy Seed Dressing, I had put almost all of the ingredients into the blender when I realized I was out of mustard! Our company was on their way and there was no time to go to the store. So I just went with it. And everyone loved it. While slightly sweeter than the original version, since it's going on greens it's not an issue. This may be a perfect variation for you if you don't like, or can't find, the salt-free mustard. It reminds me of lemonade!

INGREDIENTS:

½ cup lemon juice
½ cup water
2 ounces of dates (approximately 4 large Medjool dates)
1 Tablespoon poppy seeds
2 teaspoons chia seeds

PREPARATION:

Place all ingredients in a high-powered blender and blend until smooth and creamy. Refrigerate any unused portion.

CHEF'S NOTE:

Pour into popsicle molds and freeze for a refreshing popsicle, adding more dates when blending if needed.

LEMON POPPY SEED DRESSING

Slightly sweet, slightly tangy, this dressing is the perfect accompaniment to greens.

INGREDIENTS:

½ cup lemon juice
½ cup water
2 ounces of dates (approximately 4 large Medjool dates)
2 Tablespoons *Westbrae* salt-free stone ground mustard
1 Tablespoon poppy seeds
2 teaspoons chia seeds

PREPARATION:

Place all ingredients except for the chia seeds in a high-powered blender and blend until smooth. Add the chia seeds and briefly blend again. Refrigerate the dressing.

ONE SAUCE

Like many of my recipes, this was created from a request from one of my *YouTube* viewers who was looking for a "cheesy" sauce that didn't contain any of the usual starchy ingredients like potatoes, sweet potatoes, oats, or beans—or even the most common faux cheese sauce ingredient: nutritional yeast. This sauce is a delicious way to eat more vegetables.

INGREDIENTS:

1 12-ounce bag cauliflower
8 ounces orange bell pepper (approx. 4 cups)
8 ounces carrots (approx. 4 cups)
4 ounces sweet onion (approx. 1½ cups)
8 cloves garlic
1 Tablespoon lemon juice
1 teaspoon SMOKED paprika
1 teaspoon *Benson's Table Tasty* (or your favorite salt free seasonings)
⅛ teaspoon chipotle powder

PREPARATION:

Steam cauliflower in one cup of water. Place steamed cauliflower and water in a high-powered blender and puree until smooth. Roast the vegetables in your oven or air fry. Keep in mind that carrots take longer than the onion, garlic, and bell pepper, so either cook the carrots longer or cut them smaller. After the veggies are roasted, place in blender with the pureed cauliflower and remaining spices and puree until smooth and creamy.

ORIGINAL SENSATIONAL TAHINI-DILL DRESSING

Easy to make and very delicious. This was the dressing I first used when learning to love my greens.

INGREDIENTS:

¼ cup tahini
⅓ cup lemon juice (add zest if using fresh)
¾ cup water
¾ ounce pitted dates (approximately 1 Medjool or 3 Deglet Noor)
1 Tablespoon dried dill

PREPARATION:

Place all ingredients in a blender and blend until smooth.

ROASTED GARLIC ALFREDO

Traditional Alfredo sauce is made from cheese, butter, and heavy cream. Here the creaminess comes from cauliflower. Hard to believe it tastes so decadent.

INGREDIENTS:

24 ounces steamed cauliflower (approx. 8 cups)
¼ cup roasted garlic cloves
3 Tablespoons lemon juice
4 Tablespoons nutritional yeast
1 teaspoon *Benson's Table Tasty* (or your favorite salt-free seasoning)
10 ounces chopped onion (approx. 3 cups)
10 ounces sliced mushrooms (approx. 3 cups)
1½ pounds spiralized zucchini or spiralized butternut squash

PREPARATION:

Steam the cauliflower. Roast the garlic cloves in an air fryer for 10 minutes (or longer, if you like them more well-done) at 370 degrees F. In a high-powered blender, blend the cooked cauliflower, roasted garlic cloves, lemon juice, nutritional yeast, and *Benson's Table Tasty* until smooth and creamy. Set aside. In a large sauté pan, water sauté onion until caramelized and brown. Add mushrooms and cook until nicely browned. Add zucchini and cook for a minute or two until *al dente*. Add the sauce and stir until hot. Garnish with fresh parsley or arugula.

CHEF'S NOTE:

This sauce is delicious on pasta, steamed vegetables, and even a baked potato.

ROASTED GARLIC PESTO

Most pesto sauces are full of oil, cheese, and nuts. This one is made of veggies, so you can indulge to your heart's content. It's especially good over zucchini or butternut squash "zoodles," but also makes a delicious topping for steamed vegetables or a baked potato.

INGREDIENTS:

12 ounces cauliflower, steamed
⅓ cup roasted garlic cloves, roasted
1 cup fresh basil leaves (packed) about an ounce
2 Tablespoons lemon juice
¼ cup water

PREPARATION:

Steam the cauliflower. Roast the garlic cloves in an air fryer at 370 degrees F for 10 minutes (or longer, if you like them more well-done). Place all ingredients in a high-powered blender and blend until smooth and creamy. Refrigerate any unused portion.

SWEET AND SMOKY DRESSING

Make sure you get *smoked* paprika and not regular. It makes a big difference in this recipe. The name says it all—sweet and smoky.

INGREDIENTS:

1 cup of water
½ cup lime juice
4 ounces pitted dates
¼ cup *Westbrae* salt-free stone ground mustard
1 teaspoon chia seeds
2 teaspoons SMOKED paprika
¼ teaspoon chipotle powder

PREPARATION:

Blend all ingredients in a blender until smooth and creamy. Pour over salad and mix well. Serve chilled. Refrigerate any unused portion.

THAI PEANUT-FREE SAUCE

Back in the day, I used to LOVE Thai Peanut Sauce. I would slather it on everything from tofu to broccoli to rice. But it sure didn't love me back. Now I can have ALL of the flavor of my beloved peanut sauce with none of the guilt or fat. By using chestnuts instead of peanut butter, the sauce has 6 grams of fat instead of 72!

INGREDIENTS:

1 cup roasted chestnuts
fresh ginger (approx. one-inch knob)
2 garlic cloves
4 Tablespoons lime juice
1 Tablespoon unsweetened rice vinegar
2 ounces pitted dates
½ teaspoon crushed red pepper flakes
1 cup of water (or less)

PREPARATION:

Place all ingredients except for the water in a high-powered blender and blend until they are fully incorporated. Add up to 1 cup of water, a little at a time, until smooth and creamy. Refrigerate any unused portion.

BEVERAGES

APB SMOOTHIE

APB stands for apple, pear, bananas—but this refreshing treat is so good that you will want to put out an ALL-POINTS BULLETIN!

INGREDIENTS:

4 ounces of unsweetened apple juice
2 small soft, ripe pears
6 ounces baby spinach (approx. 10 cups)
1 ripe banana, frozen
2 cups ice
Mint leaves, to taste (optional)

PREPARATION:

Place all ingredients in a blender and blend until smooth. If your pears are not yet ripened, use jarred pears in their own juice.

CRANBERRY SPRITZER

You don't need alcohol to have a festive good time; this drink makes a delicious mocktail for the holidays or anytime you can find fresh cranberries.

INGREDIENTS:

1 cup unsweetened apple cider or unsweetened apple juice
1 Tablespoon lime juice
½ cup fresh cranberries
4 ounces of sparkling water

PREPARATION:

Place apple cider, lime juice, and cranberries in a high-powered blender and blend until smooth. Pour into two pretty glasses. Add four ounces of sparkling water to each glass. Make a toast and enjoy!

CREAMY CANTALOUPE COOLER

While these flavored vinegars are not necessary to live a healthy life-style, they sure can make it even more delicious and fun.

INGREDIENTS:

1 small cantaloupe, peeled and seeds removed
12 ounces sparkling water
2 Tablespoons Peach flavored balsamic vinegar
1 cup of ice

PREPARATION:

Blend all ingredients in a high-powered blender until smooth.

DESERT DATE SHAKE

This treat is reverse-engineered. You see, I had never even heard of date shakes until I moved to the desert. Then I couldn't wait to try them. Unfortunately, almost all the places made them with either dairy or sugar or both! And the one place that made a compliant shake charged almost ten dollars! So, of course, I bought one and tasted it to figure out how to make it myself. And now you can make your very own!

INGREDIENTS:

1 cup of unsweetened non-dairy milk
3 large Medjool dates, pitted
2 ripe bananas, peeled and frozen
1 teaspoon vanilla powder
½ teaspoon ground cinnamon
⅛ teaspoon ground nutmeg
¼ cup rolled oats
1 teaspoon chia seeds

PREPARATION:

Place all ingredients in a high-powered blender and blend until smooth and creamy. For a thicker shake, add a few ice cubes.

CHEF'S NOTE:

When I worked at the *TrueNorth Health Center*, we were not permitted to use either regular vanilla extract, as it contains alcohol, or alcohol-free vanilla extract, as it contains glycerin. Using whole vanilla beans is extremely expensive, so I began using vanilla powder. It made such a difference in flavor that I simply could not go back to using the inferior extracts. Here the vanilla powder is essential to achieve the authentic flavor of the date shakes of the desert. If you can't find vanilla powder in grocery stores, you'll find it on *Amazon*.

FOUR LEAF CLOVER SHAKE

This recipe was based on a childhood favorite, the *Shamrock Shake* from a certain fast food restaurant. A shamrock has only three leaves but a four-leaf clover has four, the fourth representing luck. And boy are we lucky that we don't go to *McDonald's* anymore! No need to wait for St. Paddy's Day; you can enjoy this healthy treat all year round.

INGREDIENTS:

1 cup of pistachio milk*
3 ripe bananas, frozen
6 ounces baby spinach (approx. 10 cups)
1 cup of fresh mint leaves (approx. an ounce)
¼ teaspoon peppermint extract (optional, for a more minty taste)

PREPARATION:

Place all ingredients in a high-powered blender and blend until smooth and creamy.

CHEF'S NOTE:

If this is not sweet enough for your palate, add a few pitted dates.

*You can buy pistachio milk in the refrigerated section of many natural foods store. Or you can make your own. Here's the recipe from my book *Unprocessed:*

Soak 2 cups raw pistachios in water for several hours. Drain and rinse well. Place in blender with 2 cups water (more for a thinner, less rich milk) and blend on high. Pour through a strainer bag and gently squeeze, separating pulp from milk.

FROZEN PINK LEMONADE

Regular lemonade has an unthinkable amount of sugar. Here the sweetness comes only from fruit.

INGREDIENTS:

4 cups of frozen purple grapes
¼ cup lemon juice (add zest if using fresh)
1 cup of ice (optional, for a thicker drink)

PREPARATION:

Place all ingredients in a high-powered blender and blend until smooth. If it's too thick, add a few tablespoons of water at a time until desired consistency is reached.

CHEF'S NOTE:

Substitute other frozen fruits like cherries, raspberries, or strawberries.

HOLIDAY EGGLESS NOG

Hannah yams are unparalleled for their subtle vanilla flavor and creaminess. Do your best to try to find them. Then roast a whole bunch, peel, and cool and freeze them for future recipes. They provide richness and creaminess without using nuts.

INGREDIENTS:

2 cups Hannah yams (a.k.a. "Jersey yams" or "White sweet potatoes"), roasted, peeled, and chilled
2 large frozen ripe bananas, peeled and frozen
½ teaspoon nutmeg (or more, to taste)
½ teaspoon vanilla powder
2 cups unsweetened, non-dairy milk

PREPARATION:

Place all ingredients in a high-powered blender and blend until smooth and creamy. Pour into a tall glass and sprinkle with more nutmeg if desired.

CHEF'S NOTE:

Japanese sweet potatoes are a good substitute for Hannah yams.

ITALIAN SODA

With only about 30 calories per tablespoon of vinegar, you can have a soda with up to 75% fewer calories than in a typical can. And Dr. Michael Greger recommends that we have two teaspoons of vinegar with every meal.

INGREDIENTS:

Sparkling water
1-2 Tablespoons Balsamic Vinegar (a fruity flavor)

PREPARATION:

Pour 8 ounces of sparkling water in a tall glass. Add vinegar and gently stir as vinegar will settle to the bottom of the glass. Add ice if desired.

CHEF'S NOTE:

I love using lemon, peach, or cherry balsamic vinegar.

MINT JULEP

Reminiscent of a drink I used to enjoy at *Disneyland*, but without the sugar and the long lines.

INGREDIENTS:

2 Tablespoons lime juice
6 ounces spinach (approx. 10 cups)
1 ounce fresh mint, about 1 cup
2 frozen bananas
1 cup ice

PREPARATION:

In a high-powered blender, blend the spinach, mint, and lime juice to a liquid. Add the remaining ingredients and serve. If you would like this sweeter, add a date or two to the blender.

SNOW CONES

I will never forget the *Snoopy* snow cone machine from my childhood. Well, now we can enjoy a healthier, sugar-free version as adults.

INGREDIENTS:

1 cup of crushed or shaved ice
1 or 2 Tablespoons of a fruity balsamic vinegar (peach, pineapple, raspberry, or strawberry)

PREPARATION:

Using a snow cone machine or your high-powered blender, crush the ice as finely as possible. Pour into a snow cone cup or other glass. Pour the vinegar over the ice and enjoy.

CHEF'S NOTE:

Unsweetened fruit juice may be used instead of vinegar, but you may need to double the amount.

DESSERTS

AIR FRY APPLE PIE (my oh my!)

INGREDIENTS:

4 cups finely chopped apple (I prefer a sweet variety of red apple)
½ cup golden raisins
1 cup unsweetened applesauce
1 teaspoon apple pie spice (or cinnamon)
1½ cups gluten-free oats
2 large ripe bananas
½ teaspoon vanilla powder

PREPARATION:

Finely chop apples and place in a bowl. Add the raisins and apple pie spice and mix well. Pour into an air fryer-safe pan. In a separate bowl, mash the banana and stir in the oats and vanilla powder. Pour on top of the apple mixture. Place in an air fryer at 370 degrees F for 20-30 minutes until top is browned.

BLUEBERRY CHIA OAT PUDDING

This would also make a terrific, easy-to-prepare-ahead breakfast.

<u>INGREDIENTS:</u>

1½ cups banana milk (made from 1 banana and 1 cup water, blended)
3 Tablespoons chia seeds
½ teaspoon cinnamon
pinch of ground cardamom
2 cups blueberries
½ cup rolled oats

<u>PREPARATION:</u>

Mix all ingredients together and refrigerate overnight. I like to use a Mason or Ball jar.

CAULIFLOWER RICE PUDDING

One day I was making my apple pie rice pudding and put all the ingredients in the *Instant Pot* except for the rice. I went to the freezer where I always have rice and, lo and behold, I had run out. I had to think fast, so I used riced cauliflower, which is available in most grocery stores now, or you can rice your own. The result was surprisingly similar to the actual rice. In fact, many people couldn't believe it was cauliflower and couldn't tell the difference! This is a great way to sneak in more veggies by having your family think it's a dessert.

INGREDIENTS:

4 cups riced cauliflower
4 cups diced apples (I prefer a sweet variety like Envy or Gala)
½ cup unsweetened applesauce
1 cup unsweetened plant milk
1 cup golden raisins
1 Tablespoon cinnamon or Apple Pie Spice
1 teaspoon vanilla powder

PREPARATION:

Place all ingredients in an *Instant Pot* pressure cooker and cook on high pressure for 5 minutes. Delicious served hot or cold. Will thicken slightly as it cools.

CHEF'S NOTE:

Try this with the Pear Whip on top (see recipe page 211).

CINNAMON BUNS

These are good for YOUR buns! There is nothing more intoxicating to me than the smell of a *Cinnabon* at the airport or mall, but a single bun contains almost 1,000 calories and over 40 grams of fat (about half of it saturated!). Now you can enjoy these guilt-free ones at home without turning into a Doughboy!

INGREDIENTS: Buns

2 cups gluten-free oats
½ cup unsweetened nondairy milk
2 large RIPE bananas
8 Deglet Noor dates, pitted
2 Tablespoons aluminum-free and sodium-free baking powder
2 Tablespoons apple cider vinegar
1 Tablespoon cinnamon
½ cup raisins (I prefer golden) or currants
1 teaspoon vanilla powder or 2 teaspoons vanilla extract

PREPARATION:

Preheat oven to 350 degrees F. Place all ingredients except raisins in a high-powered blender and blend until smooth. Stir in raisins. Fill a 12-cup silicone muffin pan and distribute the batter evenly. Bake for 30 minutes. Remove from oven and cool completely before removing from the muffin pan.

INGREDIENTS: Frosting

2 cups roasted Hannah yam flesh, cooled and peeled
¼ cup date paste* (or more, to taste)
¼ cup unsweetened nondairy milk
1 teaspoon vanilla powder or 2 teaspoons vanilla extract

PREPARATION:

Place all ingredients in a food processor fitted with the "S" blade and process until smooth and creamy. Generously frost the cooled muffins.

CHEF'S NOTE:

Due to the sticky nature of this batter, it is essential that you only use a nonstick silicone muffin pan instead of cupcake liners or you will not be able to get the papers off. Japanese sweet potatoes maybe substituted for Hannah yams, if you can't find them.

* My recipe for date paste was published in *Unprocessed*. Here it is:

INGREDIENTS:

1 pound pitted dates
1 cup liquid (water, unsweetened plant milk, unsweetened juice)

PREPARATION:

Soak dates in liquid overnight or for several hours until much of the liquid is absorbed. In food processor fitted with the "S" blade, process dates and liquid until completely smooth. Store date paste in the refrigerator.

CREAMY BLUEBERRY MILLET PARFAIT

This also makes an excellent special Sunday breakfast.

INGREDIENTS: Pudding

1 cup dry millet
3 cups unsweetened nondairy milk
1 teaspoon cinnamon
½ teaspoon cardamom
1 teaspoon vanilla powder (optional, but good)
6 Tablespoons date syrup (optional, for a sweeter pudding)

PREPARATION:

Place all ingredients in an *Instant Pot* pressure cooker and cook on high for 10 minutes. Release pressure after 10 minutes. This can be enjoyed warm or cold. Millet thickens as it cools.

INGREDIENTS: Fruit Topping

2 cups unsweetened pomegranate juice
2 Tablespoons date paste (see recipe page 200)
4 Tablespoons cornstarch dissolved in 4 Tablespoons water
1 cup wild blueberries (the small ones)

PREPARATION:

In a medium saucepan, dissolve date paste into the pomegranate juice and reduce until you have ½ cup. Slowly stir in cornstarch until mixture thickens, then gently stir in blueberries. Remove from heat.

ASSEMBLY:

Distribute pudding mixture evenly into 4-6 glasses. I like to use long stem wine glasses or martini glasses for an elegant presentation. Evenly distribute the fruit topping on each of the parfaits. Chill for a few hours until set.

CHEF'S NOTE:

This makes an elegant dessert but is also suitable for breakfast. For a delicious variation, stir lemon or orange zest into the pudding mixture. You can lightly toast the millet first if you prefer. Top with Pear Whip (see recipe page 211) if desired.

DATE NICE CREAM

My husband Charles loves a good date shake, but one day he couldn't finish it. Not wanting to waste it, I froze the leftovers and Date Nice Cream was born. And boy, is it delicious! You may have a hard time deciding which you enjoy more, the shake or the nice cream.

INGREDIENTS:

One recipe of the Desert Date Shake (see recipe page 189)

PREPARATION:

Prepare the Desert Date Shake according to the recipe and pour it into an easy release silicone ice cube tray. One that has fifteen cubes per tray will fit the contents of one date shake recipe perfectly. Freeze until firm. Release the frozen date shake cubes from the ice cube tray and run them through a *Champion Juicer* fitted with the blank plate. If you don't have a *Champion Juicer*, you can place the frozen date shake cubes in a high-powered blender, and using the tamper, add the smallest amount of unsweetened non-dairy milk possible to get it smooth and creamy.

EASY OVERNIGHT OATS

Not too sweet for a breakfast but sweet enough to enjoy as a dessert. So easy to make, this dish can be enjoyed hot or cold. Chia seeds thicken naturally and give this treat the consistency of a pudding.

INGREDIENTS:

2 cups rolled oats
2 cups unsweetened plant milk
2 cups blueberries
2 teaspoons cinnamon
2 teaspoons chia seeds

PREPARATION:

Place all ingredients into a bowl and mix well. Place in a Mason or Ball jar and refrigerate overnight.

CHEF'S NOTE:

Frozen fruit works great in this recipe. You can substitute cherries for the blueberries.

"FRIED" APPLES

These are like baked apples on steroids!

INGREDIENTS:

Your favorite apples (I like a sweet variety like the Envy or Cosmic).

PREPARATION:

Core apples and cut in half. Place on an air fryer tray and sprinkle with cinnamon. Air fry at 400 degrees F for 20-30 minutes. You could also bake in a 350 degree F. oven for about an hour.

CHEF'S NOTE:

These are yummy topped with Peach Whip (see recipe page 211)

GREAT GRAPE SORBET

Move over, frozen banana soft serve, and make way for the mighty grape! It's hard to believe that something this simple can be so satisfying. Of all the fruit sorbets, this is my absolute favorite.

INGREDIENTS:

Purple grapes

PREPARATION:

Wash grapes and remove stems. Freeze until solid. Place the frozen grapes through a Champion Juicer fitted with the blank, and enjoy immediately.

CHEF'S NOTE:

Always get the best machine you can afford. I recommend the *Champion Juicer* for the best texture but other machines such as the *Yonanas, Vitamix, Blendtec,* and *Dessert Bullet,* to name a few, will also work. If you use a high-powered blender, you will have to add a bit of liquid to get it to blend.

HOLIDAY PARFAIT

Parfait simply means perfect in French and this festive dessert certainly lives up to its name.

INGREDIENTS:

One recipe each of Pumpkin Mousse, Cherry Peary Cranberry sauce, and Pear Whip (see recipes pages 212, 173, 211)

PREPARATION:

In a clear, pretty glass, layer the parfait. Start with a layer of the Pumpkin Mousse, followed by the Cranberry Sauce, and top with the Pear Whip. Garnish with a few fresh cranberries or a fresh mint leaf.

JAM BARS

Based on a fabulous *Forks Over Knives* recipe called Strawberry Bars, these are jamtastic! Sweet enough for a dessert yet healthy enough for a breakfast. Even regular Standard American Diet eaters love them and ask for the recipe. I was serving this to company and telling them the recipe would be in our next book and they said, "this alone would be worth the price." Truly, it's one of my favorite recipes.

INGREDIENTS:

2 cups mashed ripe bananas (approx. 14.5 ounces after peeling)
½ cup unsweetened applesauce
2½ cups gluten-free rolled oats
½ cup millet, ground into a flour
1 Tablespoon cinnamon
8 ounces blueberries (approx. 1½ cups)
1 teaspoon vanilla powder
2 cups fruit-sweetened jam

PREPARATION:

Preheat oven to 350 degrees F. Peel bananas and place in a large bowl with the applesauce and spices. Mash well. (I like to use a potato masher.) Stir in the oats, millet, and blueberries and pour batter into a nine-inch square, silicone baking pan. Spread the all-fruit jam on top of the batter and bake for 40 minutes. Turn oven off and allow bars to cool in the oven with the door closed. Cut into squares. Keep refrigerated.

MACERATED BERRIES

People think you need sugar to macerate but the word actually means to soften in a liquid. And while any liquid will work, I prefer to use a reduced, fruity balsamic vinegar.

INGREDIENTS:

2 cups of fresh berries (blueberries, blackberries, raspberries, strawberries or a combination)
2 Tablespoons liquid (apple juice, balsamic vinegar, lime juice, orange juice, pineapple juice, or water)

PREPARATION:

Mix berries and liquid together and refrigerate for a few hours until soft.

CHEF'S NOTE:

These make a great topping for banana soft serve. Diced peaches are also delicious when macerated.

MINT CHOCOLATE CHIP NICE CREAM

This was my favorite ice cream flavor growing up. Now you can have a healthier version.

INGREDIENTS:

One recipe Four Leaf Clover Shake (see recipe page 190)
Unsweetened cacao nibs, to taste

PREPARATION:

Prepare the Four Leaf Clover Shake according to the recipe and pour it into an easy release silicone ice cube tray. One that has fifteen cubes per tray will fit the contents of one date shake recipe perfectly. Freeze until firm. Release the frozen Four Leaf Clover Shake cubes from the ice cube tray and run them through a *Champion Juicer* fitted with the blank plate. If you don't have a *Champion Juicer*, you can place the frozen shake cubes in a high-powered blender, and using the tamper, adding the smallest amount of unsweetened non-dairy milk possible to get it smooth and creamy. Gently stir in cacao nibs to taste.

PEAR WHIP

There is no dessert that can't be improved by this delicious topping.

INGREDIENTS:

1 25-ounce jar of pears in their own juice (or approx. 2½ cups of pears if using fresh or canned)
1 cup rolled oats
1 teaspoon vanilla powder

PREPARATION:

Place all ingredients in a high-powered blender and blend until smooth.

CHEF'S NOTE:

For a nice variation, try using a jar of peaches instead of pears. If you want more thickness, add 2 Tablespoons of WHITE chia seeds dissolved in 4 Tablespoons of liquid before blending.

PUMPKIN MOUSSE

A delicious treat for Thanksgiving, or to make any day a holiday.

INGREDIENTS:

8 ounces, pitted dates
8 ounces of orange juice
1 15-ounce can pumpkin purée (not pumpkin pie filling)
1 teaspoon cinnamon
1 teaspoon vanilla powder
⅛ teaspoon nutmeg

PREPARATION:

Soak dates in orange juice until soft. Place softened dates with the soaking liquid in a high-powered blender and blend until smooth. Add remaining ingredients and blend until smooth and creamy. Chill well before serving.

CHEF'S NOTE:

If you can't find canned pumpkin, substitute 2 cups cooked sweet potato.

PUMPKIN RAISIN MUFFINS

No need to wait for the fall to make these yummy treats. Most places now sell canned pumpkin all year round so be sure to stock up. Investing in a silicone muffin pan makes clean-up a breeze. Golden raisins instead of purple ones are a delightful variation.

INGREDIENTS:

2 large, very ripe bananas
½ cup unsweetened non-dairy milk
1 15-ounce can pumpkin puree (not pumpkin pie filling)
½ cup date paste (see recipe page 200)
2 Tablespoons ground flax seeds
1 Tablespoon Pumpkin Pie Spice
1 teaspoon vanilla powder
1 cup raisins (I prefer the golden ones)
3 cups gluten-free oats

PREPARATION:

Preheat oven to 350 degrees F. In a food processor fitted with the "S" blade, process bananas and nondairy milk until smooth. Add pumpkin, date paste, vanilla powder, flax seeds and spice and continue processing until smooth and creamy. Transfer to a large bowl and stir in the oats and raisins. Spoon an equal amount of batter into a muffin tin lined with cupcake liners or silicone baking cups. You need to fill each muffin liner with about ½ cup of batter as these do not rise. A retractable ice cream scoop works well. Bake 45 minutes.

CHEF'S NOTE:

These freeze well and make an excellent portable breakfast.

SWEET POTATO SUNDAE

This recipe proves that deprivation is simply not required.

INGREDIENTS:

Your favorite sweet potatoes or yams (Garnet, Hannah, Hawaiian, Japanese, Jewel, Stokes etc.)

PREPARATION:

Roast the sweet potatoes at 400 degrees F for an hour or longer depending on their size. Cool and then refrigerate overnight. Cut in half and air fry at 400 degrees F for 20 minutes. Top with your favorite all fruit non-dairy ice cream or Macerated Berries (see recipe page 209) or both!

CHEF'S NOTE:

Something magical happens to potatoes and sweet potatoes when you cook them and chill them before you air fry them. They taste like toasted marshmallows!

VERY CHERRY MOUSSE

I love to find ways to sneak in veggies, even in desserts!

INGREDIENTS:

12 ounces cauliflower (approx. 4 cups of florets)
16 ounces frozen cherries, defrosted
1 cup unsweetened non-dairy milk
4 ounces Medjool dates, pitted (about 8)
2 Tablespoons lime juice
4 Tablespoons chia seeds
Pomegranate arils (optional)

PREPARATION:

Steam cauliflower then drain and chill and place in a high-powered blender with the plant milk and chia seeds and blend until smooth. Add the remaining ingredients and blend again until smooth and creamy. Place in pretty glass and garnish with pomegranate arils if desired. Chill well before serving.

Recipes From Other Contributors

MACROBIOTIC PLATE

RECIPE BY: JOANNA SAMOROW-MERZER

This recipe is reprinted, with permission, from *Off the Reservation*, Glen's novel about a vegan congressman who runs for president—yes, a novel with recipes! For every meal that the congressman eats during the story, Joanna provides the recipe at the back of the book.

INGREDIENTS:

1 cup dry millet
1 dry piece of kombu (postage stamp size)
¼ cup chopped onions
½ cup butternut or kabocha squash, cut into small cubes
¼ cup daikon root, cut into match sticks
¼ cup celery root (celeriac), cut into small cubes
¼ cup chopped carrot
Burdock root (about 2 inches), peeled and finely sliced
2½ cups water
chopped scallions for garnish

PREPARATION:

Rinse the millet, then soak in water overnight together with the kombu. Discard the soaking water, and layer the millet and kombu on the bottom of a pot. Place the vegetables on top of the millet. Add the water, and bring almost to a boil, then lower the flame to a simmer, and cover the pot. Simmer for 40-50 minutes on a flame deflector to prevent burning. Remove from the stove and let sit covered for a few minutes before serving. Garnish with scallions.

RED LENTIL SHIITAKE STEW

RECIPE BY: JOANNA SAMOROW-MERZER

Reprinted, with permission, from *Off the Reservation*.

INGREDIENTS:

1 cup red lentils
2¼ cups water
4 medium fresh shiitake mushrooms, sliced
1 dry bay leaf
½ cup red onion, thinly chopped
½ teaspoon ginger powder
¾ teaspoon coriander
½ teaspoon cumin
2 Tablespoons chopped fresh parsley or purslane for garnish
1 Tablespoon chopped scallions for garnish
white pepper, to taste

PREPARATION:

Rinse the red lentils, and soak for at least 20-30 minutes. Discard the soaking water. In a pot, combine the red lentils with the water and bring to a boil, then simmer for 20 minutes. Add sliced shiitake mushrooms and onion, the bay leaf, ginger powder, coriander, and cumin, and continue simmering for 20 more minutes. In the last minute of simmering, add the white pepper and stir in chopped scallions and chopped parsley or purslane. Serve with brown rice or mashed potatoes.

MUNG BEAN CURRY

RECIPE BY: JOANNA SAMOROW-MERZER

Reprinted, with permission, from *Off the Reservation*.

INGREDIENTS:

3 cups of water
1 cup dried mung beans
2 dry bay leaves
½ medium onion, chopped
3 cloves raw garlic, minced
1 Tablespoon fresh ginger, minced
½ teaspoon turmeric powder
½ teaspoon yellow curry
2 Tablespoons chopped cilantro or sweet basil
1 Tablespoon freshly squeezed lemon juice
Black pepper, to taste

PREPARATION:

Rinse the mung beans, then soak overnight in water. The following day, discard the water, rinse the beans again, and add 3 cups of water and the bay leaves. Bring the beans almost to a boil, then reduce the flame to simmer. With a spoon, scoop up the white foam that forms on the surface of the water and discard. Then simmer covered for about 40 minutes. Add the onions, garlic, ginger, turmeric, and curry, and continue simmering for an additional 20 minutes. When it's done, add pepper to tase, lemon juice, chopped cilantro or basil, and stir. Serve over rice or other grain.

ONE PAN OF HEALTH

RECIPE BY: JOANNA SAMOROW-MERZER

This recipe and the preceding three recipes represent the kind of meals Joanna prepared as part of her regimen to overcome her autoimmune condition, diagnosed as lupus.

INGREDIENTS:

1 cup dry brown rice (or red or black)
1 Tablespoon dried hijiki seaweed
¼ cup onion, sliced
1¾ cup water
¾ cup pre-cooked cannellini beans
1 cup maitake mushrooms (if dried, soak first and reconstitute)
2 medium-sized turnips, thickly sliced and then cut in half
3 ounces arugula
1 cup cauliflower florets, cut to bite-size
1 small sweet potato, cut into french fry-size strips
A few drops of ume plum vinegar (optional)

PREPARATION:

Place a large pan on a flame deflector. Soak the hijiki for 15 minutes and rinse well. Rinse the rice and spread it evenly in the pan. Pour the water over the rice. Spread the hijiki evenly over the rice. Distribute the sliced onion evenly over the rice-and-hijiki. Next distribute the sweet potato and turnip evenly. Then distribute the maitake mushrooms and then the cannellini beans. Finally, scatter the cauliflower florets. Cover the pan. Turn on medium to high heat until the water almost starts to boil, then reduce heat and simmer, covered, for about 50 minutes until the water has evaporated. After turning the stove off, remove pot from heat and let it sit for 5 minutes before serving. Serve over fresh arugula. Optionally, serve with a few drops of ume plum vinegar.

CHEF'S NOTE:

It's good to use a glass cover in order to monitor that the water isn't boiling, and to see when it has evaporated.

GOJI MORNING

RECIPE BY: JOANNA SAMOROW-MERZER

A hearty, cholesterol-reducing breakfast.

INGREDIENTS:

5½ cups water
1 cup oat bran
1 cup spinach, loosely packed
1 ripe banana
3 Tablespoons goji berries
1 teaspoon aniseed (optional)
¼ cup blueberries, for garnish (optional)

PREPARATION:

If using the aniseed, grind it into a powder in a mortar. Cut the banana into thick slices. Bring the water to a boil in a pot, and reduce flame to a simmer. Start adding the oat bran a little at a time, stirring continuously to prevent clumping. Once all the oat bran is added, cook for 10 minutes while continuing to stir. Add the slices of banana, stir, and cook for 5 more minutes, stirring continuously. Add the goji berries and the aniseed powder (if using), and cook for an additional 3 minutes, stirring continuously. Remove the pot from the heat, then add in the spinach and stir. Sprinkle the blueberries on top, if using, and serve.

SHEET PAN ROASTED VEGETABLES

RECIPE BY: TAMI KRAMER

Tami Kramer is the creator of the *Nutmeg Notebook Whole Food Plant Based Lifestyle Blog* and *YouTube* channel. She can be found at *nutmegnotebook.com*. These roasted vegetables are simple and easy, yet big on flavor, using cumin seeds and other flavorful spices like red paper flakes. Enjoy these in a Nourish bowl with brown rice and hummus.

INGREDIENTS:

1 pound broccoli florets
2½ pounds zucchini or a combination of zucchini and yellow squash
1 large red bell pepper
2 Tablespoons aquafaba (the bean broth from cooked garbanzo beans)
2 Tablespoons fresh lemon juice
1 rounded teaspoon cumin seeds (the whole seed, not cumin powder)
½ teaspoon crushed red pepper flakes, or to taste
Freshly ground black pepper, to taste

PREPARATION:

Preheat oven to 425 degrees F. Prepare rimmed baking sheet by lining it with parchment paper or a *Silpat* mat. Cut the washed vegetables into equal size pieces so they will cook in the same amount of time. Put all the ingredients into a bowl and toss to coat them evenly with the aquafaba, lemon juice, cumin seeds, red pepper flakes, and freshly ground black pepper. Spread the vegetable mixture out evenly over the prepared baking sheet. Bake for 18-25 minutes or until the vegetables are tender.

NUTMEG NOTEBOOK'S BEST
OIL-FREE HUMMUS
RECIPE BY: TAMI KRAMER

This creamy oil-free hummus is a winner! The seasoning makes it special and the aquafaba (the liquid from the can of garbanzo beans) replaces the oil to keep it smooth and creamy.

INGREDIENTS:

1 can no-salt Cannellini Beans, rinse and drained
1 can no-salt garbanzo beans, drained but reserve the liquid
6 Tablespoons of reserved aquafaba
1 teaspoon ground coriander
½-1 teaspoon ground cumin—I used one teaspoon but start with ½ teaspoon and adjust to taste
1 teaspoon smoked paprika
½ teaspoon garlic powder
1 teaspoon black mustard seeds or 1 teaspoon prepared mustard
2-3 Tablespoons fresh lemon juice – start with two and add more to taste – I like to use three.

PREPARATION:

Place all ingredients in a high-powered blender or a food processor and blend until smooth and creamy. Store covered in the refrigerator. Serve with raw veggies for dipping.

QUINOA TABBOULEH

RECIPE BY: TAMI KRAMER

INGREDIENTS:

1 cup quinoa prewashed or rinsed then cooked
1 bunch fresh mint
1 bunch Italian flat leaf parsley
1 small red onion, diced
3 Persian cucumbers, diced
1 pound sweet cherry, sugar plum or grape tomatoes, diced
3 fresh lemons, juiced, making ½ cup fresh lemon juice
Freshly ground black pepper

PREPARATION:

To cook the quinoa in the *Instant Pot*: place 1 cup of rinsed quinoa with 1¼ cups water in the liner. Put the lid on and set the timer for 5 minutes, high pressure with natural release. When the quinoa is done, spread it out on a parchment-lined rimmed baking sheet to cool. Place in the fridge if you need to cool it down quickly. When cool, add it to a large mixing bowl.

Add the rest of the ingredients and stir gently to combine. Chill before serving. Give it a gentle stir before serving.

HEARTY LENTIL SHEPHERD'S PIE

RECIPE BY: TAMI KRAMER

This Shepherd's Pie is simple enough for a weeknight family meal but yet elegant enough to serve at a holiday meal. A thick and hearty stick-to-your-ribs kind of casserole dish that is classic comfort food.

INGREDIENTS:

Filling:
2 cups onion, chopped
1 cup carrots, diced
½ cup celery, diced
2 cups brown/green lentils, rinsed
1½ cups sweet potato, peeled, diced
1 can fire roasted diced tomatoes, no salt added
2½ cups low-sodium vegetable broth
1 Tablespoon Herbs de Provence seasoning mix or to taste
1 teaspoon sweet paprika
2 teaspoons *Table Tasty* salt substitute or your favorite no-salt substitute
Freshly ground black pepper to taste

Add after the lentil mixture is cooked:
1 cup frozen peas or corn
1 Tablespoon balsamic vinegar

One batch of Garlic Mashed Potatoes (see recipe page 228)

PREPARATION:

Plug electric pressure cooker in and turn to sauté mode. Add the onions, carrots, and celery, and stir, occasionally adding a little water if needed to prevent sticking. When onions are translucent and the carrots and celery have softened slightly, add the sweet potatoes, lentils, tomatoes, vegetable broth, Herbs de Provence, sweet paprika, *Table*

Tasty and freshly ground black pepper. Shut the sauté mode off or press cancel, depending on how your pressure cooker works. Lock the lid on the pressure cooker, be sure to set the steam valve to sealing, and set the timer for 10 minutes on high pressure. Let the pressure come down naturally.

If you have two pressure cookers, you can go ahead and make the Garlic Mashed Potatoes while the lentil filling is cooking. If you only have one pressure cooker, when the lentil filling is done, transfer it to the baking dish, wash the pot for the pressure cooker and make the Garlic Mashed Potatoes.

When the pressure has come down naturally for the lentil filling, carefully remove the lid. Add the Balsamic vinegar and the frozen peas or corn, stir well to incorporate it. Taste the filling and make any adjustments to the seasoning if needed.

Preheat oven to 350 F. Transfer the filling into a 9 x 13 inch baking dish. Top with one whole recipe of Garlic Mashed Potatoes (see recipe page 228) and spread them out evenly to cover the filling completely.

Bake the pie for 30 minutes or until heated through. Make sure your baking dish is safe to go under the broiler and, if so, broil on high for just a few minutes, watching it closely, until potatoes are lightly brown.

Sprinkle with some chopped fresh chives for a pretty garnish.

GARLIC MASHED POTATOES

RECIPE BY: TAMI KRAMER

These delicious garlic mashed potatoes are an indispensable part of Tami's Hearty Lentil Shepherd's Pie, but they also make a great side dish.

INGREDIENTS:

2 pounds Yukon gold potatoes scrubbed and cut into chunks – or your favorite kind of potato
1 cup low-sodium vegetable broth
8 cloves garlic – or to taste
2-3 teaspoons *Benson's Table Tasty* salt substitute or your favorite salt substitute
½ cup unsweetened almond milk, warmed so it doesn't cool down the potatoes
1 Tablespoon dried chives or 2 Tablespoons fresh minced chives
Freshly ground black pepper

PREPARATION:

Put the potatoes, broth, and garlic cloves in an *Instant Pot* pressure cooker, secure the lid and press manual, set time for 4 minutes. When it is done cooking, use quick pressure release. Open pot carefully as it will be hot. Do not drain the liquid, and using a potato masher, start mashing, making sure you get the cloves of garlic. Add all of the seasonings. Add the almond milk a little at a time. You may not need it all, depending on how creamy you like your potatoes. Keep mashing and adding the warm almond milk until you have the desired consistency.

CHEF'S NOTE:

Variations: You can change up the seasonings, add fresh herbs like thyme, rosemary or an Italian seasoning mix, Herbs de Provence, sun dried tomatoes. If you wish, use rutabagas or parsnips in place of half of the potatoes.

ZESTY QUINOA BEAN SALAD

RECIPE BY: TAMI KRAMER

Simple and delicious! This is the perfect recipe to take to pot lucks or make a batch for your work lunches and enjoy all week long.

INGREDIENTS:

Salad
2 cups quinoa, rinsed
2½ cups water
2 cups black beans, rinsed and drained
2 red bell peppers, diced
1 small red onion, diced
½ cup chopped cilantro
1½ cups corn, frozen, thawed

Dressing
½ cup lime juice
3 Tablespoons no-salt mustard
Zest of 1-2 limes

PREPARATION:

In an *Instant Pot* pressure cooker, add the rinsed and drained quinoa with 2½ cups water. Put the lid on, making sure the sealing vent is in the sealing position. Set time for 5 minutes at high pressure and let it come down using natural pressure release. When it is done, fluff with a fork.

Add the quinoa and the rest of the salad ingredients to a large bowl and stir until well combined. In a measuring cup, mix together the lime juice, mustard, and lime zest. Pour over the prepared salad and stir until well combined.

This can be eaten hot or cold. Refrigerate the leftovers. It can be reheated to serve it warm. Serve it cold over a bed of greens or over a big beautiful chopped salad.

CHEF'S NOTE:

Variations: If desired, add some chili powder, ground cumin, salsa, diced jalapeno, or the *California Balsamic* vinegars like *Sweet Heat, Blazin Habanero,* or *Gilroy Garlic.*

CREAMY BALSAMIC DRESSING

RECIPE BY: TAMI KRAMER

INGREDIENTS:

1 box or can of cannellini beans, no salt added, rinsed and drained
½ cup of a thick and sweet balsamic vinegar 4% acidity like *Napa Valley Naturals Grand Reserve**
4 teaspoons Dijon mustard or no-salt-added mustard
1 cup unsweetened plant milk
2-3 teaspoons Garlic & Herb no-salt seasoning or you could use 2 fresh garlic cloves

PREPARATION:

Mix all ingredients together in a blender until smooth and creamy. It thickens after chilling in the fridge.

CHEF'S NOTE:

*If you can't find a thick and sweet Balsamic vinegar, you can use a regular Balsamic and add 2 pitted dates for sweetness as long as they are not a trigger food for you.

For a slaw salad, use the white balsamic vinegar. The lighter color looks better on a slaw. The white balsamic is a lighter flavor but it still makes a yummy dressing.

DILL QUINOA AND FAVA BEANS
RECIPE BY: SHAYDA SOLEYMANI

Healthy Cooking with Shayda is best known for creating authentic oil-free Persian food and for her simple, healthy meals. You can find her on *Facebook/Instagram/YouTube* and visit her website at *Healthycooking-withshayda.com.*

INGREDIENTS:

2 cups uncooked quinoa
3 cups water
1 bunch fresh dill, chopped
1 bunch fresh parsley, chopped
½ cup dried dill
2 Tablespoons *Benson's Table Tasty* salt-free seasoning, or salt-free seasoning of your choice
3 cups frozen double peeled fava beans or frozen edamame

PREPARATION:

In a 5 quart pot, bring a pot of water to boil and put the frozen fava beans or edamame in the boiling water, and cook over medium heat for 8-10 minutes until just tender. Drain and put the beans in enough ice water to shock the beans and stop them from cooking. To remain maximum flavor, don't thaw the beans before cooking.

Put all remaining ingredients including the 3 cups of water in a 5 quart pot. Bring to a boil, reduce heat, cover and simmer until all the liquid has evaporated (about 15-20 minutes). Let it stand for about 5 minutes, then fluff with a fork. Enjoy.

TAS KABAB STEW

RECIPE BY: SHAYDA SOLEYMANI

INGREDIENTS:

1 large onion, chopped
4 garlic cloves, minced
1 large eggplant or 2 small ones, peeled and chopped
1 large zucchini, chopped
2 carrots, chopped
2 quince or Granny Smith apples or pears, chopped
4 Yukon gold potatoes, chopped
4 large tomatoes, chopped
1 Tablespoon nutritional yeast
½ teaspoon cumin
½ teaspoon coriander
½ teaspoon pepper, optional
1 cup dried prunes, chopped
1 Tablespoon tomato paste dissolved with 2 Tablespoons of hot water
Juice of 1 lemon

PREPARATION:

Premix all your spices (cumin, coriander, pepper, nutritional yeast). In a 5 quart pot, sauté the chopped onion and turmeric until the onions have softened up and are translucent. Then add the garlic and sauté for 1-2 minutes longer. Then construct a mixed layer of the ingredients. Sprinkle each layer with a bit of the mixed spice. Repeat until you have used up everything. Starting with eggplants on top of the onions and garlic, then spice, then carrots, then spice, then potatoes, then spice, then quince (or other fruit), then spice, then tomatoes, spice, and prunes. Mix the dissolved tomato paste with lemon juice and pour on top of everything. Cook on low heat, covered for 2-3 hours.

CREAMY MUSHROOM BISQUE
RECIPE BY: SHAYDA SOLEYMANI

INGREDIENTS:

3 pounds brown bella mushrooms
2.5 pounds sweet potatoes, washed and peeled (preferably Hannah sweet potatoes)
2 cups dried gourmet mix mushrooms (soaked in 6 cups water for 5 hours, to get the most flavor)
1 large onion, cut in half
8-10 cloves garlic
6 cups water from soaking the dried mushrooms
½ cup gluten-free oats
2 Tablespoons any salt-free seasoning (*Benson's* or any other)
1 teaspoon dried thyme
¼ teaspoon dried rosemary
3-4 cups unsweetened non-dairy milk
3 Tablespoons Dijon mustard or salt-free stone ground mustard
5 Tablespoons nutritional yeast
1 pound baby bellas or cremini mushrooms, sliced, reserved for the end
1 teaspoon red pepper flakes (optional)
Salt and pepper (optional)

PREPARATION:

Rinse all the dried mushrooms, then place them in a bowl and cover the mushrooms with 6 cups of water, at room temperature and allow them to soak for at least 1 hour or longer (I typically soak them for 6 hours, to get the most flavor). The longer it soaks, the more flavor it will have. Once they're finished soaking, remove the mushrooms, reserving the liquid. Then take the reserved mushrooms water and run it through a cheesecloth to get rid of any residual grit. The soaking liquid will be transformed into a mushroom broth, which is quite flavorful and we will use in the soup.

In a mixing bowl, whisk the nut milk, mustard and nutritional yeast. Set aside.

Place all ingredients except for the nut milk, nutritional yeast, and mustard in an *Instant Pot* pressure cooker and cook on high for 10 minutes. Release the pressure and add your nut milk, nutritional yeast, and mustard to the pot and purée the soup with an immersion blender right in the pot or carefully put in blender and blend until smooth. Once everything is blended, add the sliced mushrooms to the pot, close the lid and let it cook on low for at least 30 minutes or longer. Enjoy

DELICIOUS GARBANZO BEAN SALAD

RECIPE BY: SHAYDA SOLEYMANI

INGREDIENTS:

1 zucchini, shredded
2 carrots, shredded
2 Persian cucumbers, diced
1 yellow bell pepper, diced
2 cups purple cabbage, sliced
1 small onion, sliced
2 roma tomatoes, firm, diced
Some fresh mint, for garnish
2 14.5 cans of garbanzo beans, rinsed and drained
1-2 mangos, diced
Balsamic vinegar, to taste
Lime juice, to taste

PREPARATION:

Chop everything and toss into a bowl. Rinse garbanzo beans and toss into the bowl. Add some balsamic vinegar, lime juice and gently toss. Top off with some fresh mint or basil. Refrigerate a few hours before serving. Enjoy!

COLLARD GREEN WRAPS

RECIPE BY: SHAYDA SOLEYMANI

INGREDIENTS:

1 head of collard greens, ribs removed
¼ cup hummus (any oil-free hummus you like)
shredded carrots
red bell pepper, thinly sliced
red onions, thinly sliced
cucumbers, thinly sliced
avocado, thinly sliced
purple cabbage, thinly sliced
raw asparagus
raw zucchini, thinly sliced

PREPARATION:

Choose your collard leaf/leaves. Select the ones that are large enough to fill and roll, and preferably without any tears or holes. If they have a few, don't worry.

Steam your collard greens so that they become easier to roll. Don't steam for too long or the greens will become too soft; 30 seconds to a minute will do. Once steamed, put the collard greens in a bowl filled with cold water and ice to stop the cooking. Then remove and lay the collard greens on a paper towel to dry them. The rib of the collard green is very thick; using a paring knife, carefully trim that back. It will make the leaf easier to roll.

Spread the leaf out so that it's flat and then add your fillings. Start with the hummus, then add your desired veggies. Be careful not to add too much, or it will become a mess to roll. Roll the wrap like you would roll a burrito.

Serve wraps immediately and enjoy!

KHORESHT EH GHEYMEH (YELLOW SPLIT PEAS) WITH MUSHROOMS

RECIPE BY: SHAYDA SOLEYMANI

INGREDIENTS:

2 cups of chana dal (longer-cooking yellow split peas)
1 bag frozen okra
1 pound mushrooms, quartered or sliced
2 large white onions, peeled and diced
1 14.5-oz. can organic tomato sauce
28 ounce can fat-free marinara sauce
1 cup ghooreh (fresh sour grapes) OR ½ cup lemon juice
10 oz. pomegranate paste
¼ teaspoon cinnamon
1 teaspoon turmeric
1 teaspoon advieh (Persian spice)

PREPARATION:

Wash, pick out any stones and soak 2 cups of the chana dal in 4 cups of water for at least 2 hours. Put into a pot and bring to a boil, then simmer or low boil until soft, about 45 minutes. In another pot, sauté the chopped onions with turmeric; once translucent, add to the pot with the chana dal, along with the marinara sauce, tomato sauce, ghooreh or lemon juice, pomegranate paste, mushrooms, cinnamon and advieh. Let it cook for about 3 hours on low. Add the okra in the last hour. This dish is delicious on white or brown rice, topped with shoestring potatoes. Also, it's delicious on a baked potato. Enjoy.

CHEF'S NOTE:

The spices and the pomegranate paste can be found at Middle Eastern grocery stores or on my *Healthy Cooking with Shayda Amazon* favorites page.

HEARTY LENTIL SOUP

RECIPE BY: SHAYDA SOLEYMANI

INGREDIENTS:

2 cups green lentils, rinsed
1 cup red lentils, rinsed
1 medium sized white onion, diced
2 medium Yukon gold potatoes, peeled and grated
1 teaspoon dried turmeric
1 teaspoon dried red pepper flakes, or more to taste
8 cups water
3 Tablespoons tomato paste

PREPARATION:

In a 5-quart pot, sauté the diced onion with the turmeric until the onion is caramelized. Add water as needed, a tablespoon at a time. Once the onion has caramelized, add the green lentils, red lentils, grated Yukon gold potatoes, red pepper flakes, and the water. Bring to a boil, then turn down the heat to low and let it cook on low for about an hour until it has all been absorbed and it's a thick consistency. At that point, add the tomato paste and stir until it's well absorbed. Enjoy.

ZUCCHINI, BEANIE, FIT-INTO-YOUR-BIKINI NOODLES

RECIPE BY: SHAYDA SOLEYMANI

INGREDIENTS:

2 zucchini squash
1 small red onion, chopped
3 cloves garlic, minced
1 15-oz. can salt-free, fire roasted diced tomatoes
2 Tablespoons fresh basil, chopped
1 3-oz. package sundried tomatoes
1 10-oz. package sliced mushrooms
2 cups sliced carrots
1 can salt-free black beans
1 red bell pepper, sliced
2 cups chopped kale

PREPARATION:

Spiralize or julienne the zucchini to make zucchini noodles. In a sauté pan, sauté the onions on medium heat until well caramelized. Add water as needed. Once done, add the mushrooms, bell peppers, carrots, and sundried tomatoes. Once the vegetables have softened, add the cans of tomatoes and black beans. Next add the kale and zucchini. Cook for a few minutes longer until the zucchinis are slightly tender.

SOOGE'S LEMONY BRUSSELS SPROUTS

RECIPE BY: SULJO DZAFOVIC

My dog Bailey has a human best friend whose name is Suljo. No one can pronounce it so we call him Sooge. He roasted some Brussels sprouts whole in fresh lemon juice and boy were they delicious! When you use sour ingredients in a recipe you don't even miss the salt.

INGREDIENTS:

1 pound fresh Brussels Sprouts
1 cup fresh lemon juice
¼ cup finely chopped garlic
zest from 1 lemon (for garnish)

PREPARATION:

Preheat oven to 400 degrees F. Place Brussels sprouts in a single layer in a large baking dish. I use an 11" Pyrex pie plate. Pour lemon juice and garlic over the sprouts. Roast for 30 minutes. Garnish with the lemon zest.

CHEF'S NOTE:

I like to look for smaller Brussels sprouts and leave them whole. If they are large you may want to cut them in half or quarters. I added the garlic but you could skip it if you prefer.

STUFFIN' MUFFINS

RECIPE BY: MELONY JORENSON

Melony Jorenson is a dear friend of mine, and an exceptional cook. Here's what she has to say about her Stuffin' Muffins: *My favorite time of year is Thanksgiving and I loved making individual stuffin' muffins for my family and friends. I also used to love making macaroni and cheese (before meeting AJ 10 years ago). I used to make individual mac and cheese muffins as well. That way everyone gets the crunchy outside and the soft inside. One day I had a bunch of rice left over and I also just finished making some cheeze sauce from one of AJ's recipes. The rest was history. A match made in heaven. You can get as creative as you want with this recipe. That's the beauty of this kind of cooking. Bon Appetit!*

INGREDIENTS:

2½ cups brown rice
5 cups water
2-3 Tablespoons *Benson's Table Tasty* (or your favorite salt-free seasoning)
1 Tablespoon onion powder
1 Tablespoon garlic powder
1 teaspoon poultry seasoning
1 10-oz. bag chopped onions
1 10-oz. bag chopped mushrooms. Give additional chopping so mushrooms are smaller pieces than what comes in bag.
1 4-oz can chopped fire-roasted green chilis

PREPARATION:

Cook the rice in a rice cooker until done. Water sauté the onions and mushrooms, then add the fire-roasted chilis and water sauté a few minutes more. Add to cooked rice and mix well. Make your favorite non-dairy cheeze sauce. For every 2 cups of rice, add 1 cup cheeze sauce. With an ice cream scooper, fill silicone muffin tins. Bake at 350 degrees F for 40 minutes. This makes 14 muffins.

MITTY'S MASH

RECIPE BY: STEVE MITTLEMAN

Steve Mittleman is a world class comedian, host, and auctioneer, but his true passion is for all of us to be healthy on a healthy planet. Steve guest-hosted Episode 55 of *Weight Loss Wednesday* and showed us how to make his signature dish.

INGREDIENTS:

4 pounds Yukon Gold potatoes
⅜ - ½ cup unsweetened plant milk
¼ cup nutritional yeast
1 teaspoon *Benson's Table Tasty* (or your favorite salt-free seasoning)
½ teaspoon garlic powder

PREPARATION:

Place a basket or the rack that comes with your pressure cooker in the pot and fill it with water just up to the basket or the rack. Place the potatoes in the *Instant Pot* and cook on high pressure for 12 minutes. When the unit beeps, wait about another 12 minutes to release the pressure. Drain the water from the basket or insert, add the remaining ingredients and mash the potatoes right in the pot using a potato masher.

ONE POT MEXICAN QUINOA
RECIPE BY: SHARON MCRAE

Sharon McRae is a plant-based certified health coach, nutrition/cooking instructor, organizer of the Columbia MD Forks Over Knives Meetup Group, and wife and mom of three. She can be reached at www.eatwell-staywell.com. This is a delicious, quick, and easy dish you can make in minutes using simple ingredients.

INGREDIENTS:

¾ cup water
16 oz. bag frozen fire roasted or sweet corn (add frozen, no need to thaw first)
16 oz. bag frozen mixed vegetables of choice (add frozen, no need to thaw first)
1 Tablespoon Mexican/fajita/taco spice blend (salt-free preferred)
2 teaspoons garlic powder
1 can/carton black beans, drained and rinsed (or 1½ cups freshly cooked black beans)
1 cup quinoa, rinsed well if not pre-rinsed
16 oz. jar salsa (salt-free, oil-free, sugar-free preferred)

PREPARATION:

Add water, vegetables, spices, and beans in that order to an *Instant Pot* pressure cooker and stir. Then layer quinoa and salsa on top; do not stir to prevent sticking to the bottom. Set to Manual for 1 minute. Allow pressure to release naturally for 10 minutes, then quick release.

Serve as is, over a salad or bed of streamed greens, or wrap in a tortilla, lettuce or collard leaf for a delicious burrito. Also great as a salad topping or over a baked potato or sweet potato.

CHEF'S NOTE:

Optional additions and toppings: Chopped onion or scallions, avocado, lime juice, cilantro, sliced jalapeno peppers, hot sauce, chipotle
powder, smoked paprika, chili powder, cumin, oregano.

BLUEBERRY OAT GROATS

RECIPE BY: SHARON MCRAE

INGREDIENTS:

3 cups water (hot, preferably)
2 cups oat groats
2 cups blueberries (fresh or frozen)
2 ripe bananas, cut into small pieces
1 Tablespoon cinnamon
1 teaspoon vanilla powder (or 2 teaspoons alcohol-free vanilla extract)
⅓ cup raisins or goji berries

PREPARATION:

Combine all ingredients in an *Instant Pot*. Cook on pressure for 5 minutes. Allow pressure to release naturally, then let the oats rest (without opening lid) for at least one hour. Remove lid and stir well. Serve hot or cold. (Note: For added sweetness, double the raisins/goji berries or add a chopped apple.)

NUTRIENT RICH COOKIES

RECIPE BY: SHARON MCRAE

These delicious cookies are packed with nutrition. They're soft and chewy and would also make a great breakfast on the go. They're gluten-free and contain no sugar, salt, or oil. Just the delicious flavors of the fruit come through. Big hit with the kids! These are delicious straight out of the oven but leftovers should be refrigerated. We enjoy eating them reheated.

INGREDIENTS:

2 cups gluten-free rolled oats
2 ripe bananas
1½ apples (we like one Pink Lady and ½ Granny Smith)
2 medium sized carrots
3 medium sized curly kale leaves
½ cup frozen wild blueberries
1 teaspoon cinnamon
½ teaspoon vanilla bean powder (or 1 teaspoon vanilla extract)
½ cup currants, goji berries, or raisins (optional, for an even sweeter cookie)
½ -1 cup hemp or almond milk, added 2 Tablespoons at a time until mixture sticks together easily but is not too moist.

PREPARATION:

Pour oats in a large mixing bowl. Add frozen wild blueberries, cinnamon, and vanilla bean powder. In a food processor with "S" blade, blend bananas, apples, and hemp or almond milk. Pour over oats. Process kale leaves and carrots with "S" blade into small pieces and add to oat mixture. Add to the bowl and mix well.

Use an ice cream scooper or large spoon to place cookie sized portions on a silicone coated baking try (or use a *Silpat*). Bake cookies at 350 degrees F for 25-30 minutes.

Allow cookies to cool. Enjoy!

GILA MONSTER SAUCE

RECIPE BY: JEN SHIPLEY

Jen Shipley is a former lab tech who has been inspired by *Ultimate Weight Loss* to create nutritious and delicious meals for her family and friends. This is a great sauce to use over tacos.

INGREDIENTS:

8 tomatillos, husked and cut in half
1 zucchini
Pepper mixture*, all seeded (while wearing gloves) and cut in half
1 Anaheim pepper
1 poblano pepper
1 jalapeño pepper
4 cloves garlic
½ onion
2 stalks celery, coarsely chopped
¼ cup applesauce
¼ cup lime juice
2 cups fresh spinach
½ cup cilantro

PREPARATION:

Roast the tomatillos and peppers (cut side up) with the zucchini, onion, and garlic for 30 minutes at 400 degrees F. Place the roasted veggies in a blender with remaining ingredients and pulse to achieve desired consistency, either chunky like a salsa, or smooth like a ketchup. Makes about 4 cups.

*This combination of peppers will create a medium hot sauce. Feel free to substitute other peppers to achieve a milder or hotter sauce.

WATERMELON GAZPACHO

RECIPE BY: JEN SHIPLEY

Another winning recipe from Jen Shipley. This is a potluck favorite.

INGREDIENTS:

1 personal-sized watermelon, peeled and cut into large chunks
4 medium tomatoes, quartered
¼ cup onion
3 cloves garlic
Thumb-sized chunk fresh ginger
1 red bell pepper, seeded and quartered
1 jalapeño pepper, seeded and quartered (wear gloves when handling)
4 Persian cucumbers, cut into large chunks
½ cup fresh cilantro
½ cup fresh mint leaves
2 Tablespoons lime juice
Chopped chives for garnish

PREPARATION:

Combine half of the watermelon, 2 of the tomatoes, and all of the onion, garlic, and ginger in a blender and purée until smooth. Pour most of this soup into a large mixing bowl, leaving only about 2 cups in the blender. Add the remaining ingredients and pulse until ingredients are chopped to a salsa-like consistency. Pour this mixture into the mixing bowl and stir to combine with the puréed soup. This is best served well chilled and garnished with chopped chives.

SENSATIONAL SUSHI

RECIPE BY: HEATHER GOODWIN

Heather Goodwin has fought a lifetime battle with food addiction and obesity. By her 40th birthday, she weighed over 430 pounds and wondered if she would live to see 50. She went plant-based and took off the first 150 pounds and reversed many health conditions, such as type 2 diabetes, sleep apnea, and chronic pain. Then, she joined the *Ultimate Weight Loss* program and finally found relief from compulsive eating. She was finally able to reach her goal of taking off over 300 pounds. She has a *YouTube* channel called *The Butterfly Effect Plant-Based Weight Loss* and an active Facebook group of the same name where members can get support and encouragement on their health journey.

INGREDIENTS:

4 cups brown rice (make from 2 cups uncooked rice and 2½ cups water). *Lundberg* organic short-grain preferred
½ cup brewed rice vinegar
1 large cucumber, julienned
2 large carrots, julienned or shredded
1 baked sweet potato, any kind
6 sheets raw nori seaweed (find it at Asian markets or Whole Foods)

PREPARATION:

Make 4 cups of brown rice (I used 2 cups uncooked brown rice and 3½ cups water in my rice cooker and set on the brown rice setting). While still hot, add the brewed rice vinegar and stir well to combine. Lay a sheet of nori on a large flat surface. Spread rice over nori sheet evenly, leaving an inch uncovered at the top and bottom. Add a row of cucumber, a row of carrot, and a row of avocado. Roll the sushi toward you like you were rolling a sleeping bag. Cut with a very sharp serrated knife, taking care not to smash the roll. Serve with *California Balsamic Teriyaki* or *Gilroy Garlic* or wasabi and ginger or just as it is.

CAULIFLOWER PIZZA

RECIPE BY: HEATHER GOODWIN

INGREDIENTS:

Crust Ingredients for 2 crusts:
3 cups roasted white sweet potato, peeled
1 bag frozen cauliflower, thawed
1 can white beans, drained
3 cups rolled oats

PREPARATION:

Process first three ingredients in a food processor until smooth. Remove from food processor into large bowl. Add in 3 cups uncooked rolled oats and combine well.
Press into semi-thin crust. Bake at 350 degrees F for 15 minutes on silicone mat, then flip carefully and bake for 15 more minutes.

Sauce Ingredients:
1 – 13 oz. can tomato paste
1 teaspoon Italian herb mix
1 teaspoon dried basil

Toppings:
In a fry pan, add a little no-sodium veggie broth to sauté
¼ red onion sliced
3-4 mushrooms
½ red bell pepper

ASSEMBLY:

Spread sauce on crust. Add a layer of baby spinach leaves and the sautéed toppings. Bake 10 more minutes. Sprinkle with nutritional yeast and serve.

SUMMERTIME PEACH-BERRY SURPRISE

RECIPE BY: SANDRA SHOW

Sandra Show from Tustin, a member of *Feel Fabulous Over Forty*, brought this to one of our potlucks and knocked my socks off. She says she has served it to family and friends and they are truly blown away at how tasty the combination of whole foods can be! This is so delicious that I will often eat it for dessert!

INGREDIENTS:

4 Japanese sweet potatoes, roasted, refrigerated and air fried
1 pint blueberries
1 pint raspberries
6 large peaches
1 teaspoon cinnamon
drizzle of raspberry balsamic (optional)

PREPARATION:

Preheat oven to 400 degrees F. Pierce potatoes with a fork and roast for 45-60 minutes until soft, depending on the size of the potato. Once cooled, refrigerate for several hours or overnight. Slice the potatoes in half, then smash using your hand or a spatula until approximately ¼-¾ of an inch. Air fry for 20 minutes or until edges are browned and caramelized. While the potatoes are in the air fryer, cut the peaches into ½" – ¾" cubes. Gently combine the berries, peaches and cinnamon together in a large bowl. When potatoes are cooled, cut into 2" cubes and toss with the fruit mixture. Drizzle with 1-2 Tablespoons raspberry balsamic, if desired. Garnish with fresh mint.

CHEF'S NOTE:

If peaches are not in season, you can use Granny Smith apples.

WATERMELON WONDER SALAD

RECIPE BY: LAYLA RILEY

My friend Layla Riley brought this to a potluck, and I just couldn't stop eating it! I have had watermelon with fresh mint before and couldn't believe how good it also was with fresh basil.

INGREDIENTS:

Cubed watermelon
Chopped fresh basil
White balsamic vinegar

PREPARATION:

Place watermelon and basil in a bowl in the proportions you desire, drizzle with the balsamic vinegar and enjoy!

MUSHROOM SOUP WITH LEMON LIME SAUTÉED MUSHROOMS

RECIPE BY: FAITH AND WILL SCOTT

Faith and Will are passionate about living a Whole Food Plant-Based lifestyle as a family with their three children. On their blog and *You-Tube Channel Get2dRoot Health and Wellness,* they love sharing WFPB recipes with no added oil that their family enjoys. Their blog can be found at http://get2droothealthandwellness.com. This savory mushroom soup is hearty and full of flavor with a lemon-lime twist.

INGREDIENTS:

Soup Base:
1 pound white button mushrooms, sliced (or Cremini/Baby Bella)
1 large red onion, chopped
2 large celery stalks, diced
8 cloves garlic, roughly chopped
¼ cup millet
2 pounds cauliflower head (use the greens, too)
1 bay leaf
1 Tablespoon Italian herbs
1 teaspoon smoked paprika
½ teaspoon dried crushed rosemary
½ teaspoon curry
½ teaspoon chipotle pepper
4 cups water

Sautéed Lemon-Lime Mushrooms and Onions
1 pound white button mushrooms, sliced (or Cremini/Baby Bella)
1 large sweet onion, chopped
1 Tablespoon fresh lemon juice
1 Tablespoon fresh lime juice

Baby arugula (optional, as garnish)

256

PREPARATION:

Set the *Instant Pot* pressure cooker on the "sautée" mode. Add the mushrooms, red onions, celery, and garlic cloves. Place the lid on top of the pot for about 3-5 minutes to allow the pot to heat up and the natural water from the mushroom to be released. Remove the lid and allow the veggies to continue to cook, stirring occasionally until the majority of the water has cooked out (about an additional 8-10 minutes).

Add all of the spices, the bay leaf, millet, the "whole" cauliflower head and 4 cups of water to the pot. Cover and engage the lid. Be sure the steamer valve is set to the closed position. Turn the *Instant Pot* to the "Manual" mode for 10 minutes.

Juice a lemon and lime to yield 1 Tablespoon of each. Set juices aside. Place the other pound of mushrooms and the chopped "sweet" onion in a non-stick pan. Do not add any water or broth. Place the lid on the pan. Cook on medium-high heat covered for about 3-5 minutes to allow the natural water to be released from the mushrooms. Remove the lid, stir occasionally. Continue to cook for an additional 5 or so minutes until all of the water has been released and the onions are caramelized. Add both juices to the pan, stirring occasionally, continue to sauté the veggies until all juices have been absorbed. Turn the heat off and set aside.

Once the *Instant Pot* has naturally released the steam for at least 10 minutes, remove the top. Search for the bay leaf and remove it from the pot. Using an immersion blender, blend the soup to your desired creaminess. Dip some out into a soup bowl. Top with the Lemon-Lime Mushrooms and enjoy!

CHEF'S NOTE:

This soup is amazingly delicious as is, but baby arugula is a nice peppery addition. The soup will keep in an airtight glass container for 5-7 days.

EGGPLANT CHILI

RECIPE BY: FAITH AND WILL SCOTT

This eggplant chili is deliciously tasty and filling. The perfect bean-free comfort food.

INGREDIENTS:

1 eggplant, large (at least 1½ pound)
1 yellow onion, diced (about 1½ cup)
1 red bell pepper, diced (about ¾ cup)
1 green bell pepper, diced (about ¾ cup)
3 celery stalks, diced (about ½ cup)
1 carrot, medium, chopped (about ½ cup)
1 cup white button mushrooms, chopped
2 Tablespoons chili powder
1 Tablespoon Italian seasoning
2 teaspoons onion powder
2 teaspoons garlic powder
2 teaspoons smoked paprika
¼ - ½ teaspoon ancho chili pepper (use ¼ teaspoon for less spicy flavor)
½ cup nutritional yeast
1 Tablespoon liquid smoke, Mesquite

Tomato Sauce Blend
8 oz. tomato sauce, unsalted
6 oz. tomato paste, unsalted
1½ oz. Medjool date, pitted (about 3 Medjools or 6 Deglet Dates)
2 Tablespoons apple cider vinegar, raw, unfiltered
1 Tablespoon garlic, minced

Nutritional yeast (optional, as garnish)
Green onions, chopped (optional, as garnish)

PREPARATION:

Chop all veggies and set aside.

Add tomato sauce, tomato paste, dates, apple cider vinegar and garlic to blender and blend until smooth. Set aside.

Using the "sauté" mode on the *Instant Pot*, sauté all the veggies, EXCEPT the chopped eggplant, for 7 minutes. No oil is needed for sautéing. If veggies begin to stick, add 1 Tablespoon of water as needed to keep veggies from sticking.

Add all spices to sautéed veggies and stir well. Then add tomato sauce blend to sautéed veggies and stir well.

Add the chopped eggplant to the *Instant Pot* and mix well. Cook on "Manual" mode for 8 minutes. Allow the pot to naturally release the pressure for 10 minutes. Open pot and give another stir through.

Serve over a potato, rice, quinoa, or greens of choice!

CHEF'S NOTE:

Recipe inspired and adapted from *Nutritioncity.com*.

WARM BAKED APPLES WITH DATE SHAKE SAUCE
RECIPE BY: ZEL ALLEN

Zel and Reuben Allen are the publishers of *Vegetarians in Paradise*, a vegan website operating for 20 years, sharing recipes, vegan lifestyle information, and articles of vegan interest. Find them at www.vegparadise.com.

Zel came to visit me in the desert and had never had a date shake. So I made her one (recipe on page 189). She thought it would make a great sauce for baked apples and she experimented with it and it did! Since this is being served warm, we swapped the frozen bananas for additional dates.

Zel says during the cold winter months, nothing quite compares with a warm baked apple dessert that gives one that comfy, cozy feeling of home, especially when fragrant aromas begin to perfume the air as they finish baking. The exotic scents of cinnamon and cardamom flow through the house and never fail to set anticipation in motion. No need to wait for winter to enjoy this delicious dessert, though—it's delightful all year long!

For the best varieties of apples to bake, choose Granny Smith, Jonagold, Braeburn, or Honeycrisp. Tuck them into the oven, and you'll only have to wait 45-55 minutes before plunging your spoon into a delicious, homemade dessert.

INGREDIENTS:

One recipe of date shake sauce (see next page)
4 baking apples
¾ - 1 cup raisins

PREPARATION:

Preheat oven to 350 degrees F and have ready an 8-inch oven-safe baking dish. Wash the apples and core them. Put the apples into the baking dish and stuff the cavities with raisins. Sprinkle any leftover raisins onto the bottom of the baking dish and set aside. To make the Date Shake Sauce, combine the non-dairy milk, dates, vanilla extract, cinnamon, and cardamom in a high-speed blender. Blend until smooth and creamy or slightly chunky, if desired. Pour the sauce into the baking dish, filling it no more than ⅔ full. Refrigerate any leftover Date Shake Sauce to enjoy another time. Cover the baking dish with aluminum foil and bake for 45-55 minutes, or until the apples feel tender when pierced with a fork. Serve immediately, or cool the dish 10-15 minutes before serving.

INGREDIENTS: Date Shake Sauce

1 cup of unsweetened almond milk
3 large Medjool dates, pitted
2 ripe bananas, peeled and frozen
½ teaspoon vanilla powder
½ teaspoon ground cinnamon
⅛ teaspoon ground nutmeg

PREPARATION:

Place all ingredients in a high-powered blender and blend until smooth and creamy.

ENDNOTES

CHAPTER ONE: WHAT YOU NEED TO KNOW ABOUT WHAT DOC-
TORS DON'T KNOW

1. Colino S. How much do doctors learn about nutrition? U.S. News
   and World Report. https://health.usnews.com/wellness/food/articles/
   2016-12-07/how-much-do-doctors-learn-about-nutrition December 7,
   2016.
2. "Study Finds Significant Variability in Doctors' Angioplasty Death Rates,"
   press release of the American College of Cardiology, Apr. 3, 2017
3. Doll, Jacob A. et al, Assessment of Operator Variability in Risk Standard-
   ized Mortality Following Percutaneous Coronary Intervention: A Report
   From the NCDR, Journal of the American College of Cardiology, Apr.
   10, 2017, Volume 10, Issue 7, pp. 672-682, https://doi.org/10.1016/j.
   jcin.2016.12.019

CHAPTER TWO: MY STORY

1. The FH Foundation. https://thefhfoundation.org/
2. The FH Foundation. Diagnosis & Management.
   https://thefhfoundation.org/diagnosis-management
   Note: it's true that there is a genetic condition of familial hypercholesterolemia caused by a defect on Chromosome 19, most serious for the rare
   individuals who inherit the gene from both parents, but the FH Foundation's dismissal of genetic testing and discounting of the role of diet invite
   those who simply eat their way into high cholesterol to claim a genetic cause.
3. phone call with Jasmine Patel, July 1, 2019
4. I was not able to find verification for the length of Gregory's fast. It was
   at least 164 days according to this article in The Crimson: [https://www.
   thecrimson.com/article/1971/10/4/dick-gregory-pokes-fun-at-war/] and if
   he continued the fast from that point until the Paris Peace Accords were
   signed, it would have lasted in the neighborhood of 645 days.

5. Infant Nutrition Council. Breastmilk Information. https://www.infantnutritioncouncil.com/resources/breastmilk-information
6. Lyman H, Merzer G. Mad Cowboy. Simon & Schuster; 1998.
7. Lyman H, Merzer G. No More Bull! Simon & Schuster; 2005.
8. Steinfeld H, Gerber P, Wassenaar T, Castel V, Rosales M, de Haan C. Livestock's Long Shadow: Environmental Issues and Options. Rome, Food and Agriculture Organization of the United Nations, 2006 http://www.fao.org/3/a-a0701e.pdf
9. Goodland R, Anhang J. Livestock and climate change. WorldWatch. 2009; Nov/Dec: 10-19.

CHAPTER THREE: CARBS VS. ROADKILL

1. Brody JE. Unlocking the secrets of the microbiome. New York Times. https://www.nytimes.com/2017/11/06/well/live/unlocking-the-secrets-of-the-microbiome.html November 6, 2017.
2. Eberly T. Playing chicken on food safety? Atlanta Journal Constitution. https://www.ajc.com/news/local/playing-chicken-food-safety/7im32r9wNVnEugMZisphRN/ August 5, 2012. USDA Food Safety and Inspection Service. Modernization of Poultry Slaughter Inspections. https://www.fsis.usda.gov/wps/portal/fsis/topics/regulatory-compliance/haccp/haccp-based-inspection-models-project/himp-study-plans-resources/poultry-slaughter-inspection
3. Philpott T. Your chicken's salmonella problem is worse than you think. Mother Jones. https://www.motherjones.com/food/2018/08/chicken-salmonella-federal-inspection-slaughterhouse-sanderson-illness-usda/ August 5, 2018.
4. USDA Food Safety and Inspection Service. New performance standards for salmonella and campylobacter in not-ready-to-eat comminuted chicken and turkey products and raw chicken parts and changes to related agency verification procedures: Response to comments and announcement of implementation schedule. https://www.federalregister.gov/documents/2016/02/11/2016-02586/new-performance-standards-for-salmonella-and-campylobacter-in-not-ready-to-eat-comminuted-chicken February 11, 2016. All movie rights to this publication are, as far as I know, still available.
5. Neporent L. Montana bill would legalize roadkill dining. ABC News [television broadcast]. https://abcnews.go.com/Health/montana-bill-legalize-roadkill-dining/story?id=18549790 February 20, 2013.
6. Schlanger Z. It's very likely your supermarket fish isn't what you think it is. Quartz. https://qz.com/1497273/supermarket-fish-are-

mislabeled-on-a-mass-scale-new-york-state-reports/ December 16, 2018.

CHAPTER FOUR: GARY, MEET STEVE

1. Bourdain A. Kitchen Confidential. Bloomsbury; 2000.
2. Greger M. How does meat cause inflammation? [video]. NutritionFacts. org. https://nutritionfacts.org/2012/09/20/why-meat-causes-inflammation/ September 20, 2012.
3. McNamee D. Severe depression linked with inflammation in the brain. Medical News Today. https://www.medicalnewstoday.com/news/severe-depression-linked-inflammation-brain-288715 January 29, 2015.
4. Taubes G. What if it's all been a big fat lie? New York Times Magazine. https://www.nytimes.com/2002/07/07/magazine/what-if-it-s-all-been-a-big-fat-lie.html July 7, 2002.
5. Taubes G. Why We Get Fat. Alfred A. Knopf; 2011
6. Molteni M. The struggles of a $40 million nutrition science crusade. Wired. https://www.wired.com/story/how-a-dollar40-million-nutrition-science-crusade-fell-apart/ June 18, 2018.
7. https://www.arnoldventures.org/grants-list?q=nutrition
8. Diet Fiction, documentary, Michal Siewerski, director, 2019.
9. Desilver D. What's on your table? How America's diet has changed over the decades. Pew Research Center. https://www.pewresearch.org/fact-tank/2016/12/13/whats-on-your-table-how-americas-diet-has-changed-over-the-decades/ December 13, 2016.
10. CDC Report: 84.8 million U.S. adults consume fast food every day and other startling findings. ABC. October 3, 2018. https://www. abcactionnews.com/lifestyle/fast-food-consumption-cdc-report ; Fryar CD, Hughes JP, Herrick KA, Ahluwalia NA. Fast food consumption among adults in the United States, 2013-2016. Atlanta: CDC National Center for Health Statistics; October 2018. https://www.cdc.gov/nchs/products/databriefs/db322.htm
11. Why We Get Fat, p.214
12. Why We Get Fat, p.214
13. Why We Get Fat, p.176
14. Why We Get Fat, p.136
15. Why We Get Fat, p.136
16. Taubes G. The Case Against Sugar. Alfred A. Knopf; 2016.
17. The Case Against Sugar, pp. 20-21
18. email to the author, December 2, 2019

19. email to the author, May 9, 2020
20. https://www.youtube.com/watch?v=oNZsfluh0Uo

CHAPTER FIVE: THE CURIOUS CASE OF JOANNA

1. https://www.malacards.org/card/mesangial_proliferative_glomerulonephritis
2. I don't wish to give the name of the supplement in the text so as to give the impression of shilling for a commercial product, but interested readers may contact me through my website: www.ownyourhealthbook.com.
3. Hollon J, Puppa EL, Greenwald B, Goldberg E, Guurrerio A, Fasano A. Effect of gliadin on permeability of intestinal biopsy explants from celiac disease patients and patients with non-celiac gluten sensitivity. Nutrients 2015;7(3):1565-1576. https://www.ncbi.nlm.nih.gov/pmc/articles/PMC4377866/

CHAPTER SIX: SETTLED SCIENCE, PART ONE: NUTRITIONAL STUDIES

1. https://skepticalscience.com/volcanoes-and-global-warming.htm
2. Eskelinen MH, Kivipelto M. Caffeine as a protective factor in dementia and Alzheimer's disease. Journal of Alzheimer's Disease 2010;20(s1): S167-S174. DOI: 10.3233/JAD-2010-1404 https://www.ncbi.nlm.nih.gov/pubmed/20182054
3. LeWine H. Sweet dreams: eating chocolate prevents heart disease. Harvard Health Publishing, June 17, 2015. https://www.health.harvard.edu/blog/sweet-dreams-eating-chocolate-prevents-heart-disease-201506168087
4. Greger M. The safety of heme vs. non-heme iron. NutritionFacts.org, June 5, 2015. https://nutritionfacts.org/video/the-safety-of-heme-vs-non-heme-iron/
5. Campbell TC. The China Study. BenBella Books; 2005.
6. Jarasch E. New pathogens in beef and cow's milk contributing to the risk of cancer. Healthcare industry BW. https://www.gesundheitsindustrie-bw.de/en/article/news/new-pathogens-in-beef-and-cows-milk-contributing-to-the-risk-of-cancer/ June 11, 2019.
7. Snowdon DA, Phillips RL, Fraser GE. Meat consumption and fatal ischemic heart disease. Prev Med. 1984;13(5):490-500. https://www.ncbi.nlm.nih.gov/pubmed/6527990
8. High blood pressure redefined for the first time in 14 years: 130 is the new high. American Heart Association Newsroom. https://newsroom.heart.org/

news/high-blood-pressure-redefined-for-first-time-in-14-years-130-is-the-new-high Nov. 13, 2017.

9. Ophir O, Peer G, Gilad J, Blum M, Aviram A. Low blood pressure in veg-etarians: the possible role of potassium. Am J Clin Nutr. 1983;37(5):755-62. https://www.ncbi.nlm.nih.gov/pubmed/6846214

10. Vegetarian diets linked to lower blood pressure. Harvard Health Publishing, April, 2014. https://www.health.harvard.edu/heart-health/vegetarian-diet-linked-to-lower-blood-pressure; Alexander S, Ostfeld RJ, Allen K, Williams KA. A plant-based diet and hypertension, J Geriatr Cardiol. 2017 May;14(5):327–30. https://www.ncbi.nlm.nih.gov/pmc/articles/PMC5466938/

11. Pettersen BJ, Anousheh R, Fan J, Jaceldo Siegel K, Fraser GE. Vegetarian diets and blood pressure among white subjects: results from the Adventist Health Study-2. Public Health Nutr. 2012 Oct; 15(10):1909–16. https://www.researchgate.net/publication/221734212_Vegetarian_diets_and_blood_pressure_among_white_subjects_Results_from_the_Adventist_Health_Study-2_AHS-2

12. Choi EY, Allen K, McDonnough M, Massera D, Ostfeld RJ. A plant-based diet and heart failure: case report and literature review. J Geriatr Cardiol. 2017;14(5): 375–8. doi: 10.11909/j.issn.1671-5411.2017.05.003 www.ncbi.nlm.nih.gov/pmc/articles/PMC5466944/

13. Allen KE, Gumber D, Ostfeld RJ. Heart failure and a plant-based diet. a case-report and literature review. Front. Nutr. June 11, 2019. https://www.frontiersin.org/articles/10.3389/fnut.2019.00082/full https://doi.org/10.3389/fnut.2019.00082

14. Esselstyn CB. Prevent and Reverse Heart Disease. London: Penguin Books, 2007.

15. Esselstyn, Prevent and Reverse Heart Disease.

16. Esselstyn CB Jr., Gendy G, Doyle J, Golubie M, Roizen MF. A way to reverse CAD? Journal Family Prac. 2014;63(7): 356-364b.

17. ibid, p.358

18. Ornish D. Avoiding revascularization with lifestyle changes: The Multicenter Lifestyle Demonstration Project. Am J Cardiol. 1998;82(10B):72T-76T.

19. LeWine H. Fish oil: friend or foe? Harvard Health Publishing, July 12, 2013. https://www.health.harvard.edu/blog/fish-oil-friend-or-foe-201307126467

20. Levine ME, Suarex JA, Brandhorst S, et al. Low protein intake is associ-ated with a major reduction in IGF-1, cancer, and overall mortality in the 65 and younger but not older population. Cell Metab. 2014;19(3):407-17. https://www.ncbi.nlm.nih.gov/pmc/articles/PMC3988204/

21. Tang W.H.W., Wang Z., Levinson BS, et al. Intestinal microbial metabolism of phosphatidylcholine and cardiovascular risk. N. Engl

J Med. 2013;368:1575-84. https://www.nejm.org/doi/full/10.1056/NEJMoa1109400

22. Ward, T. Dean Ornish in defense of the dietary fat – heart disease link. Medscape, May 12, 2016. https://www.medscape.com/viewarticle/862903

23. Alshahrani SM, Fraser GE, Sabate J, et al. Red and processed meat and mortality in a low meat intake population. Nutrients. 2019;11(3):622. doi: 10.3390/nu11030622. https://www.ncbi.nlm.nih.gov/pubmed/30875776; Micha R, Michas G, Mozaffarian D. Unprocessed red and processed meats and risk of coronary artery disease and type 2 diabetes: an updated review of the evidence. Curr Atheroscler Rep 2012;14(6):515–24. https://www.ncbi.nlm.nih.gov/pubmed/23001745; Chen GC, Lv DB, Pang Z, Liu QF. Red and processed meat consumption and risk of stroke: a meta-analysis of prospective cohort studies. Eur J Clin Nutr. 2013;67(1):91–5 https://www.ncbi.nlm.nih.gov/pubmed/23169473

24. Zheng Y, Li Y, Satija A, et al. Association of changes in red meat consumption with total and cause specific mortality among US women and men: two prospective cohort studies. BMJ. 2019;365:l2110. https://www.bmj.com/content/365/bmj.l2110

25. Appleby PN, Thorogood M, Mann J, Key TJ. The Oxford Vegetarian Study: an overview. Am J Clin Nutr. 1999;70(3 Suppl):525S-531S. https://www.ncbi.nlm.nih.gov/pubmed/10479226

26. Rimm EB, Ascherio A, Giovannucci E, et al. Vegetable, fruit, and cereal fiber intake and risk of coronary heart disease among men. JAMA. 1996;275(6):447-51. https://www.ncbi.nlm.nih.gov/pubmed/8627965

27. Lewington S, Whitlock G, Clarke R, et al. Blood cholesterol and vascular mortality by age, sex, and blood pressure: a meta-analysis of individual data from 61 prospective studies with 55,000 vascular deaths. Lancet. 2007; 370(9602):1829-39. https://www.ncbi.nlm.nih.gov/pubmed/18061058?ordinalpos=1&itool=EntrezSystem2.PEntrez.Pubmed.Pubmed_Resultaspoonanel.Pubmed_RVDocSum

28. Simon M. And now a word from our sponsors: are Americans' nutritional professionals in the pocket of big food? eatdrinkpolitics.com; Jan. 2013 http://graphics8.nytimes.com/packages/pdf/business/AND_Corporate_Sponsorship_Report.pdf

29. Ibid., p.11

30. Melina V, Craig W, Levin S. Position of the Academy of Nutrition and Dietetics: Vegetarian diets. J Acad Nutr Diet. 2016;116(12):1970-80. https://www.ncbi.nlm.nih.gov/pubmed/27886704 https://www.eatrightpro.org/-/media/eatrightpro-files/practice/position-and-practice-papers/position-papers/vegetarian-diet.pdf

31. https://www.eatright.org/food/nutrition/dietary-guidelines-and-myplate/healthy-eating-for-women

32. Feskanich D, Willett WC, Stampfer MJ, Colditz GA. Milk, dietary calcium, and bone fractures in women: a 12-year prospective study. Am J Public Health. 1997;87(6):992-7. https://www.ncbi.nlm.nih.gov/pubmed/9224182

33. Greger M. Why is milk consumption associated with more bone fractures? NutritionFacts.org, Jan. 31, 2017 https://nutritionfacts.org/2017/01/31/why-is-milk-consumption-associated-with-more-bone-fractures/

34. Feskanich D, Bischoff-Ferrari HA, Frazier AL, Willett WC. Milk consumption during teenage years and risk of hip fractures in older adults. JAMA Pediatr. 2014;168(1):54-60. https://www.ncbi.nlm.nih.gov/pubmed/24247817

35. Levine, Morgan E. et al, Low protein intake is associated with a major reduction in IGF-1, Cancer, and overall mortality in the 65 and younger but not older population. Cell Metabolism. 2014; 19(3), 407-17. https://www.cell.com/cell-metabolism/fulltext/S1550-4131(14)00062-X

36. Chen X, Wei G, Jalili T, et al. The association of plant protein with all-cause mortality in CKD. Am J Kidney Dis. 2016;67(3): 423–30. https://www.ncbi.nlm.nih.gov/pmc/articles/PMC4769135/

37. Greger M, Stone G. How Not to Die. Flatiron Books; 2015. https://nutritionfacts.org/video/trans-fat-in-meat-and-dairy/?fbclid=IwAR0RpiXp9yQhP-V3e8h4EE6kNeBsPWil-d0fRe1FjqPMiLfB6LFeAk-GRbpo

38. Kolata G. Animal Fat is Tied to Colon Cancer. New York Times. https://www.nytimes.com/1990/12/13/us/animal-fat-is-tied-to-colon-cancer.html December 13, 1990.

39. Willett W, Skerrett PJ. Eat, Drink, and Be Healthy. Simon & Schuster; 2001.

40. https://thefhfoundation.org/diagnosis-management/diet-lifestyle-tips

41. Nestle M. Food Politics. Berkeley: University of California Press; 2002.

42. Barnard ND, Long MB, Ferguson JM, Flores R, Kahleova H. Industry funding and cholesterol research: A systematic review. Am J Lifestyle Med. Published online Dec. 11, 2019. https://journals.sagepub.com/doi/abs/10.1177/1559827619892198

43. http://www.vegsource.com/news/2019/02/more-nut-industry-lies-exposed-part-5-of-nuts.html

44. Johnston BC, Zeraatkar D, Han MA, et al. Unprocessed red meat and processed meat consumption: Dietary guideline recommendations from the Nutritional Recommendations (NutriRECS) Consortium. Ann Intern Med. 2019;171:756–64. https://annals.org/aim/fullarticle/2752328/unprocessed-

45. red-meat-processed-meat-consumption-dietary-guideline-recommendations-from

46. Leung Yinko SS, Stark KD, Thanassoulis G, Pilote L. Fish consumption and acute coronary syndrome: A meta-analysis. Am. Journal of Medicine. 2014;127(9):848-57. https://www.amjmed.com/article/S0002-9343(14)00355-6/pdf

CHAPTER SEVEN: SETTLED SCIENCE, PART TWO: COMPARATIVE ANATOMY

1. Mills MR. The Comparative Anatomy of Eating. http://adaptt.org/archive/Mills The Comparative Anatomy of Eating1.pdf
2. Dunn R. How to Eat Like a Chimpanzee. Scientific American. https://blogs.scientificamerican.com/guest-blog/how-to-eat-like-a-chimpanzee/ Aug. 2, 2012.
3. Yong E. Male chimps trade meat for sex. National Geographic. https://www.nationalgeographic.com/science/phenomena/2009/04/08/male-chimps-trade-meat-for-sex April 8, 2009; Chimps Trade Meat for the Chance of Sex. Science Magazine. https://www.sciencemag.org/news/2009/04/chimps-trade-meat-chance-sex April 8, 2009.
4. Rehkamp S. A Look at the Calorie Sources in the American Diet. USDA, Economic Research Service, Dec. 5, 2016. https://www.ers.usda.gov/amber-waves/2016/december/a-look-at-calorie-sources-in-the-american-diet/

CHAPTER EIGHT: HOW TO EAT WELL AND STICK AROUND

1. Jillette P. Presto: How I Made Over 100 Pounds Disappear and Other Magical Tales. Simon & Schuster, 2016.
Note: As you might expect from a brash and often raunchy magician, Jillette's book is a funny personal weight-loss account, not a scientific volume. Still, it does contain considerably more science than "The Red Meat Papers" published in the Annals of Internal Medicine.
2. Pawlowski A. "Spud Fit": Man Loses 115 Pounds Eating Nothing But Potatoes for a Year. Today. https://www.today.com/health/spud-fit-man-loses-weight-eating-only-potatoes-year-t106144 Dec. 19, 2016.
3. Chef AJ with Merzer, G. The Secrets to Ultimate Weight Loss. Hail to the Kale Publishing; 2018, pp.45-46.
4. Presto: How I Made Over 100 Pounds Disappear, p.92.
5. Benji Kurtz and I first used these terms in our book, The Plant Advantage (Vivid Thoughts Press, 2015)

CHAPTER NINE: PUBLIC POLICY

1. Ogden CL, Carrol MD, Kit BK, Flegal KM. Prevalence of Obesity in the United States, 2009-2010. NCHS Data Brief No. 82, Jan., 2012. CDC National Center for Health Statistics https://www.cdc.gov/nchs/products/databriefs/db82.htm

2. CDC National Center for Health Statistics https://www.cdc.gov/nchs/fastats/obesity-overweight.htm

3. CDC: U.S. deaths from heart disease, cancer on the rise. American Heart Association News. https://www.heart.org/en/news/2018/05/01/cdc-us-deaths-from-heart-disease-cancer-on-the-rise August 4, 2016.

4. Saiidi U. Average life expectancy in the US has been declining for 3 consecutive years. USA Today. https://www.usatoday.com/story/money/2019/07/09/u-s-life-expectancy-decline-overdoses-liver-disease-suicide/1680854001/ July 9, 2019.

5. Shute N. Fat Doctors Make Fat Patients Feel Better, And Worse. Shots: Health News From NPR. https://www.npr.org/sections/health-shots/2013/06/05/188920874/fat-doctors-make-fat-patients-feel-better-and-worse June 5, 2013.

6. Gupta S. More Treatment, More Mistakes. New York Times. https://www.nytimes.com/2012/08/01/opinion/more-treatment-more-mistakes.html July 31, 2012.

7. U.S. Food and Drug Administration. Preventable Adverse Drug Reactions: A Focus on Drug Interactions. https://www.fda.gov/drugs/drug-interactions-labeling/preventable-adverse-drug-reactions-focus-drug-interactions March 6, 2018.

8. U.S. Department of Health and Human Services. What is the U.S. Opioid Epidemic? https://www.hhs.gov/opioids/about-the-epidemic/index.html

9. National Institute on Drug Abuse, NIH. Opioid-Involved Overdose Deaths. NIH, National Institute on Drug Abuse, Ohio Opioid Summary. https://www.drugabuse.gov/opioid-summaries-by-state/ohio-opioid-summary March 2019.

10. Zampa M. How Many Animals Are Killed for Food Every Day? Sentient Media https://sentientmedia.org/how-many-animals-are-killed-for-food-every-day

11. Erskine, Eliza, "Jane Goodall Says Humanity Will be 'Finished' if we Don't Alter our Food System Post Coronavirus," 6/7/20, OneGreenPlanet.org, https://www.onegreenplanet.org/environment/jane-goodall-says-humanity-will-be-finished-if-we-dont-alter-our-food-systems-post-coronavirus

Recipe Index

About The Authors

GLEN MERZER

Glen began his career as a stand-up comic in San Francisco. He gave up performing after a couple of years of middling success and devoted himself to playwriting. Three of his plays have been published by Samuel French. Two of his plays were presented at the John F. Kennedy Center for the Performing Arts, and two were produced Off-Broadway, but his best plays have been seen nowhere at all. Glen wrote for network television for ten years before turning his attention to writing books.

Glen is co-author, with Howard Lyman, of *Mad Cowboy* and *No More Bull!*, and co-author, with Chef AJ, of *Unprocessed* and *The Secrets to Ultimate Weight Loss*.

Glen's one novel, *Off the Reservation*, is the story of a vegan congressman from Bloomington, Indiana, who runs for president. (The novel contains 20 vegan, oil-free recipes by Joanna Samorow-Merzer.) *The Progressive* magazine chose it as one of its "Favorite Books of 2015," and called it "a sardonic roller-coaster ride of a campaign seen through the eyes of a truth-telling vegan idealist who makes Bernie Sanders look positively plastic." *Off the Reservation* was also named to Kirkus Reviews' "Best Books of 2015." *Kirkus* called it a "fast-paced, wryly comic, and vastly satisfying political satire."

Glen can be found at www.ownyourhealthbook.com.

CHEF AJ

Chef AJ is the host of the television series *Healthy Living with CHEF AJ,* which airs on Foody TV. A chef, culinary instructor and professional speaker, she is author of the popular book *Unprocessed: How to Achieve Vibrant Health and Your Ideal Weight,* which chronicles her journey from an obese junk-food vegan faced with a diagnosis of pre-cancerous polyps, to learning how to create foods that nourish and heal the body. Her latest bestselling book *The Secrets to Ultimate Weight Loss: A Revolutionary Approach to Conquer Cravings, Overcome Food Addiction and Lose Weight Without Going Hungry* has received glowing endorsements by many luminaries in the plant-based movement.

Chef AJ was the Executive Pastry Chef at Santé Restaurant in Los Angeles where she was famous for her SOS-free (sugar, oil, and salt-free) and gluten-free desserts that use the fruit, the whole fruit and nothing but the whole fruit. She is the creator of the *Ultimate Weight Loss Program,* which has helped hundreds of people achieve the health and the body that they deserve, and is proud to say that her IQ is higher than her cholesterol. In 2018 she was inducted into the Vegetarian Hall of Fame. She has been a vegan for 43 years.

For more information, go to www.chefajwebsite.com or *https://www.youtube.com/c/ChefAJ.*

Made in the USA
Middletown, DE
18 October 2020